dwelling places

dwelling places

WORDS TO LIVE IN EVERY SEASON

Lucinda Secrest McDowell

ABINGDON PRESS
NASHVILLE

DWELLING PLACES
WORDS TO LIVE IN EVERY SEASON

Copyright © 2016 by Lucinda Secrest McDowell

Macro Editor: Ramona Richards

Library of Congress Cataloging-in-Publication Data

Names: McDowell, Lucinda Secrest, 1953- author.
Title: Dwelling places : words to live in every season / Lucinda Secrest McDowell.
Description: First [edition]. | Nashville, Tennessee : Abingdon Press, 2016. | Includes bibliographical references.
Identifiers: LCCN 2015045589 (print) | LCCN 2015048631 (ebook) | ISBN 9781501815324 (binding: pbk.) | ISBN 9781501815331 (e-book)
Subjects: LCSH: Meditations.
Classification: LCC BV4832.3 .M348 2016 (print) | LCC BV4832.3 (ebook) | DDC 242—dc23
LC record available at http://lccn.loc.gov/2015045589

16 17 18 19 20 21 22 23 24—10 9 8 7 6 5 4 3 2 1

MANUFACTURED IN THE UNITED STATES OF AMERICA

Copyright page continued on page 293.

If you are weary of wandering,
Hungry for a true home,
Longing for serenity and refuge,
And eager to live an authentic story
filled with grace and mercy . . .
These words are for you.

My dwelling place will be with them,
I will be their God, and they will be my people.

~ Ezekiel 37:27

Before the winds that blow do cease,
*Teach me to **dwell within Thy calm:***
Before the pain has passed in peace,
Give me, my God, to sing a psalm.
Let me not lose the chance to prove
The fullness of enabling love.
O Love of God, do this for me:
Maintain a constant victory.

~ Amy Carmichael (1867–1951)
"Constant Victory"

Contents

dwell

FALL

∽∽∽∽∽∽∽∽∽∽∽∽∽∽∽∽∽∽∽∽∽∽∽∽

. . . But mixed His music with my human cry,
Till somewhere from the half-withdrawing wood
Sound of familiar footsteps: Is it Thou?
*Master, where **dwellest** Thou? O speak to me.*
And He said, "Come and see."

∽∽

~ Amy Carmichael
"Where Dwellest Thou?"

1. dwell

*God's dwelling place is now among the people, and he will **dwell** with them. They will be his people, and God himself will be with them and be their God.*

~ Revelation 21:3

One word.

In the days preceding the New Year, one word kept clamoring for my attention from surprising places: *dwell*.

I read it in my psalm for the day: "Whoever dwells in the shelter of the Most High / will rest in the shadow of the Almighty" (91:1). I noticed *dwell* on the masthead of a glossy magazine all about clean living spaces. I uttered it as an admonition to someone—"Don't dwell on your past mistakes."

It was hard not to notice it, so I became curious and finally turned to God in prayer. I whispered, "OK. Dwell. Please reveal what You want me to learn from this word."

So as my word-for-the-year marinated in heart and mind, I embraced both meanings of dwell: 1. *to live* and 2. *to focus*. It soon became obvious that all too often I *live* amid hurry and obligation, dwelling in anxiety and surrounded by noise. And where was my default *focus*—circumstances, lists, self-preservation, tasks, things?

No more.

Throughout the Bible God calls His people to dwell with Him constantly. He offers us a refuge and shelter, and He fills it with a beauty and peace that is restorative. And, best of all, He sends Jesus Christ to dwell in our hearts and make His home with us forever!

Would you like some of *that* in your life?

First we need to acknowledge that God is the only One who can provide such a life for us. Moses, that great wanderer, knew this. God had long ago promised to be with him wherever he journeyed. So even though he was often a stranger in a strange land, Moses was confident in his true dwelling: "Lord, you have been our dwelling place / throughout all generations" (Psalm 90:1).

And this same God invites us to dwell with Him!

In the original language of the Old Testament, the Hebrew word for dwell is *yashab*, which is translated "to dwell, to sit down, to remain." How can we possibly do this? Sitting down is considered unproductive. We are a culture on the move! Believe me, friend, I know the challenges of making time for close communion with God in prayer and study—that's why I'm suggesting one word a day as our focus.

We can do that!

After all, we have certainly dwelled everywhere else: we give our time and resources to other places, people, and projects without a second thought. Yet all along, God is there with us, offering us His continual presence no matter where our journey might lead. Do you have a difficult appointment today? He'll go with you. Do you cry yourself to sleep at night? He's beside you, holding you close. His constant presence is the greatest gift of all.

Today you can truly make "the Most High your place of residence" (Psalm 91:9 CEB). You can dwell with a firm knowledge of His presence with you always. Will you join me in discovering all the dwelling places God has for us throughout every season?

☙

My child, I know you are exhausted running from this to that. And perhaps you regret that you have not taken more time to draw near to Me. But it's never too late. I'm still here, and I long to offer you a refuge—a respite from your busy life. Will you choose to dwell with Me? All you have to do is say "Here I am, Lord." Or you could even groan. Just come. And remain. Sit still. I love you.

2. quietness

Therefore, the Lord God,
the holy one of Israel, says:
In return and rest you will be saved;
quietness and trust will be your strength—
but you refused.

~ Isaiah 30:15 CEB

Daddy hallucinated while recovering from brain surgery. He clearly heard the voice of baritone Doug Oldham singing the gospel song "There Is a Quiet Place." The lyrics, which speak of a peaceful dwelling where one meets God and finds strength far from the rapid pace, were a clear sign from God. He was a successful businessman in midlife; now it was time to build in more rest and relaxation.

He had survived the brain tumor. Now he would make the life change.

So from his hospital bed, Daddy purchased (sight unseen) a mountain cottage by a babbling brook three states away and christened it "Quiet Place." After the song. And this dwelling place was a life-changer. For more than a quarter century our extended family built precious memories in that Montreat, North Carolina, sanctuary—and a few of them were even fairly quiet!

Do you need a "quiet place"—somewhere to go and experience God's peace and presence? Do you deliberately carve out hours or days when there is no noise, no music, no technology, and no interruptions to dispel the sounds of silence?

Or are you like the Israelites in today's verse who have yet again turned away from their God in order to pursue all the world has to offer? The prophet Isaiah is begging them to return and find strength through quietness and rest. Yet they refuse. Do you? I know why I refuse: because it's simply not natural to be alone and quiet and still. And yet it is a restorative spiritual discipline.

Ruth Haley Barton elaborates, "To be in solitude is to choose to do nothing. For extensive periods of time. All accomplishment is given up. Silence is required to complete solitude, for until we enter quietness, the world still lays hold of us. When we go into solitude and silence we stop making demands on God. It is enough that God is God and we are his."[1]

It is in the quietness that we hear the still, small voice of God. He is longing to speak to us, but our lives are too filled with the cacophony of the world and chatter of our own voice to actually hear. Dr. Richard Peace urged his students to "develop a taste for silence, a comfort in the midst of silence." How could you and I do that today?[2]

It will take some strategy, for sure. Carving out a place and time with no distractions. Turning off smartphones, pagers, computers, iPods, iPads. And then putting ourselves in a position of receiving—with open ears, open hands, open hearts—all that God wants to say. It will seem awkward and almost impossible at first. But, if you're like me, the silence will soon become a wanted friend, a comfortable dwelling place.

In this quietness, we create space for God's activity, God's agenda, God's words rather than filling every minute with our own.

What will He reveal to you today?

―――――――――――

My child, hush. Settle down and rest. Breathe. Block out every other sound except the quietness that will descend upon your weary soul. I know it's hard. I know you have so much on your mind and heart that needs immediate attention. But it will wait while you linger here with Me and allow your soul to catch up with your body. Close your eyes and hear My whisper through the trees. I am here. All is well.

3. soul

use as communion

*My **soul** yearns, even faints,
    for the courts of the LORD;
my heart and my flesh cry out
    for the living God.*

~ Psalm 84:2

Have you ever had that feeling?

You know, the one in which you're desperately hungry—or is it thirsty?—for *something*. But nothing sounds good, and you really don't feel like eating or drinking, but there's this *craving*.

And so you do something to fill up: eat, shop, gamble, clean, read romance, collect, drink, work out, cook—something! But it never does fill you up.

Because that part of you that yearns to be filled? That's your soul. And our verse today provides the only answer to this need: the "living God."

Longing. Wanting. Desiring. These words are repeatedly associated with the original Old Testament Hebrew word for soul: *nephesh*. That's why the word is so often translated in the context of mouth or stomach or throat. The Bible talks about a soul being hollow or empty or hungry or thirsty—never satisfied.

What is your soul craving today? Security, love, significance?

Only God can satisfy. That's why the psalmist declares, "Your faithful love / is better than life itself! / I'm fully satisfied— / as with a rich dinner" (Psalm 63:3, 5 CEB).

In His earthly ministry Jesus also spoke to our souls when He warned us that pleasing our appetites alone will cause us to lose our souls: "For what is the use of a man gaining the whole world if he loses or forfeits his own soul?" (Luke 9:25 JBP) Being successful in the outside world doesn't help if our inner world collapses.

John Wesley is known for asking everyone he encountered, "How is it with your soul?"

Be honest. How would you answer? Is your soul dry? Empty? Flourishing? Rested? Only you know about the inner life that no one else sees. Perhaps it is time for making soul care a priority.

Because the most important thing about us is not what we do; it's *who we become.*

The late Dallas Willard spent a lifetime encouraging believers to understand the importance of soul care: "What is running your life at any given moment is your soul. Not external circumstances, not your thoughts, not your intentions, not even your feelings, but your soul. The soul is that aspect of your whole being that correlates, integrates, and enlivens everything going on in the various dimensions of the self. The soul is the life center of human beings. You're a soul made by God, made for God, and made to need God."[3]

Best of all, your soul is His heart's delight.

My child, you polish up nicely, and folks like what they see. But I alone know the child within who is sometimes fearful, frequently overwhelmed, and occasionally despairs of life ever becoming manageable. It is my truest desire and deepest joy to nurture the care of your precious soul. Will you allow me access? May you find refuge as I draw you close into my sheltering nest. Be filled.

4. grace

*For it is by **grace** you have been saved, through faith—and this is not from yourselves, it is the gift of God—not by works, so that no one can boast.*

~ Ephesians 2:8-9

The best gift I ever received was grace. In fact, it quite literally changed my life.

Unfortunately, I had been a Christ follower for many years before I actually opened this precious gift I'd been carrying around and made it my own. I knew grace was part of the package deal for salvation, but I never understood that grace was God's gift we don't deserve and can never earn and can never lose.

So I kept trying to please God and get everything "just right" so that He might love me more and consider me worthy. *Striving* was my dwelling place, and *despair* was my landing place every time I failed at perfection. Until one day, in His mercy, God stooped down (the Hebrew word for *grace* means "to stoop") and lifted me up.

He reminded me that I am already loved, already accepted, already chosen for kingdom work, not because of anything I have done, but simply because I am His own. And that, dear friend, is the Gift of Grace.

Because we live in a world of reward and punishment, it is difficult to grasp the idea of receiving something we don't deserve. And yet that's the very nature of grace as illustrated in today's verse: "not by works, so that no one can boast." Perhaps this acronym says it best—God's Riches At Christ's Expense.

Frederick Buechner explains,

> The grace of God means something like: Here is your life. You might never have been, but you are because the party wouldn't have been complete without you. Here is the world.

Beautiful and terrible things will happen. Don't be afraid. I am with you. Nothing can ever separate us. It's for you I created the universe. I love you. There's only one catch. Like any other gift, the gift of grace can be yours only if you will reach out and take it. Maybe being able to reach out and take it is a gift, too.[4]

I used to dwell in a place of judgment, performance, rules, hurry, and approval. Nothing was enough. I could never rest; there was always more to do. Grace reminds me that my love and the outpouring of my life for the kingdom flow from knowing with confidence that, though I am not worthy, as God's child I am totally received and loved.

Do you need more grace in your life? The great news is it is already here for you if you are a child of the King. Just like when I'm home in the South and order a big breakfast at the diner. When I choose bacon and eggs on the menu, the plate always arrives with grits as well. "Honey, you don't have to special order grits. Down here they just come with!" the waitress cheerfully explains.

Grace "comes with" your commitment to Christ. So, open the gift and dwell in the love. Then, be sure and pass it along to others.

───────────────

My child, it's time to stop trying so hard and simply release yourself to Me. Unclench your fists and open your hands for the gift I so long for you to appropriate in your life: My grace, My favor, My unconditional love. As you do, may your whole being wash clean with a peace and sweet aroma of gratitude and grace to all whom you encounter. I am enough.

5. prayer

I cry out to you, LORD: Come to me—quickly!
  Listen to my voice when I cry out to you!
*Let my **prayer** stand before you like incense;*
  let my uplifted hands be like the evening offering.

~ Psalm 141:1-2 CEB

The sanctuary was filled with incense, the sunbeams through the windows reflecting the vapor as a cloud settling on the praying congregation. This Orthodox church was nearest to where we were house-sitting out in the country, so we had chosen to worship with this particular band of believers that Sunday. Turns out it was their twenty-fifth anniversary, and thus a two-and-a-half-hour service!

As I listened to the familiar scriptural prayer in an unfamiliar chant, I understood today's verse anew. For the Hebrews, incense symbolized an ascent to God. The prayers of God's people rise upward like the smoke from the incense, filtering through the atmosphere as an offering. Then the fragrance fills the holy space as God's presence hovers over and around us.

Prayer is our privilege—a lifeline to the Creator and Sustainer of the universe. An opportunity to communicate our worship, our gratitude, our concerns, our desires, our questions to the One who hears. And answers.

For my own evening prayer offering, I like to use a version of an ancient practice first suggested by Ignatius of Loyola in the sixteenth century: the prayer of Examen. Basically this is a time at the end of the day when we reflect on our day before God, in order to detect His presence and determine His direction for us.

Would you like to try this?

Picture yourself sitting with Jesus and talking through the details of your day. In some ways, this is merely an expansion of what we used to do with our four young children at the supper table. We asked each to share

"God-sightings" and at least one difficult situation that happened. It's all about being more attentive to our own actions and responses and to God's continual presence in our daily lives. All in the spirit of prayer.

Here are some guidelines for starting an evening prayer of Examen:

> As you begin to pray, still and quiet yourself. Give thanks for some of the specific gifts God has given you today. Then ask the Holy Spirit to guide and direct your thoughts as you prayerfully review your day. Let the details play out like a short movie. Pay attention both to the things that gave you life and to the things that drained you. Notice where the Spirit invites you to linger and ponder.[5]

- Where did you see God in your life today? When did He seem absent?
- In what situations did you respond with grace and mercy? Were there also times of disobeying or resisting God?
- When did you feel most alive and empowered? What made you feel drained or discouraged?
- What needs to be confessed? For whom do you need to pray as a follow-up to a conversation or a prompting from the Spirit?
- How will you live tomorrow in God's presence and power?

As night falls and rest beckons, may you know your prayers and your life "are a Christ-like fragrance rising up to God" (2 Corinthians 2:15 NLT).

〰️

My child, how I love hearing your voice lifted up to Me in prayer. Not because I don't know your deepest thoughts or concerns, but because I want you to come to Me and voice them. This communion with one another is precious and will make a difference in your life. Bring each person you care about to My throne of grace. Because I will always answer.

6. courageous

*Be strong and **courageous**. Do not be afraid; do not be discouraged, for the LORD your God will be with you wherever you go.*

~ Joshua 1:9

There are no coincidences.

My work for today is to write about the word *courageous*.

And I just got the call that author and missionary Elisabeth Elliot has passed "through gates of splendor" and is finally Home. As her daughter tells me of her mother's final moments I realize that the courage with which she faced all of life never left her—even at the end.

I remember her saying to me, "Courage is not the absence of fear, but the willingness to do the thing we fear."

Elisabeth not only believed but also wholeheartedly lived today's Scripture promise "the LORD your God will be with you wherever you go." And that was the secret of her courage:

- To continue ministry in the jungles of Ecuador at age twenty-eight after her young husband had been speared to death, along with four other missionaries.
- To take her toddler daughter, Valerie, to live and share Christ among the very tribe who had killed her husband.
- To communicate her unique story through thirty books, speaking, and radio so that others might be drawn to a deeper walk with God.
- To walk the journey of death from cancer with her second husband.
- To make family a priority and embrace her roles as wife, mother, and grandmother.
- To have confidence to be her authentic self, regardless of cultural pressure.

- To pour into the lives of countless people to whom
  she offered a prayer, an admonition, a blessing,
  word of advice, or a prophetic pronouncement.

When God told Joshua to be courageous it was at a crucial juncture in his life. After forty years of wandering in the desert, Joshua was now tasked to lead forty thousand Israelites (most of whom had never seen water) across the rushing Jordan River into Canaan. How could they cross to dry land? And, if indeed God would make a path, how could Joshua convince them to put their feet into the water, trusting the way would open?

When I was privileged as a young seminarian to live with Elisabeth Elliot—type her manuscripts, drive her to the airport for speaking engagements, and help with housekeeping—it was at a crucial juncture in my life. I needed courage to study and venture forth into the world with my own voice, to respond to God's unique call.

Elisabeth told me back then that it was my duty to write for God in response to the gift He had bestowed on me. And so I do. My time with her also firmly established my lifelong desire to become more and more like Jesus as I chose to follow her constant advice: "do the next thing." Today, on my writing retreat out in the country, I wanted to stop working on this manuscript and grieve the loss of my remarkable mentor. To remember and reflect.

But after a while I could hear Elisabeth's quiet, yet firm, voice, "That's enough sentimentality, Cindy. Now go back to your writing."

And so I shall. Be courageous. And share the legacy.

My child, I know that living in your world takes a lot of courage. And so I send some special people to help show you the way. Be sure to ask questions and listen and learn from those who have experienced so much. And then pass along the legacy of courage and encouragement as you continue further along the journey. Never forget that whether you are stepping into a river or a jungle, I am with you always. Do the next thing.

7. presence

*"My **Presence** will go with you, and I will give you rest."*
~ Exodus 33:14

You are not alone. This was God's promise to Moses, and it's one we can count on today.

Kevin better understood God's continual presence after a tandem sky-diving experience: "Though I couldn't see my instructor—he was strapped to my back—as we jumped from 13,500 feet and whipped through the sky at 120 miles per hour I knew he was there. After 60 seconds of freefall, he pulled the chute, and we soared. Every twist and turn we made, we made together. We were on the same trajectory."[6]

John Ortberg says that "our deepest calling is the 'with God' life (Him dwelling in His people) and then what we do with that to touch a hurting world." In other words, be filled so that you are empowered to go out and fill others!

Is yours a "with God" life? Because He is most definitely strapped on your back if you are a Christ follower. Whether you are languishing on a hospital bed, building a school for children who are orphans, figuring out how to pay your bills, or whipping through the sky at 120 miles per hour, you are *with God* and He *with you*, like a tandem skydiving instructor.

And God's presence makes the perfect dwelling place for our soul: "The 'with God' life is not a life of more religious activities or devotions or trying to be good. It is a life of inner peace and contentment for your soul with the Maker and Manager of the universe. The 'without God' life is the opposite. It is death. It will kill your soul."[7]

This truth doesn't change just because you don't sense a connection. Not *feeling* the presence? All you have to do is invite Him back, acknowledging that your efforts of going it alone have failed: "I have set the LORD continually before me; / Because He is at my right hand, I will not be shaken" (Psalm 16:8 NASB).

This is simply one way of paying attention to the Constant Companion in our life. Brother Lawrence, a monk in the twelfth century, called it "practicing the presence of God" and illustrated with his simple life that he could pray and focus on God in the midst of service among the pots and pans. We can do the same, but it will require us to live intentionally:

- Awaken each morning with a heart of gratitude and expectancy for what God will do both in you and through you.
- Use household objects or gifts as "prayer prompts" for others. For instance, there's a glass bluebird on my windowsill given to me by a dear friend living in a Muslim country. Every time I pass the bird I send up a prayer for her.
- Ask to see others as God sees them.
- When driving alone or sitting alone, picture Jesus in the seat next to you and pour out your heart in honest conversation.
- Fill your mind with hymns and songs of praise, Scripture, and prayers and offer up these words in worship wherever you may be.

My child, you are not alone. I am always closer than you think. And though I won't intrude, I am available to lift you up, clear the path, hold your tongue, or just hold you. Let go of everything else and cling to Me. And we will soar. Together. Far beyond your wildest dreams.

8. strength

*How thankful I am to Christ Jesus our Lord for choosing me as
one of his messengers, and giving me the **strength** to be faithful
to him.*

~ 1 Timothy 1:12 TLB

A year ago, young Dr. Kent Brantley, medical missionary in Monrovia, Liberia, was diagnosed with Ebola—a horrific disease that had already killed dozens of his patients. In the ensuing weeks and months, the world held its collective breath as Brantley was evacuated to the United States, treated with experimental drugs, and miraculously healed of this scourge that killed thousands last year, primarily in western Africa. Throughout the ordeal, he and his family—followers of Christ—exhibited faith, grace, and tremendous strength.

It is the same kind of strength that Christ Jesus provides all those He chooses to be "his messengers."

This summer as the Brantleys returned to Liberia, he recalled needing that strength, even at the beginning of the epidemic:

> Ebola didn't just kill our patients, it stripped them of their
> dignity. Ebola humiliated its victims by taking away control
> of their bodily functions. We constantly changed diapers and
> sheets and cleaned up patients, and we fed them when they
> could no longer do so themselves. Unable to cure their disease,
> we focused on treating their sense of isolation. No families.
> No friends. No familiar faces. No human contact. But I had
> determined to display compassion over fear.[8]

Eventually the day came when another fully protected doctor stood outside Brantley's bedroom window, because he could not come into the contaminated home, and gave the news that he now had the virus: "I was so sick at that point. . . . I am a husband and a father, and my thoughts turned to my beautiful wife and children back home in the United States. I might not see them, much less touch them, ever again."[9]

Needless to say, this year's homecoming was a mixture of emotions—both reliving the trauma and great loss and remembering with gratitude the many who helped them and those who survived. Even now Liberia, Sierra Leone, and Guinea (where my own daughter lived for several years with the Peace Corps) are still discovering new cases of Ebola every day. They need our continued support and prayer.

Where do you need strength today? It is probably not in the same place where Dr. Brantley did, because you are called to be a messenger in a different milieu—your own vocation, your own family, your own community. You are facing your own crises and challenges. But if you call out for strength, He will meet you right where you are.

> Bless the LORD
> because he has listened to my request for mercy!
> The LORD is my strength and my shield.
> My heart trusts him.
> I was helped, my heart rejoiced,
> and I thank him with my song.
> The LORD is his people's strength;
> he is a fortress of protection for his anointed one.
> (Psalm 28:6-8 CEB)

Yes, the Lord is His people's strength.

My child, when you are weak, I am strong. And My strength is made perfect in your weakness. All you have to do is call out for Me and trust Me. If I have chosen you as a messenger to the world, I will always be beside you to guide and provide. Be strong. Be courageous. You, too, may be used to heal a hurting world.

9. hiding place

*You are my **hiding place**;*
you will protect me from trouble
and surround me with songs of deliverance.

~ Psalm 32:7

It was only a cupboard behind a false wall in the bedroom of a devoted Christian spinster named Corrie ten Boom. But this temporary dwelling place became the literal lifesaver of many Jewish people and Dutch resistance workers during World War II.

The hiding place.

As a college student I heard Corrie tell the story of how she and her family built their hiding place to protect those being hunted by Nazis. How they freely shared their rations and home with Jewish people at great risk. And how the suspicious gestapo arrested her family and sent them to various concentration camps where all died except Corrie.[10]

My own Dutch relatives, the van Seventers, were also part of this resistance movement of Christians who harbored Jews during the war. And, like the ten Booms, their names are listed in the Holocaust Museum in Jerusalem (Yad Vashem) as "righteous Gentiles." These families' nonviolent resistance was their way of living out their Christian faith.

A place to hide from danger is important in the lives of more than just war victims. What about ordinary men and women like you and me? What about kings?

As King David was on the run for his life, he turned to the God whom he knew would protect and deliver him: "In the shelter of your presence you hide them / from all human intrigues; / you keep them safe in your dwelling / from accusing tongues" (Psalm 31:20).

King Saul pursued David because, even though Saul knew he was anointed to be the next king, he simply could not bear the fact that David's current popularity outshone his own. Yet David knew where to hide: "When the wicked came against me / . . . They stumbled and fell. / For in the time of trouble / He shall hide me in His pavilion; / In the secret place of his tabernacle" (Psalm 27:2, 5 NKJV).

He chose a cave. First Samuel 24 tells the story of David going to the desert of En Gedi because it was full of caves. And though they were used by local people for housing and tombs, soon they became places of refuge. Can you imagine how dark and wet and cold and stale such dwellings were? Add to that the devastation of being hunted by a former mentor and hearing the dogs barking after you, while you wonder, *Will they find me this time?*

But hiding places can also be a catalyst for new life if we survive them, just like all those hiding in the ten Boom home escaped that day even after the family was arrested. You see, we have every reason to believe that while he was hiding in the darkness, David was communing with his God.

Hiding places can become dwellings of redemption and new life if we cling to the One who is right there with us. In a cave. In a cupboard. Wherever we may be.

❧

My child, are you hiding from something? Perhaps a long-ago pain inflicted so deep that no one else sees? Perhaps a fear of an unknown future? Perhaps from imagined catastrophe or real threat? Please know that you can run to Me. I am your hiding place. And I will fill you with songs of deliverance. There is safety here. Just come.

10. calm

Jesus was sleeping at the back of the boat with his head on a
cushion. The disciples woke him up, shouting, "Teacher, don't
you care that we're going to drown?" When Jesus woke up, he
rebuked the wind and said to the waves, "Silence! Be still!"
Suddenly the wind stopped, and there was a great **calm**.

~ Mark 4:38-39 NLT

It was called the perfect storm.

Three fierce storms converged into one, creating an almost apocalyptic situation in the Atlantic Ocean in which boats encountered waves of one hundred feet, the equivalent of a ten-story building. Stronger than any in recorded history, the storm hit the coast off Gloucester, Massachusetts, in November 1991.

Because this particular event formed with such suddenness, the National Weather Bureau didn't even have time to name it and barely had time to send out a warning to all vessels at sea. In his book *The Perfect Storm*, author Sebastian Junger explained that the crew of the fishing vessel the *Andrea Gail* never received that warning. They had no idea of what was about to hit them.

Have you ever been unexpectedly broadsided with a "perfect storm" in life?

The disciples in our text today find themselves in the middle of one. High waves are breaking into the boat, filling it with water. Yes, their Master was with them, but they felt He didn't care because He was sleeping and seemed absent during their turmoil.

Do you ever feel that Jesus is "sitting this one out" on one of your worst days?

I have. That's when the "why" questions arise and the panicky accusations start:

"Don't you even care

- that my child is making poor choices?"
- that I can't pay my bills?"
- that this expensive medical treatment isn't making me any better?"
- that the world is going crazy?"

Of course He cares. Jesus is full of compassionate calm and wants us to dwell there as well: "The LORD is full of compassion and mercy" (James 5:11); "God is gracious—it is he who makes things right, / our most compassionate God. / God takes the side of the helpless; / when I was at the end of my rope, he saved me" (Psalm 116:6 MSG).

Words such as chaos, confusion, and cacophony could describe our world today. Yet those three *C* words are the exact opposite of what God brings to me in the middle of my storms. Calm. In our story today it only takes a few words from the Most High and the storms ceased.

Do you crave calm?

Jesus can speak that into your life: "Speak through the earthquake, wind, and fire, O still, small voice of calm."[11]

> Calmly we look before us—we fear no future ill,
> Enough for safety and for peace, if Thou art with us still.[12]

Surprise storms are inevitable in this life. Panic is optional. Call out for Him now. And be prepared to dwell in calm.

∽✒∽

My child, I know your boat is rocking and that it sometimes feels as though you are going to drown—from all the overwhelming responsibilities, from your regret, from the noises and voices that clamor for your attention and pull you away from Me. And so I speak into your life and order all to be still. Receive the calm I offer. It's for your soul.

11. love

Fill us full every morning with your faithful **love**
so we can rejoice and celebrate our whole life long.

~ Psalm 90:14 CEB

Sometimes I secretly wonder if there is enough of God's love to go around. And what if you end up getting more of it than I do?

The good news is that God's love is endless and limitless: "As high as heaven is above the earth, / that's how large God's faithful love is for those who honor him" (Psalm 103:11 CEB). The Old Testament Hebrew word in these verses today is *hesed*, which is usually translated "loving-kindness," "everlasting love," or "faithful love."

Here this word is used twice in an effort to help us grasp God's loving intentions toward us: "I have loved you with a **love that lasts forever**. / And so with **unfailing love**, / I have drawn you to myself" (Jeremiah 31:3 CEB). Do you believe this? Or do you find it hard to grasp that you could be the recipient of such love? Perhaps that's because we've been wounded by faulty human love.

Perhaps another person has disappointed us. If someone who once promised to love us let us down, we may now view all love with suspicion, wondering if it will last. Human love is convenient and limited; when the object of love no longer satisfies the current need, love is ended. But God's love—His *hesed*—is not only unlimited and eternal but also a commitment for always.

And yes, there is plenty to go around. Augustine of North Africa once said that God loves each one of us as if there was only one of us. We're *all* the beloved—infinitely and lavishly and unconditionally loved. Paul prayed we would have "the power to understand, as all God's people should, how wide, how long, how high, and how deep his love is. May you experience the love of Christ, though it is too great to understand fully" (Ephesians 3:18-19 NLT).

A favorite fictional character, Hannah, put it this way: "Think about a beach on a sunny day. My soaking up the warmth and sunlight doesn't take anything away from anyone else on the beach. And someone else baking in the warmth and sunlight doesn't take anything away from me. God's love isn't limited. When will I really believe that?"[13]

"O the deep, deep love of Jesus, vast, unmeasured, boundless, free! Rolling as a mighty ocean in its fullness over me! Underneath me, all around me, is the current of Thy love."[14]

We can know this with confidence: "In the Scriptures, the couplet 'unfailing love' never occurs in the context of a man's love for a woman, a parent's for a child, a friend's for a friend. But always in the way God cares about us. God's love is unfailing."[15]

My child, what will it take for you to understand that your truest identity is that you are My beloved? I love you. And My love is unconditional, boundless, and everlasting. Open your hands and let go of all the broken pieces of past loves. As they flutter to the ground, keep your hands open. For yes, I will fill you every single morning with love.

12. spirit

*Don't you know that you yourselves are God's temple and that
God's **Spirit** dwells in your midst?*

~ 1 Corinthians 3:16

The Holy Spirit nudged me to go out into the garden of the convent before lunch. And so, I left the rest of my staff and ventured out only to find an elderly nun working there. As I visited with her I discovered she was in her eighties and about to return home to Ireland after a year's sabbatical. What could I say to encourage her, for surely that's why I had been prodded toward this remote section of the retreat center?

I began to build a bridge, seeking to find common ground—me a Protestant with this Catholic sister. I asked her what being on sabbatical at the convent meant and found to my delight that one task was to read a book a week and report to her spiritual director.

"You mean you've just read fifty-two books? What was your favorite?" I asked, hoping she would mention the latest Henri Nouwen I had just finished, since he was my favorite Catholic author.

To my shock she replied, "*Amazed by Grace* by McDowell. It changed my life."

It was the first book I ever wrote.

I don't know who was more surprised that day—Sister Alphonsina, in discovering this stranger in the garden was the author of her new favorite book, or me, discovering that God had somehow used my words to encourage this precious reader. Needless to say, there were both tears and laughter as we embraced each other and God's grace.

What if I had ignored the prodding of the Spirit? Both of us would have missed a blessing.

We read in God's Word that this third person of the Trinity, the Holy Spirit, is sent to live within us and give us divine discernment, power, and comfort.

This Spirit is available to every believer. Will you be attentive to His nudging and His working within you?

If you're not sure exactly how that works, perhaps Amy Carmichael's poem can best explain the Spirit's indwelling:

Upon the sandy shore an empty shell;
Beyond the shell infinity of sea;

O Saviour, I am like that empty shell,
Thou art the Sea to me.

A sweeping wave rides up the shore, and, lo,
Each dim recess the coiled shell within

Is searched, is filled, is filled to overflow
By water crystalline.

Not to the shell is any glory then:
All glory give we to the glorious Sea.

And not to me is any glory when
Thou overflowest me.

Sweep over me Thy shell, as low I lie;
I yield me to the purpose of Thy will,

Sweep up, O conquering waves, and purify;
And with Thy fullness fill.[16]

Be filled.

My child, don't let the Holy Spirit be a complicated stumbling block to your understanding of ways in which I fill your life. I am God the Father, Jesus His Son, and also the Holy Spirit. This Trinity is a mystery. Just open yourself and allow Me to dwell in you. Then, act on My promptings and live in My power.

13. joy

Splendor and majesty are before him;
*strength and **joy** are in his dwelling place.*

~ 1 Chronicles 16:27

This year a friend died way too soon. Steve Hayner's life had intersected with ours throughout the years and at numerous points—not the least of which was preaching our wedding homily. But in the process of dying, Steve, along with his wife, Sharol, taught us how to live.

Joyfully.

When our mutual friend, Tim, visited his bedside and asked Steve for final words of advice, he received this answer:

> Life is a whole lot less complicated and a whole lot more joyful than I'd ever imagined. The grace and love of God permeate more of life than we dare to realize. Often I've taken life and myself way too seriously, and God never meant life to be lived that way. It's meant to be lived with joy and playfulness. The outcome is good and terrific. I wish I'd played more. But now I'll have lots of opportunity to grow into that. As C. S. Lewis says, "Joy is the serious business of Heaven."[17]

Steve signed every communication "joyfully," and his life affected countless numbers of people during his ministries as pastor, president of Columbia Seminary and InterVarsity, and board chair of International Justice Mission and World Vision. I'm grateful Steve and Sharol were generous enough to share the struggles and victories of his last days with us through their book *Joy in the Journey*.

And now his whole life is signed with joy.

Joy is God's dwelling place, and He wants to share that with us. This joy is a pervasive sense of well-being that is deeper and broader than any pleasure. It is an element of inner transformation into Christlikeness and the outer life that flows from it. Jesus urged joy in his closest friends: "I have said these things to you so that my joy will be in you and your joy will be complete" (John 15:11 CEB).

So often joy is accompanied by strength, as our verse indicates. Surely this was the case with the Hayners, and it is true for you and me as well, "The joy from the LORD is your strength!" (Nehemiah 8:10 CEB). Christ is dwelling in us, giving us exactly what we need.

Jennifer Kennedy Dean, who also walked her young husband through death, prays thus, "Jesus, let my life house You. Make Yourself at home in me. Recreate me so completely that only You are evident. The evidence of Your indwelling presence is true joy. Not so much high emotion as calm and settled contentment. When nothing in my life seems reason for rejoicing, I still find myself rejoicing."[18]

G. K. Chesterton puts it this way: "Joy, which was the small publicity of the pagan, is the gigantic secret of the Christian."[19]

Friends, let's keep a secret no longer, spilling out joy everywhere we go!

My child, may you be filled with My joy, which is a whole lot more satisfying than mere happiness. May this joy be a settled contentment in the midst of whatever comes your way. May you smile and relax, knowing that we are in this together and I am the Giver of joy. And may you find great delight in sharing joy with all around you. There is enough.

14. home

*Then Christ will make his **home** in your hearts as you trust in him.*

~ Ephesians 3:17 NLT

I adjusted my radio dial, but the singing still sounded dreadful. Some choral group was ruining Leonard Bernstein's "Somewhere" from *West Side Story*.

I soon discovered why.

The NPR announcer introduced the Dallas Street Choir—a group that changes members daily. In fact, the director had practiced with fifty-seven different homeless singers just in the last few weeks leading up to this concert. On this particular night two dozen of them were dressed up in donated tuxedoes and black evening gowns, ready to perform at the Dallas City Performance Hall to a standing-room-only crowd.

Homeless no more.

Well, at least for this evening when each singer had been given an overnight stay at a fancy hotel and a chance to be accompanied by mezzo-soprano Frederica von Stade. Now that I'm really listening, the quality of the music greatly improves as her voice comes alongside theirs in searching for "a place for us, a time and place for us."[20]

Where can we truly be at home? Perhaps we are asking the wrong question. *With whom* can we finally be at home? Paul told the church in Ephesus that "in him you too are being built together to become a dwelling in which God lives by His Spirit" (Ephesians 2:22). And today's verse gives the most startling announcement: Christ wants to make His home in us!

I first understood this good news when as a teenager I read Robert Boyd Munger's booklet, *My Heart—Christ's Home*. In this allegory, Christ is invited into each area of the heart as though it were a room in a house—dining room, recreation room, bedroom, kitchen, and living room. Each activity for those areas is submitted to Christ as Lord. Finally, the deed and title are turned over to the new owner. This marvelous picture helped me understand what happens when we allow Jesus to dwell in us.[21]

Many have wandered homeless for a long time and waded through lots of other sketchy real estate, only to find that there is a "place for us somewhere" and it is in Christ and He in us. Our true home.

Have you spent time in a far country—a place of noise and push and shove? Do you know that God wants to welcome you home to dwell in His peace and serenity?

> We need not be afraid. God's arms are stretched out wide to take us in. God's heart is large enough to receive us. Welcome to the living room of God's love, where we can put on old slippers and share freely. . . . Welcome to the study of God's wisdom, where we can grow and stretch and ask all the questions we want. Jesus is the doorway into this home that is the heart of God, and prayer is the key that by grace through faith unlocks the door. Welcome home.[22]

My child, stop wandering. Come home. You who are weary, come home. I am waiting for you. I have your room ready. Let's dwell together. Me in you and you in me. Forever. It's not too late. Take one step today. I'm right here.

15. mountains

*I raise my eyes toward the **mountains**.*
  Where will my help come from?
My help comes from the LORD,
  the maker of heaven and earth.

~ Psalm 121:1-2 CEB

I was not prepared for the awesome splendor of the Grand Teton Mountains.

The pictures on calendars, postcards, and paintings paled in comparison to the real deal. Standing in their presence I was totally overwhelmed with the creativity of "the maker of heaven and earth."

Sometimes words are inadequate to describe God's creation. But as I "raised my eyes toward the mountains" a few came to mind: *majestic, formidable, untamable, stately, beautiful, towering, grandeur, unwavering, foundational, life-giving, mammoth*, and *splendid*.

And *thanks*.

As a child I first fell in love with mountains by spending summers in the Blue Ridge—forever known to me as "God's Country." But since then I have been privileged to backpack on the Appalachian Trail, rappel in New England's White Mountains and the Adirondacks, ride cable cars up the Swiss Alps and New Zealand's Remarkables, trek through Washington's Cascade Range and the Scottish Highlands, and even enjoy a bit of Rocky Mountain High (I call it "altitude sickness").

This summer in Grand Teton National Park I was reminded of John Muir's words, as the park system was evolving in 1901: "Climb the mountains and get their good tidings. Nature's peace will flow into you as sunshine flows into trees. The winds will blow their own freshness into you, and the storms their energy, while cares will drop off like autumn leaves."[23]

To paraphrase today's psalm: "Look to the mountains and receive help from the Lord, their Creator." The mountains draw our eyes skyward toward the One who is all powerful: "You establish the mountains by your strength; you are dressed in raw power" (Psalm 65:6 CEB). As the soft, white clouds rest on top of the rocky crags and peaks I am reminded of their Maker's dual character so often contrasted in gentleness and power, mercy and judgment, humanity and divinity.

Today's familiar words from the psalmist remind us that although we often turn to nature for inspiration and help, it is nature's creator—God—who provides the help we need.

One outdoorsman captured this variance well:

> The wilderness often mirrors so much of what happens inside a man—tough slopes, rough waters, and fierce mountain winds symbolize hard and painful life passages, while clear skies at a peak's summit, smooth green rivers, and a warm campfire at night symbolize the opposite. The wild is not only a place for physical and emotional renewal. It is one of God's chosen instruments for coming to grips with what has damaged our souls, so that our spirits can be revitalized and the whole world made new. Whether by prayer and repentance, or by praise and thankfulness.[24]

When David was in distress, he cried out to the God who dwells in His holy mountain: "Send your light and truth—those will guide me! / Let them bring me to your holy mountain, / to your dwelling place" (Psalm 43:3 CEB). Whether or not you can see a majestic mountain today, you are only one cry away from God's dwelling place. Look up.

My child, you spend so much time looking down, fooling around with technology, or wringing your hands from circumstances. Today I invite you to look up and call upon Me. As you drink in the vastness of My glorious creation, may you also welcome the limitless help I so long to give you. You are missing much down there. Look up. I'm here.

16. content

*I have learned how to be **content** in any circumstance. I know
the experience of being in need and of having more than enough.*

~ Philippians 4:11-12 CEB

When is enough enough? Apparently, only after "just a little bit more."

We live in a cluttered culture. One *New York Times Magazine* story reported that "the United States has 2.3 billion square feet of self-storage space—more than 7 square feet for every man, woman and child. A 2006 UCLA study found middle-class families in Los Angeles 'battling a nearly universal over accumulation of goods.' Garages were clogged. Toys and outdoor furniture collected in the corners of backyards. 'The home-goods storage crisis has reached almost epic proportions.'"[25]

While I don't have a storage unit, I certainly have way more stuff than is necessary down in my basement! Why can't we just be content with what we already have?

No wonder the latest craze is decluttering.

Or "konmariing," That's a word that you will hear soon if you haven't already. It derives from the bestselling book *The Life-Changing Magic of Tidying Up* by Japanese cleaning consultant Marie Kondo (she calls her method "KonMari," which is a mash-up of her names). The basis is that every object in our household should have its place and be returned to it religiously after it is used. That sounds suspiciously like what my mama used to say: "A place for everything and everything in its place."

One KonMari customer, Jamie Gutfreund, says "There's also an emotional aspect to decluttering and even a spiritual one. Like meditation and yoga, decluttering appeals to overscheduled Americans seeking calm and focus."[26]

That's the crux of the matter: we are hoarding stuff, hoping it will fill that hole in our soul that craves calm and focus and peace. But the more we gather, the less we are satisfied and content. That's because we are going after the wrong source—that is, stuff instead of the Savior.

The apostle Paul was wise in sharing with us the importance of learning how to be content. In the original New Testament Greek, this word is *autarkes* and is translated to mean "adequate or needing no assistance." Why can't we appreciate "adequate"?

Here's the vision Kondo offers in her book: "I have time to experience bliss in my quiet space, where even the air feels fresh and clean; time to sip herbal tea while I reflect on my day . . . the space I live in is graced with only those things that speak to my heart. My lifestyle brings me joy."[27]

You don't have to rush out and buy her book. God, the original "cleaning consultant," offers you a place to dwell that is full of all those very things because it is full of Him and His love. And with that we can be content "in any circumstance," as our verse suggests.

So go throw out a bunch of unneeded junk; it will make you feel better. But also, be sure to attend to the cleansing of your heart and soul. Where God dwells.

My child, your life, your home, and your heart are often too full of stuff that doesn't belong there. And the messiness of all that causes unrest. I long to help you know that I am enough. That all I send your way is all you truly need for joy. What are you willing to get rid of today? Let's dispose of it together.

17. refuge

How priceless is your unfailing love, O God!
  *People take **refuge** in the shadow of your wings.*
                                    ~ Psalm 36:7

I awaken to the sound of heavy rain encompassing me. This second-floor sleeping porch contains one piece of furniture: a large bed surrounded on three sides by floor-to-ceiling windows, setting me high among the trees.

Sliding down into the soft sheets, I pull up the covers, thankful for my cozy refuge from the outside world. Nothing, it seems, can touch me here.

For the first time in my life, I have the sensation of being in a nest, dwelling in the shelter of God's wings. And I remember that in the original language of the Old Testament, the Hebrew word for "to dwell" is sometimes translated as "to nest."

"He will cover you with his feathers, / and under his wings you will find refuge" (Psalm 91:3-4). I recall how baby chicks rush under the mother hen at the first sign or sound of danger. They can nestle into a sense of safety and security.

I believe this is exactly how God wants me to feel about Him—my true Refuge.

Nesting in my bed, I think back to the previous week when I had been reading a favorite book to my precious grand-girl: *Are You My Mother?* by P. D. Eastman. The story reinforces the sheltering refuge of the home nest to those who are lost and wandering. In that story, after asking every creature she encountered, "Are *you* my mother?" the baby bird finally ends up safely back in the nest and realizes that her mother is the one who nourishes her and shelters her.[28]

So often I relate to the psalmist's yearnings, "I long to dwell in your tent forever / and take refuge in the shelter of your wings" (Psalm 61:4). David wants God to be his forever nest. He's had enough of running and hiding and maneuvering and outwitting. He just wants to snuggle under those wings and be safe.

Is this the longing of your soul as well?

If so, all you have to do is call upon the name of the Lord. And that's pretty simple. It can even sound something like, "God, are you there?" or, "Dear God, help me." Or you could just groan and He will understand. King Solomon rejoiced that "the LORD's name is a strong tower; / the righteous run to it and find refuge" (Proverbs 18:10 CEB).

Hannah Whitall Smith discovered this the hard way when tragedy came: "The secret of His presence is a more secure refuge than a thousand Gibraltars. I do not mean that no trials come. They may come in abundance, but they cannot penetrate into that sanctuary of the soul, and we may dwell in perfect peace even in the midst of life's fiercest storms."[29]

It's time to stop asking everyone you meet some version of "Are *you* my refuge?" And start dwelling—nesting—under the shelter of the One who knows you best and loves you most.

My child, come in closer and let me draw you to Myself in a Mother Hen embrace. You are not alone. You are in the best place possible—the nest of My presence, My love, My care. Here I will nourish you and protect you. Here I will strengthen you for when it's time to fly off and do amazing things. But remember to always return to Me for refuge. I am home.

18. truth

*We will lovingly follow the **truth** at all times—speaking truly,
dealing truly, living truly—and so become more and more in
every way like Christ.*

~ Ephesians 4:15-16 TLB

I am so tired of current events being viciously argued over social media.

There, I said it. Did I step on your toes? Are you going to make a nasty comment about my politics or my family or whether or not I'm really a Christian?

Yes, I know issues are important. And yes, I do care about being salt and light for the Kingdom. But have you seen the steady digression into judgment and self-righteous bantering online lately?

May I ask, Isn't there a way we can lovingly lift up God's truth in the same manner as Paul exhorts us in today's verse: becoming more and more in every way like Christ?

Someone once told me that compassion is the "tact" that accompanies truth. And by modeling Christlike compassion, we go far in valuing the other person at the moment he or she most needs to hear the truth.

The original New Testament Greek word here is *alethia*, which refers not only to ethical truth but also to truth in all its fullness and scope as embodied in Christ. Paul's passion was that people would not only understand who they are in the vertical relationship with Christ but also express their new identity in their horizontal relationship with each other.

Yet we are rapidly becoming a culture in which there is not a clear definition of truth. It used to be that everyone recognized at least some "absolute truth," that is, something was true for all people, even if they didn't know it. These days the majority appear to embrace "relative truth," that is, something is true for one person but not true for another.

No wonder folks are confused! And no wonder we see rampant lying on the part of people who are supposedly trustworthy: news anchors, sports heroes, political leaders, teachers, and clergy.

Today I learned two new words: *Crowdpounding* is when the online community rages against something that was said, Tweeted, or blogged, with an avalanche of vindictive words spewed on the screen. *Crowdaffirming* is the same but in a vehemently positive way, which also can get out of control. Who wants to be part of a "crowd-anything"? We are called to be individuals and to answer to God as such.

There is guidance from the Spirit: "When the Spirit of Truth comes, he will guide you in all truth" (John 16:13 CEB). And there is Christ as our model: "Grace and truth came into being through Jesus Christ" (John 1:17 CEB).

But how does this help you and me in our conversations today?

Os Guinness speaks to this issue:

> We Christians must seek to communicate in a way that is shaped by the One who sends us, and therefore by the pattern of the Incarnation, the Cross, and the Holy Spirit . . . God's truth requires God's art to serve God's end. Any Christian explanation or defense of truth must have a life, a manner, and a tone that are shaped decisively by the central truths of the gospel.[30]

So true.

———————————

My child, I suspect there are times where you even wonder what is really true. And how can you stand up for truth without giving in to the world's tactics? Today's cultural shifts seem to threaten the foundations of truth that you have always trusted. Just remember, I am still God. And I will help guide you in all truth. Always.

19. singing

The LORD *your God is in your midst—a warrior bringing*
victory.

> *He will create calm with his love;*
> *he will rejoice over you with **singing.***

~ Zephaniah 3:17 CEB

I never planned to sing in public. But God had other ideas.

And so, when nudged by the Spirit, my faltering voice softly sang over the group the words of an old hymn: "Every day the Lord Himself is near me, / With a special mercy for each hour; / All my cares He fain would bear and cheer me, / He whose name is Counselor and Power."[31]

By the time the verse was over and I seamlessly moved into a closing prayer, I was no longer conscious of my singing quality—only that I had offered a joyful noise unto the Lord. And since that time, God has made it clear that I am to "get over myself" and not be concerned about the actual sound that comes out of my mouth, merely the spirit with which I sing over my audiences in order to draw them deeper into the presence of God for prayer.

I had already been doing this for years in my own morning times of devotion; my hymnal was kept alongside my prayer book and Bible. I often discovered the richness of meaning in so many of these precious songs. Singing them had frequently "primed the pump" when I wasn't sure exactly how to pray or for whom.

Thus, in the past ten years, only in obedience to God, I have chosen to sing over each group where I speak, remembering three important promises from today's verse. First, our victorious Lord "is in your midst." He is right here beside us! Is that a comfort to your heart? Second, He will "create calm with His love." Do you need calm today? Love? Know beyond a doubt that your God desires to bring it into your life through His presence.

Third, God is rejoicing over you and me "with singing!" Did you know that He is pleased with you? So much so that you bring Him joy? Be honest, when was the last time someone sang over you just because he or she loved you? Perhaps you are thinking of when you were a small child and one of your parents sang you to sleep. Did that make you feel comforted, safe, loved?

In my favorite children's devotional, *Thoughts to Make Your Heart Sing*, Sally Lloyd-Jones says, "We forgot our song long ago, when we turned and ran away from God. But Jesus has come to bring us home to God—and give us back our song. The whole world's singing a song. Have you heard it? 'God loves us. He made us. He's very pleased with us.'"[32]

And so, in order to help others remember the song, I will swallow my pride and joyfully sing over those God sends my way—perhaps even you.

What will you sing today?

My child, I long to hear you sing. No matter that you don't always remember the words. No matter that you can't carry a tune. I created music for glory and praise and want it to be part of your life. And now, as you enter this new day or enter a night of rest, will you listen carefully? For, dear one, I am singing over you. With great joy.

20. still

Be *still*, and know that I am God.

~ Psalm 46:10

It was a large white tent on a campus in the middle of greater Los Angeles.

The surrounding world was fast and loud; inside the tent was slow and quiet.

The Stillness Tent.

Fuller Seminary erected it on their quad during Lent with the invitation to "visit the Stillness Tent—a space for us to write, reflect, and pray." Organizers felt that the community needed a visual interruption to call them to stillness. They believed the tent would be something that people naturally stumbled upon—hard to ignore in the major thoroughfare of the campus. And they did.

Director of the Chapel Jenn Graffus said it accomplished what they wanted: "Even on the weekends, I've seen people lying around inside it just resting—we don't do that naturally. Stillness is not just about being quiet—there's something deeper to stillness than silence. We tend to minimize rest, but it's okay to experience God by slowing down and enjoying creation. It's been an interesting experiment for our community."[33]

While most of us don't have access to a stillness tent, we are commanded to "be still." So how's that working for you?

Being still is not usually our default posture; we must deliberately train ourselves in this ancient spiritual discipline. Saint John of the Cross used a helpful word picture that instructs us in the quieting of all physical and emotional senses: "My house being now all stilled."

What could you do to *still* your own dwelling place today?

Sharon Garlough Brown created a memorable book series that combines the best of fiction and spiritual direction, beginning with *Sensible Shoes*. The spiritual director in this story is pointing out to four disparate women the importance of spending time growing deeper with God:

> We don't need to retreat to a far-off place or abandon our daily lives to encounter God. But we do need training in how to discern the movement of God's Spirit in ordinary and every-day circumstances. We need designated time for stillness and listening. It takes time to identify the baggage we've been carrying that weighs us down. The Spirit of God is always speaking to us, but we need to slow down, stop, and give more than lip service to what God is saying.[34]

What will you do today to slow down and be still? Where will you go? And when you're in that place, what will be your posture: comfortable seating, open hands, a peaceful heart? Do it as an act of obedience. End up with a blessing. "Be still, my soul: thy God doth undertake, To guide the future, as He has the past. Thy hope, thy confidence let nothing shake; All now mysterious shall be bright at last. Be still, my soul: the waves and winds still know, His voice Who ruled them while He dwelt below."[35]

My child, thank you for choosing to set aside this time with Me. Because you are being still and focused and receptive—even if only for a few moments—I will honor your obedience. I will speak to you. I will guide you. I will meet you in this still place. I promise.

21. holiness

*Therefore, since we have these promises, dear friends, let us purify
ourselves from everything that contaminates body and spirit,
perfecting **holiness** out of reverence for God.*

~ 2 Corinthians 7:1

"We never thought in our wildest dreams that we would ever want to
be a holy person."

When I read these words by spiritual disciplines author Richard Foster,
I was a bit shocked. When did wanting to be holy get such a bad rap? Why
is *holiness* such an unpopular word in our day, smacking of exclusivity?

Doesn't Jesus call us to seek holiness? Of course. And Paul supports that
in our verse: "perfecting holiness out of reverence for God."

And yes, Foster is totally on board: "We never thought in our wildest
dreams that we would ever want to be a holy person. But now that is *exactly* what we long for, to be holy in a strong, winsome, vigorous sense.
Interactive communication with God is becoming a natural way of life,
as is our ability to listen. We are owned by God and we are responding
accordingly."[36]

I guess the question becomes, are you and I seeking holiness? Or are we
worried that we will have to give up happiness in the process?

Counselor Leslie Vernick believes that "God calls us to be holy but He
also made us to be happy. Holiness leads to wholeness and wholeness leads
to happiness."[37]

These admonitions of Paul are not to make us miserable. He exhorts us
to "purify ourselves from everything that contaminates body and spirit"
because that is for our own good—that is what will ultimately make us
whole. And holy. And perhaps, even happy.

How can we master the delicate dance of holiness and authenticity?
How can our behavior be set apart to honor God while we are approachable

human beings obviously in need of grace? I know this is possible or God wouldn't have ordained it so.

Some people argue that living a holy life is harder in the twenty-first century than it was back in the first century. I think that's because we have more choices that are readily available to us; technology opens doors that we can easily slip through without anyone knowing. We are pulled and overloaded. So, yes, it's a challenge.

But it can be done: "In spite of the fact that holiness entails a certain amount of attention to particulars, which can vary enormously from one era or culture to another, it boils down to two foundational underpinnings that hold true for every century: Trust and Obey. The first century heart is the same as the twenty-first century heart—desperately in need of saving, stubbornly selfish—and fairly disinclined to trust and obey God."[38]

So what can we do in order to progress further along this path? Here are two constants: "1. Prayer and Meditation; and 2. Simple Obedience to what He has said."[39]

Trust and obey. There's no other way.

My child, holy does not mean holier-than-thou. The one who lives a set-apart life does the exact opposite of lording over others in a haughty way. If anything, the more godly you are, the more in touch you are with your own unworthiness. But I want you to know that it honors Me when you walk this path. And I will help you every step of the way.

22. ordinary

When they saw the courage of Peter and John and realized that
*they were unschooled, **ordinary** men, they were astonished and*
they took note that these men had been with Jesus.

~ Acts 4:13

She could not have been more ordinary.

Gladys was a poor student and had quit school by age fourteen. She grew up to be a London parlor maid with few prospects. But then God got ahold of her heart, and after hearing about the needs in China, she was determined to serve Him there.

Only no mission board would accept her.

In 1929, China Inland Mission declared she was not qualified and her educational background was too limited. So Gladys Aylward decided to reserve a one-way train ticket to China and every month made a small payment to the travel agency. By age thirty, she was on her way, not knowing where, what, or with whom she would minister but determined to serve God there.

Through a miraculous journey across Russia and many war zones, Gladys arrived in this very foreign country, ready to take on the world. Years later, she said: "I had two childhood heartaches: 1. Everyone else had golden curls and I had short dark hair. 2. Everyone else kept growing but I stopped at four foot ten inches. I always wished things were different. But when I got off the train in China I was shocked to discover that everyone else around me was short with dark hair. I was home."[40]

Gladys's first mission was at the Inn of the Eight Happinesses where she watched over orphans and had a government job of inspecting feet to help educate women on the new law banning foot binding. This gave her an "in" with the community, and from then on she became one of them.

By the time war came, she had adopted several children and bravely escorted hundreds of orphans safely across the mountains and the Yellow

River. There were churches and believers throughout the Shanxi Province when she finally left China.

An ordinary woman living an ordinary life? Perhaps. But her story became a best-selling biography by Alan Burgess: *The Small Woman*.[41] Screen star Ingrid Bergman (who was definitely not short) played Gladys Aylward in the Hollywood movie, *Inn of the Sixth Happiness*.

Most important was her spiritual legacy, of course.

Our God takes an ordinary person and does extraordinary things through her or him.

Peter and John, for instance. In today's Scripture, their courage is applauded at the same time it is observed that "they were unschooled, ordinary men." What was the deciding factor that catapulted them into the extraordinary? "These men had been with Jesus." And it showed.

What could an ordinary person like you (or me) do if we spent more time with Jesus? Short, dark-haired parlor maid Gladys gives us one answer.

What will our story reveal?

My child, you may feel ordinary and nothing special, but I assure you that, to Me, you are uniquely gifted for the life I have planned. As you live out your story on the stage of human reality, you will be supernaturally empowered for extraordinary Kingdom work. And others will notice that you are pointing to Me.

23. abide

Abide in Me, and I in you. As the branch cannot bear fruit of itself unless it abides in the vine, so neither can you unless you abide in Me.

~ John 15:4 NASB

I grew up in south Georgia surrounded by a vine that was lush and green with fragrant blossoms. It also grew like wildfire and was practically impossible to destroy.

Kudzu.

Some of you are nodding in recognition, and others are ignorant of the scourge of this beautiful vine. Evidently, at the 1876 Philadelphia Centennial, the Japanese brought kudzu to their pavilion and the U.S. Soil Conservation Service came up with the bright idea of promoting it as the answer to soil depletion and erosion during the 1920s and 1930s. Which was all fine and good until it took over everything in sight and became "the plant that ate the South."

Though they can be a huge nuisance, vines are also incredibly strong. Kudzu has a tap root that grows down twelve feet, and the vine itself can grow as much as six hundred feet a year. The only way to destroy it is to go underground and cut off the crown root. Whether or not you like kudzu, you have to admire the reach of this vine.

Our Lord, Jesus Christ, called himself the True Vine, and on the long walk to the Garden of Gethsemane, He spent His final conversation with His disciples telling them an allegory about how they as branches needed to stay close to Him.

He called the process "abiding," which is the same thing as dwelling. In fact, this command to abide was so significant that this word is repeated no less than eight times in John 15. Abiding in Christ is living out our union with Him in faith, baptism, love, obedience, and Eucharist. This image of vine and branches reveals that life flows from the Vine to the branches, indicating that our abiding in Christ is not static, but dynamic and vitalizing.

In New Testament Greek, the word *abide* is a present imperative verb, indicating continual action. We must be grafted into the vine for a lifetime. Perhaps that's why I find myself singing quite frequently this favorite hymn: "Abide with me; fast falls the eventide; The darkness deepens; Lord, with me abide; When other helpers fail and comforts flee, Help of the helpless, oh, abide with me."[42]

Mark Batterson says, "We cannot do something for God if we aren't with God." And he elaborates with five reflections of the meaning of abide:

- *To stay overnight*—Sometimes we need to press into the presence of God a little longer.
- *To hold fast*—Every time we pray, we gain a position in the spiritual realm.
- *To stand still*—Sometimes we must stand on the Word of God and trust His promises.
- *To be moved*—We cannot abide in the Word of God and not be moved to action.
- *To tarry*—We must tarry in the Word of God and engage in prayer.[43]

Do you want to be fruitful and strong, and maybe even take over the world with the fragrance of Christ? Then stick close to the crown root of the Vine. Nothing can touch you there.

My child, cling to the Source of all the nutrients you will ever need in order to flourish in life. That's your Vine and I'm here, attached to you all the way. I will give you strength and you will bear fruit. All you need to do is stay close. Abide, dear one.

24. beauty

One thing I ask from the LORD,
*   this only do I seek:*
that I may dwell in the house of the LORD
*   all the days of my life,*
*to gaze on the **beauty** of the* LORD
*   and to seek him in his temple.*

~ Psalm 27:4

I have heard the angels sing.

At least, when I hear our choir, under the superb direction of David Spicer, sing "How Lovely Is Thy Dwelling Place" by Johannes Brahms, I close my eyes and experience all the beauty and peace and serenity of being in Heaven. It seems as though I am actually gazing on the beauty of the Lord in His dwelling place.

Beauty personified will be finally dwelling in the house of the Lord. But He sends us glimpses of that beauty here on earth as well.

I have never seen a field of sunflowers in Tuscany. And I've never been in Texas in the spring when the fields are covered in bluebonnets. But today I saw an outcropping of purple and blue lupines covering the wilderness in Wyoming, and their beauty almost made me cry.

It was a beauty that I first learned to appreciate many years ago on my first trip to Maine—the home of Alice Rumphius, the lupine lady. In her delightful book *Miss Rumphius*, Maine author Barbara Cooney tells of a little girl who so enjoys hearing her grandfather's stories, she declares to him that when she grows up she also wants to go to faraway places and live by the sea.

But he tells her she must do a third thing: "You must do something to make the world more beautiful." Alice had no idea what that could be. She grew up, became a librarian, and traveled to many exotic places. After retiring to a cottage by the sea, one day she noticed a field of lupines and had a grand idea.

All summer Miss Rumphius wandered over the countryside flinging handfuls of lupine seed, despite the fact that people called her "that crazy old lady." But the next spring fields and hillsides were covered with blue and purple lupines. Miss Rumphius had done the third, most difficult thing of all!

This sweet story ends with the elderly "Lupine Lady" telling stories to children in her parlor. As her grandniece talks about traveling and living by the sea herself, her great-aunt Alice exhorts her to do a third thing: "You must do something to make the world more beautiful."[44]

God is the Creator of all beauty.

What will you do to help make your world more beautiful? Both inside and out.

My child, beauty is all around you and calls to your heart. This gift comes from Me but is given so that you might pass it along to others. Everywhere people are affected by the ugliness of the world's sinful choices. What will you do today to offer My beauty to them? Plant those seeds. I'm behind you all the way.

25. gentleness

*Let your **gentleness** show in your treatment of all people. The*
Lord is near.

~ Philippians 4:5 CEB

We welcomed a new baby into our extended family this week. Beatrice is precious and perfect, with ten fingers and ten toes. She is rosy and healthy, for which we are all most grateful. But she is still tiny and fragile.

So everyone treats her with much gentleness.

Even I know to be gentle with newborns. It's with everyone else that I seem to have trouble.

Sometimes I can just hear God admonishing me, "Cindy, take it down a notch." Or, "Lower your voice." Or even, "Keep Calm and Carry On!" (Who says God doesn't quote the British?)

I confess, my default manner is not gentleness. In fact, my tone of voice with all its urgency (I prefer to call it "passion") is sometimes mistaken for harsh instead of enthusiastic. Imagine!

But I long to let my "gentleness show." A soft touch. A whispered endearment. A kind word of encouragement and support.

Often when we think of people who model a depth of spiritual life, we are struck by their gentleness: "Their eyes communicate the residue of solitary battles with angels, the costs of caring for others, the deaths of ambition and ego, and the peace that comes from having very little left to lose in their life."[45]

What if, in our "treatment of all people," we used the same gentle manner with babies and with frail and elderly great-grandmothers? As though they might break if handled too harshly.

The truth is we all break rather easily.

And the louder the words we hear, the more defensive we become. King Solomon knew this quite well when he warned, "A gentle answer deflects anger, / but harsh words make tempers flare" (Proverbs 15:1 NLT). Harsh words can crush a spirit and shut down a soul. Kind words can mend a broken heart or plant a dream.

What gentleness can you offer to others today?

- the clerk at the checkout counter
- the colleague at work
- the unruly child who clamors for attention
- the spouse who is sometimes overlooked

Take heart, no matter whether you are predisposed or not to being a gentle person: "Put on my yoke, and learn from me. I'm gentle and humble. And you will find rest for yourselves" (Matthew 11:29 CEB). With Christ dwelling in us, being yoked to us, we can learn from the best of the best.

Not only is He gentle, but also "The Lord is near."

My child, even though you sometimes feel like "a bull in a china shop," I have great hopes for you cultivating the wonderful gift of the Spirit that is gentleness. The first step is to have a sincere desire toward this kind of treatment of all people. Reach out and discover how I empower you to bless them in ways you cannot even imagine.

26. faithful

*The LORD is trustworthy in all he promises
and faithful in all he does.
The LORD upholds all who fall
and lifts up all who are bowed down.*

~ Psalm 145:13-14

The park ranger promised me it would happen at this exact moment. And as I stood with hundreds of people from all over the world, our long-awaited anticipation was rewarded with a true spectacle.

Old Faithful.

The famous geyser at Yellowstone National Park that erupts about every ninety minutes, shooting up as high as 184 feet, lasting as long as five minutes. Without fail. As I joyfully witnessed the plumes of boiling water and steam bursting skyward in a majestic show of power and beauty, I couldn't help but think of the original Old Faithful.

God.

The One by whom other forces of nature shrink in importance, no matter how predictable they are. Even though God's faithfulness is constant, it is often surprising. There's no scheduling *His* appearance—only that He will be faithful to every promise.

Perhaps you and I are not unlike those Yellowstone tourists—finding ourselves waiting around, thinking we know exactly how and when God will choose to come through with His power and promise. We have set aside this time in our lives and are ready. Only, instead of a prompt appearance, we discover that the God of the Universe will not be managed or manipulated. He is:

- Faithful in putting together families; just not
  always in the traditional fashion.

- Faithful in providing financial resources for our needs; but perhaps not all our wants.
- Faithful in walking beside us through every calamity, though the journey often involves painful detours.

Still, we can rely on His character. Our verse today reminds us that God not only is "faithful in all He does" but also can be trusted to keep His promises. He will lift us up when we fall and help us stay upright when we wobble. When I struggle with faith, I remind myself of the acronym for FAITH I learned so long ago: Forsaking All, I Trust Him.

Where do you need God to be faithful in your life today? Take a moment and write down two areas and then pray over them by singing the familiar hymn "Great Is Thy Faithfulness."

My child, you can trust Me. I have been faithful to countless generations before you, and I shall most certainly be there for those who come after you. You see, I never change. While my ways and my will are not predictable in time and manner, my character remains. Faithful. True. Loving. Merciful. Count on it.

27. trust

*Happy are those who **trust** in the LORD,*
   who rely on the LORD.
They will be like trees planted by the streams,
   whose roots reach down to the water.
They won't fear drought when it comes;
   their leaves will remain green.
They won't be stressed in the time of drought
   or fail to bear fruit.

~ Jeremiah 17:7-8 CEB

Let's face it, the prophet Jeremiah may have had some trust issues. And for a good reason.

This man was called to the unenviable prophetic ministry of urging the rebellious Israelites to repentance for nearly fifty years without any significant positive response! How could he trust those who publically humiliated him, put him in the stocks, threw him in a cistern, and forced him to flee for his life? On top of all that, he was grossly misunderstood.

He learned that trusting other people, favorable outcomes, or popular numbers was a dead end. And so he trusted God. He remained faithful to his calling as a prophet and endured discouragement and pain to the end.

His wrestling is why Jeremiah could write such life-giving words to us today about the benefits of trusting God. He is worthy. We can truly "rely on the Lord." And when we make a conscious effort to place our trust in the Lord—not people, not institutions, not things—we exhibit the same strength as trees planted by streams:

- We have a deep root system for nourishment.
- We are not afraid of drought.
- We are not stressed by circumstances.
- We are always fruitful.

Do you find it hard to trust these days? Or is your trust misplaced? If so, when replenishing rains stop, you will dry up and stress out, and your efforts will become fruitless.

What is the alternative? To stay near to the Source of life, just as trees do when they are planted by streams. Because their roots go deep, the lack of surface rain (outward circumstances) has no derogatory effect. They remain green.

I want to stay fresh and fruitful. Would you also like to dwell in trust?

Perhaps a study of the original Old Testament Hebrew word here will reveal something helpful. In Hebrew the word for "to trust" is *chacah*, a verb which literally means to seek refuge or put trust in God. Its noun form, *machacah*, is actually interchangeable with our English word *refuge*. So when we speak of trust, we are also speaking of a safe dwelling place.

One of my friends discovered that refuge of trust as her dying husband began to receive hospice care. She shares that singing this simple song helped: "Trusting as the moments fly, Trusting as the days go by, Trusting Him what'er befall, Trusting Jesus, that is all. Singing if my way be clear, Praying if the path be drear; If in danger, for Him call, Trusting Jesus, that is all."[46]

I somehow think Jeremiah would approve.

❧

My child, there are many who seek your trust. But they make promises they cannot keep. They will let you down and then toss you aside. But you can trust Me. You can find your refuge in My place of nourishment, if you stay close to Me. It is a simple choice, even though it's not an easy one. Just as Jeremiah. But always know you are right. I am here. Trust Me.

28. sanctuary

I pray that the LORD answers you whenever you are in trouble.
    Let the name of Jacob's God protect you.
*Let God send help to you from the **sanctuary***
    and support you from Zion.

~ Psalm 20:1-2 CEB

"Sanctuary! Sanctuary! Sanctuary!" yelled Quasimodo from the top of Notre Dame Cathedral after rescuing the gypsy Esmeralda. He thought she would finally be safe in the sanctuary of the Cathedral. Sadly, he was wrong.

What a memorable scene from Victor Hugo's *The Hunchback of Notre Dame*—and the catalyst for me first learning about the medieval sanctuary law. Criminals or debtors who wanted to escape arrest could plead for asylum at a cathedral if they arrived before being caught by authorities. At the point of entry, the bell was rung in order to announce that a felon sought sanctuary.

Governments recognized sanctuary laws for several centuries throughout Europe, but due to many instances of violation the laws disappeared by the seventeenth century. Countries had adopted the ancient belief that sacred spaces were impenetrable. Someone "in sanctuary" had entered a holy place that could not be violated, and under its influence, he might spiritually transform.

> Once inside, the criminal confessed his crime to a priest, surrendered his weapons, paid a nominal fee, and donned a black gown. He lived in a railed-off alcove above the southwest tower, and within thirty-seven days decided whether to stand trial or leave the country. If a criminal chose to "quit the kingdom," the law afforded him nine days to exit England's borders, traveling solely on the king's highways. For the journey, he wore nothing on his head and a long white robe. He carried a wooden cross.[47]

What does this ancient custom have to do with us in the twenty-first century? There are biblical parallels, as evidenced in our Scripture today. Here the psalmist is praying for someone in trouble, that they may receive help and protection—sanctuary—from God. And sanctuary was key in the rescue of the children of Israel: "You will bring them in and plant them / on the mountain of your inheritance— / the place, LORD, you made for your dwelling, / the sanctuary, Lord, your hands established" (Exodus 15:17).

What are you running from? Where are you running to?

Do you believe that the God of grace will open wide the door and welcome you in? "He accepts us however we arrive: sweaty from the escape, wild-eyed with fear, the blood-stench of crime on our sleeves, and doubting that sanctuary from sin—our haunting spiritual crimes—actually exists. But God doesn't banish us from His kingdom or force us to stand trial. Wearing robes of white, carrying the sign of the cross—the mark of the King's forgiveness—we can begin again."[48]

Today most of us use *sanctuary* to refer to a sacred place, like our house of worship. But it has also come to mean a safe haven—whether for animals, refugees, or other asylum seekers. As you think of those who need a "safe haven," share with them God's divine plan of rescue and sanctuary.

━━━━━━━━━━━━━━━━━━━━━━
∾⟡⟆

My child. Many are running from the consequences of a life of bad choices, or perhaps just bad luck. And they often seek shelter from those who want to use their desperation to exploit them. But I offer sanctuary to all who will come and seek a new life, a fresh start with Me. Yes, I will hear those calls for help and open wide the door. You know where I am. Tell them.

29. rest

My people will live in peaceful dwelling places,
  in secure homes,
  in undisturbed places of rest.

~ Isaiah 32:18

Driving through Pebble Hill Plantation I saw the road sign that caused me to grind to a halt: "Slow Down. I Mean It!"

Pansy Poe, the owner of this beautiful estate outside my Georgia hometown, had signed her name to give it more authority.

Actually, God could have authored that sign as well.

I believe He sends signs warning me to "slow down" all the time, but I'm usually running by too quickly to notice. According to our verse today, He longs for His people to dwell in slowness and peacefulness and security and rest.

Or, as one seasoned pastor advises, "You must ruthlessly eliminate hurry."

When was the last time you really rested? Hard to do, isn't it? Our environment is constantly depleting us with noise, distractions, and the compulsion to always be in a hurry. We are just too busy to rest.

"Busyness does not mean you are a faithful or fruitful Christian. It only means that you are busy, just like everyone else," claims a young pastor and father of six who struggles with finding true rest. "It's not wrong to be tired. It's not wrong to feel overwhelmed. It's not wrong to go through seasons of complete chaos. What is wrong—and heartbreakingly foolish and wonderfully avoidable—is to live a life with more craziness than we want because we have less Jesus than we need."[49]

Do you want more of Jesus and His rest?

I believe our greatest threat is distraction. Did you know the root of this word is the Latin word *distractus*, which literally means "to draw or pull apart"? No wonder we feel torn in every direction!

The author of *Sanctuary of the Soul* says that we have noisy hearts: "The fact that our schedules are piled high and we are constantly bombarded by multiple stimuli only betrays that we have succumbed to the modern mania that keeps us perpetually distracted. The moment we seek to enter the creative silences of meditative prayer, every demand screams for our attention."[50]

How can we quiet our hearts and discover these "undisturbed places of rest"?

Unplug. Sign out. Turn off. Hang up. Be "closed for the weekend." Clean up your surroundings so fewer projects call out your name. Put sleep and "nothing" on your agenda and then keep those appointments. Determine your greatest distractions and energy-drainers and decide to be proactive about curbing their power over you.

And then go to Jesus and rest in His care: "Faith means resting—relying—not on who we are, or what we can do, or how we feel or what we know. Faith is resting in who God is and what He has done. And He has done everything."[51]

Slow down. I mean it!

❧

My child, I long to give you rest, but you need to stop what you're doing in order to receive this gift. The world simply cannot offer the security and peace that your soul craves. But if you deliberately choose this life, it will become possible. Take the first step now. Just breathe. Relax. I've got it covered. Rest, dear one, rest.

30. same

*Jesus Christ is the **same** yesterday, today, and forever!*
~ Hebrews 13:8 CEB

"I just wish everything would stay the same. I'm so tired of change I could scream!" was a comment I overheard recently while standing in line at the computer store.

Oh, yeah.

On a recent trip to Seattle, our family discovered huge changes since we last lived there about thirty years ago. Renting a condo in the same cozy little Scandinavian neighborhood of Ballard—our home when the kids were little—was an eye-opener. More people everywhere, largely thanks to companies such as Microsoft, Expedia, and Amazon moving in. There were more cars on the streets and constant traffic. Sky-high real estate prices. Endless recreational choices. And wealth. Lots of wealth.

My husband, a Washington native, found himself longing for the Seattle of the past. But change is here to stay. Pretty much everywhere.

Except for our Lord who remains "the same yesterday, today, and forever!"

In our turbulent world full of crisis and upheaval, nothing seems permanent. In a culture that seems to be drifting politically, economically, personally, and spiritually, Jesus Christ is our only secure anchor. He is ever the same—immutable: "I the LORD do not change" (Malachi 3:6). He is everlastingly "the Father of heavenly lights, with whom is no variableness, neither shadow of turning" (James 1:17 NASB).

But we are fickle people. We tend to change jobs, churches, spouses, and even worldviews as often as we change clothes. How we long for something that lasts, that can be counted on! "How we long to point to something—anything—and say, 'This works! This is sure!' But if it is something other than God Himself we are destined for disappointment. There is only one ultimate guarantee. It is the love of Christ. The love of Christ."[52]

And if you know this love—have this love deep in your heart—you can face the changes that come, without looking back in regret or looking forward in anxiety.

One of my favorite hymns declares, "Before the hills in order stood, Or earth received her frame, From everlasting Thou art God, To endless years the same."[53]

Andrew Murray confirms, "All that He was yesterday, He is today. All that He has been on His throne, in sending down His Spirit, in working mighty things in and on behalf of His Church, in revealing Himself in joy unspeakable to trusting soul, in meeting and blessing you who read this He is today. All that He is, He can be to you today."[54]

My child. I know it would be more comfortable if you never had to adjust to changes and seasons. And yet that is the nature of the world in which you are called to live. The great news is that you have Someone who you can count on to always be the same. I will be with you to help you navigate all the new. Count on it.

shine

ADVENT

~~~~~~~~~~~~~~~~~~~~~~~~~~~~~~~~~~~~~~

Jesus our Lord,
By the virtue of Thy grace,
*In the **shining** of Thy glory*
Let us see Thy face.

~ Amy Carmichael
"The Glory of That Light"

1. thankful

*Let us be **thankful**, and so worship God acceptably with reverence and awe.*

~ Hebrews 12:28

To me, thankfulness is not so much an act as an orientation.

Each day we are encouraged to face what life brings, receive it, and, no matter how challenging, give thanks. According to our verse today, this act of gratitude helps us "worship God acceptably with reverence and awe."

Thanksgiving is a good time to renew our faith in God's goodness: "We can speak all the lofty phrases we want about God's sovereign goodness, but the proof is in the thanking. The Bible tells us to give thanks *for* all things and *in* all things. Only thankfulness on this scale is an incontestable sign we believe what we say."[1]

The daily discipline of thanking God can change a life.

Just ask Ann Voskamp, author of the *New York Times* best-selling *One Thousand Gifts*. She believes that remembering to give thanks is the crux of Christianity: "For months of naming blessings, these words have spurred me on, that gratitude was the preeminent attitude of the Christ-follower. But I had never seen that gratitude truly is the foremost quality of a believing disciple precisely because gratitude is what births trust . . . the true belief."[2]

A life of *eucharisteo* becomes a choice. That Greek word is translated "to be grateful; to give thanks." We can choose to whine, grumble, complain, or even just neglect looking for God's good gifts. Or we can discipline ourselves to recognize them. The more we do it, the more naturally we do it: "When we practice giving thanks, we practice the presence of God and it is always a practice of the eyes. We don't have to change what we see. Only the way we see."[3]

This year Sharol Hayner will be facing her first Thanksgiving and Christmas alone. Over the last year of her husband's life, she chose to practice thankfulness:

Even in the worst of times, there is always something for which to be thankful. Today I'm thankful for an amazing hospice doctor who comes and sits with us and explains what's going on physically for Steve but also asks questions about our emotional and spiritual journeys. I'm grateful for e-mails and texts from so many who have felt nudged to pray for us. Yes, it's a time for grief, but it's also a time for gratitude. As one friend says, grief and gratitude mixed together create joy. How true this is.[4]

Will you make an effort to live thankfully today? During the Advent season? All year?

- Set a goal to notice and announce/record three of God's gifts each day.
- Keep out a large jar filled with paper slips of recorded thanks.
- Make simple ornaments for your tree, commemorating God's special gifts this year.
- Give to someone else who is needy, as an expression of thanks to God.
- Worship God with thanksgiving.

"Praise to the Lord! O let all that is in me adore him! All that hath life and breath, come now with praises before him. Let the amen sound from his people again; gladly forever adore him."[5]

My child, when you choose a lifestyle of thanksgiving, you honor and glorify Me. You also show the world that outer circumstances do not dictate your inner beliefs. Thank you for trusting that I am indeed in control and the good Giver of all.

2. shine

*Let your light **shine** before others, that they may see your good
deeds and glorify your Father in heaven.*

~ Matthew 5:16

I don't want to just survive the holidays; I want to *shine.*

Don't you want the season to be different this year? Not as hectic or
harried? Not as full of stress and "shoulds"? More purposeful and peaceful?
Brighter and more beautiful, but in a low-key way? I'm thinking of words
like *simplicity* and *serenity.*

You, too?

Ready to let go of the debt and duty. Happy to keep the lights and
shimmer. In fact, I want every single corner to shine, not necessarily with
a designer tree or sequined sweater, but with sweet contentment. In thinking of such possibilities, my heart bursts into praise: "Shine, Jesus. Shine.
Fill this land with the Father's glory."

But, of course, my deepest prayer is, "Shine on me."

For until I am filled with that light inside, I can never reflect it to those
around me. Or, as the apostle Paul put it, "Nothing between us and God,
our faces shining with the brightness of his face. And so we are transfigured
much like the Messiah, our lives gradually becoming brighter and more
beautiful as God enters our lives and we become like him" (2 Corinthians
3:18 MSG).

In *Finding the Messiah*, author Jane Rubietta observes,

> If you have arrived at Advent, at the coming, with doubts,
> dragging chains of disbelief, disenchantment, and discourage-
> ment, welcome. You are not alone. And if you enter this season
> with a harried heart and a furrowed brow, welcome. You are
> not alone. If your moanings feel louder than the quiet, subtle
> hope tucked behind the noise of the world's Christmas season,

then welcome. You are not alone. And that's the good news, isn't it? That in this darkness, in this aching nighttime, we are not alone. Christ comes. Christ pierces the darkness with His light.[6]

Our dwelling place is God's presence. Out of that place of refueling and reigniting, we then go forth to mingle with a damaged and desperate culture. "Among these people you shine like stars in the world" (Philippians 2:15 CEB).

One symbolic way our family enjoys keeping the shine in our season is the tradition of lighting candles each day. Advent wreaths can be purchased at hobby stores and gift shops. But all you really need is a circle of four candles and a place in the middle for the Christ candle. Candles can be any color, or you can use the traditional colors of three purple/blue and one pink. Each week, a new candle is lit. The first Sunday, we light a purple candle for Hope; the second Sunday, another purple candle for Love; the third Sunday, the pink candle for Joy; the fourth Sunday, a purple candle for Peace; and on Christmas Eve, the center white candle for Christ. With each lighting, we read Scripture and sing a Christmas carol.

Decide today how you will choose to spend these next weeks. As you focus on each of our Advent words, may you discover all the places God will brighten your world.

෨ඏ෪

My child, in My eyes, you already shine beautifully. Because I see what's inside you. But I know you also want to be a bright light in your home and workplace, your church and community during this special time of year. Draw near to Me each day and you will shine. Go ahead, light the candle.

3. emmanuel

*"Look, the virgin shall conceive and bear a son,
and they shall name him, **Emmanuel**,"
which means, "God is with us."*

~ Matthew 1:23 NRSV

She had arrived at the retreat with a friend. On the very first night I could tell she felt out of place, perhaps wondering how this gathering of women would unpack our topic, "Breathe—Making Space for God in Your Full Life." I longed for her—and all of us—to grasp that God "is with us" all the time!

So, in the opening session, as I laid out the foundation of our need to draw close to the One who loves us most, an image came into my thoughts from a children's book, *Winnie the Pooh*.[7]

> One of my favorite scenes in the Pooh stories is when little Piglet sidles up to Pooh and grasps his hand. When Pooh asks what's up, Piglet merely responds, "I just wanted to be sure of you."
>
> Friends, tonight God is longing for you to come close and put your hand in His. To be sure that He's there by your side—even on those days when you feel most alone.

I closed the session and during refreshments was surprised to find that same visitor making a beeline for me. Tired from travel, I nonetheless looked her in the eye and opened my heart to whatever challenges or questions she might have.

"How did you know?" she asked.

Puzzled, I watched as she slowly hiked up her pants leg to reveal a large tattoo covering her entire calf. It was that very illustration from the original *Winnie the Pooh* book—when Piglet is holding Pooh's hand!

"Now I *know* I'm supposed to be here," she said.

By the end of the weekend she, too, had reached for the lifeline—God's hand.

Aren't you grateful that ours is not a distant God who simply looks down from heaven and, seeing His creation struggling, shouts words of encouragement to hang in there?

Instead, He actually came down to be with us and hold our hand. In the form of tiny, helpless baby Jesus.

Emmanuel—God with us.

While singing "O Come, O Come, Emmanuel," one woman reflected,

> How many people standing here in this church are trying to stand through cancer and divorce and debt and the sharp edge of life that's cutting their heart right open and they're singing through this Christmas, but they're really bleeding quiet? We sing it like a plea, "O come, O come, Emmanuel" . . . God with us and for us and in us and holding us and this is the Christmas miracle that outlasts all of time. The miracle of Christmas is that we get more than proof of God's existence. We get the experience of God's presence.[8]

You can experience God with you today. Just sidle up to Him and reach for His hand.

৩৩৫

My child, I love you that much. To send My only Son down to earth to live among you so that you would know that I know. And We are with you even now—the Father, Son and Holy Spirit—through a mystery of incarnation. So, even when you're the one searching or hurting, keep singing. And I will come.

4. wait

But me! I will keep watch for the LORD;
*I will **wait** for the God of my salvation;*
my God will hear me.

~ Micah 7:7 CEB

Imagine waiting more than four hundred years for an answer to prayer!

That's what God's chosen people had to do—waiting in the dark, hoping for deliverance. Perhaps singing their own version of "Come, Thou long expected Jesus, born to set Thy people free; from our fears and sins release us, let us find our rest in Thee."[9]

In between the Old Testament and the New Testament, the heavens seemed closed to the nation of Israel. God appeared to be silent. They thought nothing was happening. And certainly their prayers for a Messiah seemed to fall on deaf ears.

Yet, in reality, God was still at work, bringing about the perfect political and religious setting for the appearance of His Son. Because the Romans were in power, Jesus was put to death in response to Jewish religious factions of the day. Because Christ came at that exact time, the highway system of Rome allowed the message of His resurrection to spread. And through the writing of the New Testament in the Greek language, the Gospel was proclaimed in a tongue nearly everyone could understand.

God's timing is always best. Even if it means we have to wait. We can be assured that "God will hear me."

During those waiting years, the Jews were unwilling subjects of the Roman Empire. They wanted more than just limited freedom to worship and hope. As they read the prophecies of the Old Testament, they dreamed of the Messiah who would finally restore them to a powerful nation as in the time of King David. Surely this person would be a mighty warrior, a strong and larger-than-life hero!

No one was looking for a helpless, newborn baby.

What are you waiting for these days?

For that feeling to go away? You know, the one that keeps reminding you that you're not enough and never will be, the one where you are searching for something that will make everything else fall into place, but it's just beyond reach.

God knows. He desires good things for us, but often His timing is not in sync with ours:

> We orient our lives to speed. We want faster computers, fast food, instant coffee. We want what we want now, so waiting becomes hard. Waiting in our prayer life and waiting for Christmas become disciplines we return to every December. For what do we wait? Do we wait for a baby to be born? Do we wait for peace to dwell in the whole world and in our fractured, busy lives? Do we wait for the rebirth of joy, a rekindling of hope?[10]

Here are some steps I find helpful during those excruciating waiting times:

- **W**rite down your prayers and concerns for this situation.
- **A**ssure God you truly desire His will in His way.
- **I**ntercede in prayer for others you know who are also waiting.
- **T**ake the next step that has been made clear to you.

Keep watch. God will show up.

My child, the waiting process is excruciating, isn't it? Whether it's just one day waiting for test results, or four hundred years waiting for rescue, it's all about clinging to the promise. My Word is full of promises for you—some you may have already realized, others will potentially be fulfilled in days ahead. But don't waste your wait. I'm coming.

5. genealogy

*This is the **genealogy** of Jesus the Messiah . . .*
    Salmon the father of Boaz, whose mother was Rahab,
    Boaz the father of Obed, whose mother was Ruth,
    Obed the father of Jesse,
    and Jesse the father of King David.
David was the father of Solomon, whose mother had been Uriah's
wife.

~ Matthew 1:1, 5-7

In the South where I grew up, everyone cared about who your "people" were.

And they had all the patience in the world to hear every single detail of the family tree. Fortunately, my Mama and my Mamalu (that's what I called my maternal grandmother whose "people" lived in a house next to the Big Oak, our hometown's most important landmark) were experts at researching and recording genealogy.

I discovered that our family was sufficiently documented for me to be eligible as a Daughter of the American Revolution (DAR) and as a member of the more elite Colonial Dames.

I say all this because I know that some of you like to skim over the Matthew account of the genealogy of Christ. And yet, this list is rich with story and meaning, just like the Secrests, Hastys, and Chastains of my own kin. These names were put in the Bible for a reason, though we may actually find a few of them a bit shocking.

Jesus' "people" were a mixed bunch. And yet, God chose each one of them for His family. Let's consider three women in this list—perhaps an unlikely group of mothers. Boaz was the child of Rahab and Salmon. Yes, that Rahab, the harlot. The one who helped Joshua and Caleb escape and thus saved her family during the fall of Jericho. Rahab turned from her former life of running a house of ill repute inside the city wall, to being a God-honoring wife and mother.

Her son, Boaz, married a foreigner, Ruth the Moabite, who was a widow from an alien culture. Yet she was willing to risk being a stranger in a strange land in order to support her mother-in-law, Naomi, one of Boaz's relatives. Thus, she, too, began a new life and commitment to God, and she gave birth to Obed. Obed's son was Jesse, whose son was David, the shepherd boy who grew up to be king.

And we all know that David, though "a man after God's own heart," was not perfect. In fact, it was from his union with Uriah's wife, Bathsheba, that his son Solomon was born. Bathsheba made mistakes and paid dearly with the loss of her first child by David but is still counted as worthy in the lineage of Christ.

Families are imperfect but still can be used in God's plan. Something else we find in the South is that there can be a whole extended family made up of folks who aren't exactly related, sometimes known as "kissin' kin."

"All my childhood friends had aunts and uncles who weren't really kin, as well as people who joined their people on every family occasion, so much so one tended to forget they weren't linked by blood. There are wide-reaching benefits to this familial fluidity, not the least of which is what it teaches our children. That the safety net is large. That love isn't confined."[11]

Whether officially your "people" or just "kissin' kin," open the doors wide and embrace them all.

❧

My child, if you know Me as your Heavenly Father, then you are in My forever family. And this family was not built on bloodlines, but on each person's salvation through the blood of Christ. My love is not confined to those who can document wealth or intelligence or royalty. Everyone has the same opportunity to come to the family reunion. Go out and invite them.

6. bethlehem

*As for you, **Bethlehem** . . .*
>   *though you are the least significant of Judah's forces,*
>>   *one who is to be a ruler in Israel on my behalf will come*
out from you.
>   *His origin is from remote times, from ancient days.*
>>   ~ Micah 5:2 CEB

Visiting Bethlehem was a shock. The barbed-wire fences and armed guards. The poverty and hunger and desperate beggars. The crumbled buildings and shattered lives that lay as debris from a decades-long struggle of Arab versus Jew.

"What happened to 'O little town of Bethlehem, how still we see thee lie?'" I wondered, two thousand years after the birth of Christ.

But Bethlehem has always defied expectations. The prophet Micah, speaking seven hundred years before the nativity, pointed out that this village was definitely on the bottom of the must-see list in Judah—"least significant." And yet today, thousands still make the pilgrimage to the site of the holy birth, now marked by the Church of the Nativity.

People like me, praying, "Turn us again to the place when, with quietness You wrap up Your truth and promise, Your love and salvation in the Child born in a rude stable . . . Bring us to Bethlehem, to the place where He was homeless but where we are truly at home."[12]

In that one moment God chose to elevate the lowly. His plan defied both reason and protocol. Instead of a major city, He chose a rural village in which to send the "ruler" who was a baby instead of a warrior king. Yet how appropriate that the One who said, "I am the bread of life" (John 6:35), should be born in Bethlehem, whose name means "house of bread."

What can Bethlehem symbolize for us this season?

Do you sometimes feel small? Is your day filled with tasks that appear to be insignificant? Were you once told you'd never amount to anything?

Take heart. If the Creator and Sustainer of the universe can choose a small town as the setting for the birthday of a King, then He most certainly can choose you and me to make a difference for the Kingdom in countless ways.

Or perhaps you feel you are in the wrong location. You were never meant to end up here. I often wonder if Mary felt that way when she had to lay Jesus in a feeding trough because they had traveled to be counted in a census: "But our God is so big that He even uses the decrees of pagan governments to accomplish His purposes, so the birth of the Savior happens in the very place prophesied about centuries before. God is never surprised by inns with no vacancy."[13]

Today Bethlehem is a divided town, full of turmoil and confusion. It was not always so. And shall not always be. Let us continue to make our Advent journey to Bethlehem.

It may yet shine again with light—a dwelling place for the homeless soul.

"Yet in thy dark streets shining, the everlasting Light. The hopes and fears of all the years, Are met in thee tonight."[14]

My child, my Light still shines in dark places. I have not forgotten Bethlehem, even in its darkest days. And I will not forget you. No matter how small and insignificant you may feel, to Me you are important. Take heart as you remember that amazing plan that made Bethlehem unforgettable. And know I am the same God to you today.

7. gift

*Thanks be to God for his indescribable **gift**!*

~ 2 Corinthians 9:15

There is at least one Christmas gift incident I'd rather forget.

At least I'm ashamed at the immature and selfish way I handled it. You see, after much thought and sacrificial financial investment, I gave someone what I believed to be the perfect Christmas present.

And that person didn't like it.

Well, at least they didn't respond in the glowing appreciative manner I had envisioned. In my disappointment I confess that I sulked, hosted a self-pity party, and vowed to give that person just a brown paper bag next year. "Who needs gift-giving anyway?" I muttered.

Who indeed?

God, the One who started the whole thing, after all, by sending His only Son as a Gift to us at Christmas, decided to teach me a few things. He reminded me that the very essence of a gift is that the giver wants to bestow it on someone with no strings attached. No promise to use it or wear it or play it; no reciprocal gift; and no obligatory thank-you note of appreciation.

In other words, a gift is *free*!

Can I truly give like that this Christmas? Can you?

While our gift-giving shouldn't be contingent on a favorable response or appreciation, most of the time people do express their thanks. But that's just icing on the cake. At Christmas, we receive the best Gift of all—Jesus! God loved us so much that He gave His Son (John 3:16). God is a giver, for sure. It's part of His nature: "every good and perfect gift is from above" (James 1:17).

Rather than list the gifts you *want* this year, why not write a list of the gifts you *have* already received—from both God and others? Then make two responses:

First, thank Him for your many gifts. One way is to write Him a thank-you note in your journal or on your nicest stationery.

Second, offer yourself as a gift back to the Giver: "What can I give him, poor as I am? If I were a shepherd, I would bring a lamb; if I were a Wise Man, I would do my part; yet what can I give him: give my heart."[15]

Yes, this is indeed a time for gifts.

My child, I know that you delight in gift-giving during this festive season. But I want to caution you to keep a perspective on why you are giving: as an expression of love and care rather than a need to be recognized. Creative gifting is also way to honor Me by not going into debt. You have already received the Best Gift of all. Now, give yourself to others.

8. song

*I will praise God's name with **song**;*
I will magnify him with thanks.

~ Psalm 69:30 CEB

Sometimes a song can save a life.

Just ask Ira Sankey, longtime song leader for nineteenth-century evangelist Dwight L. Moody. He will never forget one Christmas Eve as he was traveling by steamboat up the Delaware River when someone asked him to sing. As Sankey sang "Saviour, Like a Shepherd Lead Us," a man with a rough, weather-beaten face came up to him.

"Mr. Sankey, did you ever serve in the Union Army?"

After he answered in the affirmative, the man continued, "And were you possibly doing picket duty on a moonlit night in 1862?"

Much surprised, Sankey falteringly answered, "Why yes." The stranger said,

> So was I, but I was serving in the Confederate Army. When I saw you at your post I raised my musket and took aim. I was standing in a shadow, but you were lit by the moon. At that instant, you raised your eyes to heaven and began to sing, and I took my finger off the trigger. "Might as well let the guy sing before I kill him."
>
> The song you sang then was the same one you just now sang, "We are Thine, do Thou befriend us, Be the guardian of our way." When you had finished singing, it was impossible for me to take aim at you again. I thought, "The Lord who is able to save that man from certain death must surely be great and mighty" and my arm dropped to my side.

Needless to say, Ira Sankey spent the rest of his life singing.[16]

Are you celebrating Advent each day with a song? If not, why not? There are so many wonderful Christmas carols that have come to us through the years, and every time we sing one, we do exactly what our text encourages today: "praise God's name with song" and "magnify him with thanks."

My family loves Christmas carols, and they play in our home constantly during the season. In our annual Family Christmas Interview, I ask several questions from each family member. About five years ago, one of the questions was, "What is your favorite line from a Christmas carol?" McDowell family answers were:

- **Mike**—"And our eyes at last shall see Him, through His own redeeming love."
- **Cindy**—"The hopes and fears of all the years are met in Thee tonight."
- **Justin**—"He rules the world with truth and grace!"
- **Tim**—"Christ by highest heaven adored, Christ the everlasting Lord!"
- **Fiona**—"Truly He taught us to love one another, His law is love and His Gospel is peace."
- **Maggie**—"A thrill of hope the weary world rejoices, for yonder breaks a new and glorious morn!"
- **All**—"Fa la la la la, la la la la!"

What would you favorite line be? Think about it. Then sing the whole carol, including every single verse, aloud to the Lord. It may just save your soul—if not your life—today.

My child, music is one of My most favorite creations, and I long for it to fill your heart and your life, especially during this season. When you sing, you share of My faithfulness and cause others to ponder the true meaning of Christmas. So, let go of inhibitions and join in the throng through the years. Alleluia! Amen!

9. glorifies

And Mary said:
"My soul **glorifies** *the Lord*
    and my spirit rejoices in God my Savior,
for he has been mindful
    of the humble state of his servant.
From now on all generations will call me blessed,
    for the Mighty One has done great things for me—
    holy is his name."

~ Luke 1:46-49

Listening to the freshman girls talking at school, I'm struck with how young, naive, and self-absorbed they seem. As a substitute teacher, I'm pretty "invisible" and thus privy to all sorts of conversation around me, some of it shockingly graphic. Yet I am also overcome with a tenderness that wants to spare them the awkward and scary process of growing up.

Then it suddenly hits me that they are the same age as Mary was when the angel Gabriel announced she would be the mother of the Savior of the world.

Which makes Mary's response in our verse today all the more amazing.

Today's Scripture is part of Mary's *Magnificat*—also known as the "Canticle of Mary" or "Ode of the Theotokos." *Magnificat* is a Latin word that means "my soul magnifies or glorifies." These beautiful words occur during Mary's visit to her cousin Elizabeth when she is praised for her faith. Mary turns all the praise back to God.

Earlier He sent the angel Gabriel to tell her that, though she is a virgin, she will conceive by the Holy Spirit and bear the Son of God, calling Him Jesus. At first, Mary's response is what we might guess, "How will this be since I am a virgin?" (Luke 1:34). But upon further explanation that "nothing is impossible with God," Mary submits in obedience, "I am the Lord's servant. May your word to me be fulfilled" (Luke 1:38).

As a girl, I learned the Westminster Shorter Catechism, which begins with the question, "What is the chief end of man?" The answer? "To glorify God and enjoy Him forever." This foundational tenet of the faith has stayed with me my whole life.

Have you ever asked the question, "How can I glorify God?"

Here is the answer I've discovered through my spiritual journey. I bring God glory when I do something that could never be done without His power and presence inside me. Then, since it was so obviously God and not myself, He is glorified.

I'm a hot mess, an ordinary person, a sinner. Alone, I blow it, but with God in me, I am empowered to do that which will point to Him and His glory.

"In the blink of an eye, Mary was taken out of her ordinary life. . . . Her spirit rejoiced and her soul proclaimed God's greatness. Joy bubbled up from her innermost being. She had a role in salvation's story."[17]

In the novel *Two Steps Forward*, Mara has made many bad choices and tells her spiritual director that she's not perfect. Katherine replies, "None of us are. That's what grace is all about. But like Mary, you've received a very special calling from God. Like Mary, you've been chosen to be the dwelling place of the Most High. By God's grace. God's favor."[18]

What has God called you to be and do? How will you glorify Him?

My child, you are not so different from that teenaged Mary I called so long ago. She had no idea that I would fill her with My Son and My Spirit. But she believed that I in her could accomplish the impossible. I can do that through you as well. And the world will witness My glory.

10. celebrate

*Let's have a feast and **celebrate**.*

~ Luke 15:23

I missed my thirty-second birthday celebration.

And if there ever was a year I needed a party, that was it.

In the preceding months I had become a wife for the first time, moved a thousand miles north from San Francisco to Seattle, adopted three children, and was about to observe my first wedding anniversary while my husband was at a ministry meeting in Texas!

May 23 dawned rainy as usual in my new Northwest home as I drove four-year-old Fiona to her playgroup—a wonderful gathering of little girls from our church who played together with two different moms each week.

This particular week Sharol was the hostess, and since someone else was the helper I didn't even consider going inside with Fiona. I was too busy having a pity party.

So I drove to a nearby cafe and spent two hours drinking coffee and working myself into a grand depression: *No one loves me, no one understands me, and no one knows it is my birthday in this new place.*

Imagine my horror when I picked up Fiona and discovered that Sharol and the other moms had put together a lovely brunch to honor me on my first birthday in Seattle! Of course, it was a surprise party, and by the time my little girl walked into the house where everyone was waiting, I was already in the car and not to be found (no cell phones back then).

I missed the celebration!

The beauty, the food, the caring, the love, the gifts—they were all there especially for me, but I was too caught up in myself and my own neediness to be present.

Soon we will celebrate the birthday of Jesus Christ.

The expectations of the season are that we be full of joy and festivity with lots of gifts to give and people to remember us in special ways. But for some folks it has been a hard year. It might be easier to just crawl off into a corner and host a pity party.

Don't do it!

Don't miss this celebration because it's for you. God gave us the ultimate Gift of His Son, Jesus Christ, to show us His great love!

This is our party. We are the recipients of this most treasured Gift. But we have to show up, accept God's offering to us, and then bask in His love.

What are the temptations each Christmas that might cause you to miss the joy and wonder of it all? Ask God to help you focus on others and not just your own situation.

Will you carve out moments to sit by a fire and listen to Christmas music or read a classic Christmas story or attend a candlelight service? If you realistically accept your own limits for where you are now, then you will be better prepared to intentionally celebrate the birth of Christ in the ways you find most meaningful and most satisfying.

Don't forget to celebrate!

〰〰

My child, sometimes it seems easier to avoid others and hide away, licking your wounds. And yet, your world is full of people who want to care and help, but perhaps you need to take the first step. Go to that neighborhood gathering or church event or maybe ask a new acquaintance out for coffee. Do the things that cause your heart to celebrate My birth. For I am now here for you. Forever. Don't miss it.

11. afraid

*An angel from the Lord appeared to him in a dream and said,
"Joseph son of David, don't be **afraid** to take Mary as your
wife, because the child she carries was conceived by the Holy
Spirit."*

~ Matthew 1:20 CEB

Joseph was scandalized.

He had just learned that his fiancé, Mary (with whom he had not had intimate relations), was pregnant. And full of joy.

It was the ultimate betrayal and mockery of him as an honorable man. She could actually have been subjected to punishment by stoning. But something in Joseph still loved Mary and "because he didn't want to humiliate her, he decided to call off their engagement quietly" (Matthew 1:19 CEB). If he had followed through with this, the Christmas story would have been totally different.

God sent an angel to Joseph to convince him of the miracle that was in progress and offered these words: "don't be afraid to take Mary as your wife." Perhaps it wasn't so much that Joseph was "scared" as that he felt embarrassed, ostracized, and shamed.

Isn't this what happens when we become the brunt of malicious gossip? Fear steps in and offers us any excuse for a way out.

"Don't be afraid" (or "fear not") is a favorite message sent by God through angels, not only to Joseph, but perhaps even to you and me.

- *Don't be afraid* to get medical tests for that symptom you're experiencing.
- *Don't be afraid* to apply for that scholarship or financial aid.
- *Don't be afraid* to tell your husband that it's time to go for marital counseling.

- *Don't be afraid* to ask for help.
- *Don't be afraid* to admit you were wrong.

Because . . .

Because God has a plan. There is so much more to the story than you can possibly imagine. In fact, if the rest of the story is as incredulous as Joseph's ("because the child she carries was conceived by the Holy Spirit"), you could never have made it up.

How many times has being afraid prevented you from discovering life-changing gifts and opportunities? Do you really care more about what other people think than what God is calling you to be and do?

One of my favorite aphorisms, which I drilled into my children is, "Nobody ever died from embarrassment." In other words, sometimes we have to go forward even if it's a bit sketchy and the world will misunderstand us. It helps to remember Who has called us and what He hopes to do in and through us.

Elisabeth Elliot felt this when she was traversing the jungles of Ecuador to live with the tribe who had just speared her husband and four other missionaries to death. She confessed to being in a place "full of things I was afraid of and did not know how to cope with." Though tempted to give up, she realized that "without a clear understanding of the ultimate objective, the immediate objectives make no sense to us. But if we bear in mind that we shall, beyond any doubt whatsoever, finally dwell in the house of the Lord, settle down to stay in His presence, then the intermediate pastures and waters, even the valley of the shadow, are understood. They are stations and landings along the journey and they will not last long."[19]

My child, don't be afraid. I am with you always. I was with Mary and Joseph in their unique calling and I will help you respond to the unexpected with a similar joy and faith. I want you to dwell in this confidence and assurance. You are in the right story, after all. And I am writing the script.

12. time

*I listened to you at the right time, and I helped you on the day of salvation. Look, now is the right **time**! Look, now is the day of salvation!*

~ 2 Corinthians 6:2 CEB

She thought she had all the time in the world.

With the kids now married, the grandbabies were starting to arrive, and she was planning all kinds of fun things to do with them—tea parties, museum trips, a grandparents' camp week each summer. Only two more years and she could retire from teaching and they could now travel as a couple and perhaps even get more involved at church—sing in the choir or join a Bible study. And maybe she would finally write that book. Yes, this season of life would be perfect for exploring spiritual things.

Then a phone call changed everything.

A routine checkup had been anything but routine, and within six months cancer had ended her life. There was, quite literally, no more time.

Are you waiting for the right time to get close to God? To explore spiritual things?

"Teach us to use wisely / all the time we have" (Psalm 90:12 CEV). And what exactly is "all the time we have?" Now. Today. Tomorrow is not promised to us, but God has given us the gift of today. And our verse suggests that "now is the right time!" For what? "Now is the day of salvation!"

Vital to the Christmas story is Simeon, a righteous and devout man who lived in Jerusalem and believed that God had promised he would not die until he had seen the Lord Christ. And so he waited for the proper time. When Joseph and Mary brought baby Jesus to the temple, "Simeon took Jesus in his arms and praised God. He said, 'Now, master, let your servant go in peace according to your word, / because my eyes have seen your salvation. / You prepared this salvation in the presence of all peoples. / It's a light for revelation to the Gentiles / and a glory for your people Israel'" (Luke 2:28-32 CEB).

The time had come. For salvation. For light. For shining. And Simeon was ready.

Are you ready to shine? If you're not sure you have the Light within, you can gain assurance today with a simple prayer:

> Dear Jesus, thank you for loving me and coming on that long ago Christmas. I'm sorry that I have tried to live on my own terms, resulting in sin against You. But I don't want to waste any more time. Please forgive me. Thank you for dying on the cross so I could live freely here and eternally with You in heaven. I invite you to make Your home in my heart and help me grow so I can serve and glorify You forever. Thank you for the great gift of salvation. For me. Today. Amen.

We are children of God. Whether you just now prayed that prayer or have been following Christ for awhile. John says that to all who receive Him and believe in His Name, Jesus gives them the right to become children of God (John 1:12). So celebrate this special time and mark it down for your whole life. You, like Simeon, have witnessed the true Light and can now shine for others.

"O come to my heart, Lord Jesus, There is room in my heart for Thee."[20]

My child, you are truly My child. And I am so grateful that you place your time in My hands. Every minute is precious and once it's gone, it cannot be retrieved. So My prayer for you is that you embrace the moments and the days, using them to glorify Me and touch a hurting world. What a light!

13. angel

Suddenly a great assembly of the heavenly forces was with the
angel *praising God. They said, "Glory to God in heaven, and*
on earth peace among those whom he favors."

~ Luke 2:13-14 CEB

Arseny and Alexei were left to freeze to death.

In their Siberian Gulag prison, they had been sent to the unheated sheet metal Isolation Shack. Sentenced to forty-eight hours in complete darkness with a temperature of less than minus 30° F, they would most certainly be two corpses by the time the guards opened the door two days later.

Arseny, a priest / monk imprisoned by Stalin for nineteen years for practicing his faith, asked Alexei to join him in prayer. Miraculously, as Father Arseny prayed, the isolation chamber became filled with light and warmth, and two men wearing bright robes appeared.

Angels.

Alexei, who was not religious, felt his body slowly warm, and he began to breathe deeply and fell asleep. When knocks on the door awakened him two days later, he saw that Father Arseny was just concluding his prayers. Soon the angels disappeared. As the light receded, the dark cold shack returned to its original state. Two shocked guards opened the doors to find their prisoners alive and well and smiling serenely.[21]

Angels are spiritual beings created by God who help carry out His work on earth. Proclaiming. Providing. Protecting.

Christmas is full of angels.

Gabriel appears to Mary to tell her the good news of God choosing her to give birth to His Son. Another angel appears to Joseph in a dream to reveal why his fiancée is pregnant and to encourage him to marry her anyway. An entire host of angels appear to the lowly shepherds in the fields to announce the Savior's birth. And various angels are used as God's messengers to the world.

The word *angel* actually comes from the Greek word *aggelos*, which means "messenger." The matching Hebrew word, *mal'ak,* has the same meaning. Their proclamations are often variations on "Fear not," "Glory to God," and "Peace on earth."

Legion of angels ("a multitude of heavenly hosts") sing "Glory" to celebrate Christ's birth. Angels exist to praise God: "Praise him, all his angels; / praise him, all his heavenly hosts" (Psalm 148:2). And even to the final book of the Bible, they are gathered in worship: "All the angels were standing around the throne. . . . They fell down on their faces before the throne and worshiped God" (Revelation 7:11).

In today's verse the angels also call for "on earth peace among those whom he favors." Angels desire to help bring peace and protection: "For he will command his angels concerning you / to guard you in all your ways" (Psalm 91:11).

As you place an angel on your Christmas tree, think of the angels that very first Christmas. And join in their song, "Hark! The herald angels sing, 'Glory to the newborn King;' Peace on earth, and mercy mild, God and sinners reconciled! Joyful, all ye nations rise, Join the triumph of the skies; With the angelic host proclaim, 'Christ is born in Bethlehem!' Hark! the herald angels sing, 'Glory to the newborn King!'"[22]

My child, angels are My voice. I send them for protection, defense, declaration, encouragement, and simply to call you into praise. Embrace the stories of how angels spoke marvelous truth to the people I chose to use that long-ago Christmas. And be aware that, even now, you are surrounded by heavenly beings.

14. generations

So, even in my old age with gray hair,
don't abandon me, God!
*Not until I tell **generations** about your mighty arm,*
tell all who are yet to come about your strength,
and about your ultimate righteousness, God,
because you've done awesome things!

~ Psalm 71:18-19 CEB

An African proverb states, "When an old man dies, a library burns to the ground!"

Think of what stories, knowledge, laughter, wisdom, perspective, and testimony we miss when we neglect to include older generations in our daily lives. And what better time than now to give them a place of honor and to actually ask them to share stories of God's faithfulness.

Author Catherine Marshall once said that her most memorable Christmas was the one in which her elderly father gathered everyone around and said he didn't want to inject a somber note, but he suspected it would be his last Christmas: "I've had a most wonderful life. Long, long ago I gave my life to Christ. Though I've tried to serve Him, I've failed Him often. But He has blessed me with great riches—especially my family. I want to say this while you're all here. Even after I go on into the next life, I'll still be with you. And, of course, I'll be waiting for each one of you there."[23]

Marshall remembered that scene in the living room "like a jewel of a moment set in the ordinary moments that make up our days. For that brief time, real values came clearly into focus."[24]

And now, since I am currently in my "third trimester of life" (as my same-age friend Maggie calls it), may I kindly suggest that during your holiday season, you make a point of including people from all generations in your gatherings, outings, and worship?

Mix it up and help the younger folk understand that the oral stories we pass down are valuable. How many times have I heard my friends say, "I wish I had asked Daddy this or that when he was still alive."

And to those of us who are older, let's make a special effort to be gracious, even if we are ignored or our contributions aren't requested. Let's just be glad to share life and light with those around us. For as long as we can.

Canadian pastor Mark Buchanan offers a few ways to live in your current season: "When you're young and in spring, do something dangerous. When your children are young, be with them. When you're fiftyish, sixtyish, and moving into fall, say yes to every young person who wants your time. When you're old and in winter, worship with all that's in you and even if it takes your last breath, speak blessing on the next generation."[25]

My child, I am with you now, whether you are in the springtime or winter of life. I will never abandon you, especially during your old age. But there will be changes and limits, which may cause concern for you. Just remember that all you need, I will provide. So, go out and share your stories and, in the process, you will share Mine.

15. child

*For unto us a **Child** is born,*
Unto us a Son is given;
And the government will be upon His shoulder.
And His name will be called
Wonderful, Counselor, Mighty God,
Everlasting Father, Prince of Peace.

~ Isaiah 9:6 NKJV

One night in 1741, a bent old man shuffled listlessly down a dark London street. George was starting out on one of the aimless, despondent wanderings that had become a nightly ritual for him. His mind was a battleground between hope based on his past glories and despair based on his unknown future.

George Frideric Handel couldn't help but think of his up-and-down life.

For forty years, he had written stately music for the aristocracy of England and Europe. Kings and queens had showered him with honors. Then court society turned against him, reducing him to poverty and illness. For a while, he experienced a recovery in health and fortune, until his patroness, Queen Caroline, died. As Handel sank deeper into debt, his heart sank deeper into depression.

Trudging into the warmth of his apartment that night, he discovered a package had been delivered—a commission to write a sacred oratorio. He would have preferred writing another opera. That is, until he began to read the words he was asked to set to music: "He was despised and rejected of men"; "Wonderful, Counselor, the Mighty God, the Everlasting Father, the Prince of Peace": and "I know that my Redeemer Liveth."

As these words came alive with meaning and purpose, so did Handel. He became consumed with writing and then jumping up and running to the harpsichord. At times, he would stride up and down the room, flailing the air with his arms and singing at the top of his lungs, "Hallelujah! Hallelujah!" the tears running down his cheeks.

People thought he was going mad.

For twenty-four days he labored like a fiend with little rest or food. Then he fell on his bed exhausted, with his new score, "Messiah," laying on his desk. At the very first performance of "Messiah," the king and queen attended and spontaneously stood in reverence when the "Hallelujah Chorus" began. That custom has continued to this day.

Handel never again succumbed to despair. Age sapped his vitality, he went blind, but his undaunted spirit remained to the last. "Unto us a Child is born, unto us a Son is given" became words that gave him new life. And through his oratorio, George Frideric Handel lit a torch that still shines.[26]

This Child whom we celebrate during Christmas has great power to rescue those who are at the end of their rope. To offer a lifeline which restores purpose and passion to a discouraged soul. To anoint with power so that even the most feeble of humans can make a divine offering back to the Giver.

What will your "Messiah" be this year?

My child, are you also wandering the streets of an up-and-down life where no sooner do you find your balance, then all gives way beneath you? I am here to remind you that with the Child of Christmas comes fresh hope and new beginnings. Hallelujah!

16. neighbor

*You will love your **neighbor** as yourself. No other commandment
is greater than these.*

~ Mark 12:31 CEB

Someone once said that the two most beautiful words in the English language are *come in*. When was the last time you opened your door and said those words?

I'm embarrassed I don't do more for my neighbors. We've lived in this house a few years now, and I still haven't hosted a neighborhood Christmas Tea the way I did for twenty years in our old neighborhood.

Why is that? Was it easier to reach out when our yards were full of kids and bikes and dogs? Can I blame it all on this season of life?

Perhaps I'm just human. It's too easy these days to come home from work tired and peopled-out and just cocoon inside for the evening. Or at least until we go out to our evening event.

Are you too exhausted or overextended to reach out to your neighbors? In our verse today, Christ commands that we do just that. Even though it does tend to be one of the busiest times of the year, holidays can be a perfect opportunity to reach out.

For a long time, I struggled with the concept of hospitality, primarily because I confused it with entertaining. But there is a difference. Entertaining focuses on what *I* have to offer—the beautiful home, the delicious food, and creative decorations. Hospitality may include all those elements, but the focus is on making the *other person* feel comfortable and at ease—wanted.

Hospitality requires an open heart and a gracious spirit. The writer of Hebrews encourages us, "Don't neglect to open up your homes to guests, because by doing this some have been hosts to angels without knowing it" (Hebrews 13:2 CEB). In other words, we as hosts are often the ones who receive the blessing when others come to call!

There are ways to show hospitality without having an elaborate Christmas party. Create and deliver gift baskets to neighbors. Include them in your Christmas card list. Invite them to join you for a candlelight service at your church. My friends, the Schoenlys, host an annual Christmas Carol Sing in their home, and people look forward to it every year.

In his final discourse, Jesus said, "In My Father's house are many dwelling places" (John 14:2 HCSB). He was using a wonderful illustration of hospitality: "God's gracious welcome to a new home beyond time and death. A literal house may not await us in heaven, but the verse evokes a sense of warmth and hospitality. God has prepared a place for us; a table waits for us. God's love and welcome do not end with death. This is hospitality without measure."[27]

You may be asking the question, "Who is my neighbor?" And the answer is, of course, anyone who needs to hear the good news that Christ is born—God with us. That opens the playing field to those we encounter at work, in the market, and elsewhere, not just the ones with whom we share an address.

Is it time for you to say, "Come in"?

My child, I have welcomed you with an acceptance and grace that I hope makes you feel at home in Me. And now I ask you to do the same for others. There are so many people out there who have not been invited anywhere for such a long time. And the holidays can be especially lonely. Don't wait until you have it all together. Just reach out. You will receive a blessing in the process.

17. how long

How long, LORD? Will you forget me forever?
How long will you hide your face from me?
How long must I wrestle with my thoughts
and day after day have sorrow in my heart?

~ Psalm 13:1-2

Are you in agonizing sorrow or deep pain right now?

One Sunday a parishioner told Nashville pastor Scott Sauls that he was unimpressed by the fact that he was such an excellent preacher.

Before the pastor could even react, the man went on, "The moment I decided to trust you was when you revealed you have struggled with anxiety and depression. Then I knew you were my pastor."

Sauls says it finally dawned on him, "As a pastor and as a man, my afflictions may end up having greater impact than my preaching or my vision ever will. It is helpful to remember that nearly all of the Psalms were written from dark, depressed, wrecked, and restless places."[28]

Perhaps your own groans of "how long" deafen your ears to the Voice that whispers, "I came to be with you, the one I love"?

Statistics reveal that the days between Thanksgiving and New Year's Day are the most fragile for those already experiencing emotional or physical loss and pain. And if you are not that person, perhaps you are standing next to someone who is.

In the fifteenth-century carol, "Lo, How a Rose E'er Blooming," Jesus is incarnate as the flower gift from God who comes to us in the midst of darkness and lightens every load.

We know He did that for King David. In today's text, he cries out to God four times but later in the psalm is able to profess hope and trust in God, even by singing. He joins other biblical characters who struggled and lamented:

- Hannah had bitterness of soul over infertility and a broken domestic situation.
- Elijah felt so beaten down that he asked God to take his life.
- Job and Jeremiah cursed the day that they were born.
- Jesus said that His soul was overwhelmed with sorrow and wept when His friend died.

Sauls's blog post has already been reshared over twenty thousand times, giving some indication of the chord it struck with readers. Pastor Scott concludes, "Suffering has a way of equipping us to be the best expressions of God's compassion and grace. It has a way of equipping us to love and lead in ways that are helpful and not harmful. A healer who has not been wounded is extremely limited in her/his ability to heal. Damaged does not mean *done*."[29]

Friend, we, too, may be *damaged*, but we are not *done*.

Today, may you come close to this Christ child who was also "a man of sorrows, and acquainted with grief" (Isaiah 53:3 ESV). He knows what your life is like. He came to sit with you in sorrow, to guide you in bewilderment, and to give you hope to take the next step.

Emmanuel—*God with us*—is the great good news for all who weep today.

My child, I also wept. I even asked my Father to take away my cup of suffering. And so when I hear your cries of "how long," I do understand. Know that I am here to sit with you in your sorrow or pain. And then to redeem all loss in My way and My time.

18. stars

Look up to the skies.
*Who created all these **stars**?*
He leads out the army of heaven one by one
and calls all the stars by name.

~ Isaiah 40:26 NCV

Question: How many stars are there in the universe?

Answer: 100 billion stars in the Milky Way galaxy.

And that's just what we can see.

However, scientists tell us that there are possibly 10 trillion galaxies in the universe.

"Multiplying that by the Milky Way's estimated 100 billion stars results in a large number indeed: 100 octillion stars, or 100,000,000,000,000,000,000,000,000,000 stars, or a 1 with 29 zeros after it. That number is likely a gross underestimation, as more detailed looks at the universe will show even more galaxies."[30]

I can't even wrap my mind around that staggering number. More than that, as I realize the Creator of the stars "calls all the stars by name," I am filled afresh with awe and wonder. This same God is the One who used a very special bright star to fulfill the prophecy of the birthplace of His Son: "A Star shall come out of Jacob; / A Scepter shall rise out of Israel" (Numbers 24:17 NKJV).

A star on top of the Christmas tree is one of many symbols of Christmas that hearkens back two thousand years ago when that first star appeared, in order to guide the wise men to worship the newborn king: "O star of wonder, star of light, Star with royal beauty bright, Westward leading, still proceeding, Guide us to thy perfect Light."[31]

Scientists and astrologers have spent the past two centuries coming up with theories and explanations for that star—what it was actually made of, where it was in the sky, and how everything came together at just the right time to serve as a beacon.

Curiously, the magi seem to have been the only ones who understood the star's meaning: "Whatever the exact mechanism, the fact that the star led the magi to Christ is evidence that God uniquely designed the star for a very special purpose. God can use extraordinary means for extraordinary purposes. Certainly the birth of our Lord was deserving of honor in the heavens."[32]

We, too, are called to shine, in order to guide others to the source of life: "Those skilled in wisdom will shine like the sky. Those who lead many to righteousness will shine like the stars forever and always" (Daniel 12:3 CEB).

Lord, hear our prayer:

> God of the winter sky, place a star on the horizon, for our world needs the assurance of Your shining presence. Shine gently on those who grieve. Shine brightly on all who struggle for bread to eat, land to till, work to do. Shine with a strong light on all those who struggle for justice, who work for peace, who bind up the wounds. God of the winter sky, place a star above me so that I may go into the New Year with your light to guide me. Amen.[33]

My child, raise your eyes to the heavens and see all the stars I have created. Even though there are many, many more than you can see, I assure you that each one has a name. And I know it. So, don't you think I know you by name? I know your needs, your concerns, and your struggle to be a shining light where you are. Be confident. You are shining a path to Me.

19. everyone

If it is possible, as far as it depends on you, live at peace with everyone.

~ Romans 12:18

Let's face it. Great-uncle Horace is not going to change this year.

He will still be obnoxious, drink too much, and end up snoring in the recliner during the family Christmas gathering. Yes, he's a piece of work.

But he's *your* family's piece of work! Extended families during the holidays. Can someone say, "It's complicated"?

Even if we didn't have all the drama with in-laws and outlaws and custody and visitation, we would still find ourselves with a living room full of people with varied views on everything from religion to sports to politics and even the traditional menu for the holiday meal.

May I make a suggestion for this year?

Don't dread it. And don't skip it. Embrace the mix! Do what the apostle Paul encouraged in today's verse: "as far as it depends on you, live at peace with everyone." You and I can choose to be kind and diplomatic and full of grace when such challenging annual events come along. We can't control the response of others, but we can control our own attitudes and behavior.

Jesus said, "Blessed are the peacemakers" (Matthew 5:9). Unfortunately, our world is defined by our many conflicts. But we need to bring the focus in tighter to our personal worlds: "Little arguments, petty responses later regretted, disagreements blown out of proportion, and hurt feelings, nurtured and fed, occur in abundance. Let peace begin with me. . . . The focus is on what I can do to be an instrument of [Jesus'] peace."[34]

But what if *you're* the misfit—the "piece of work" at the party?

In her novel *An Endless Christmas*, Cynthia Ruchti's character felt that way. Katie believes she cannot marry Micah because his family seems perfect, so she tells him she is "the opposite of what you need. Bad ancestry.

Bad decisions. Bad credits. Bad debts." But as Micah's family acts graciously amid myriad catastrophes, something shifts in Katie's heart.

> Weeks ago, a scene like this would have sent her into mourning over how far the sweetness was from the kind of family Christmas she'd known in her growing-up years. . . . She allowed herself to feel the full impact of the enduring love that hemmed the Christmas story.[35]

C. S. Lewis once commented that there are two kinds of love:

> We love wise and kind and beautiful people because we need them, but we love (or try to love) stupid and disagreeable people because they need us. This second kind is the more divine because that is how God loves us: not because we are loveable but because He is love, not because He needs to receive but He delights to give.[36]

Love. Peace. It's all been given to us. Now it's the season to return the favor.

My child, please stop trying to orchestrate everything about your life with the hopes that all circumstances and people will be perfect. Everyone is flawed in some way, but everyone also has much to give. Your job is to give what you have to offer—out of the grace and acceptance I've already showered on you. Don't try to change someone. That's my role. Just love.

20. hope

*May the God of **hope** fill you with all joy and peace in faith so
that you overflow with hope by the power of the Holy Spirit.*

~ Romans 15:13 CEB

It is said that human beings can live for forty days without food, four days without water, and four minutes without air. But we cannot live for four seconds without hope.

Where do you find hope?

If you look for it in institutions, they will fail you. If in the economy, you're in trouble. Even if your hope is based on a precious loved one, they, too, may let you down. What is really needed is a Source of hope, and our verse today reminds us that Source is God. He is reliable, worthy, unchanging, and absolutely powerful: "Our hope is set on the living God, who is the savior of all people" (1 Timothy 4:10 CEB).

Are you fearful? Are you hopeless? Jesus is the answer to those very real needs.

This would have been good news to Jeremiah, known as the "weeping prophet."

He didn't cry because his life was so bad. He was moved to tears for the people who had rejected God—the same God who made them, loved them, and sought repeatedly to bless them.

By the time he wrote Lamentations in 586 BC, Jerusalem had fallen and Jeremiah knew that these people's sin and selfishness would result in suffering and exile. He felt great empathy and sympathy for them. That's why he cried—his heart was broken with the things that break God's heart.

Can you relate to the plight of the Israelites in such a dire time? Have you ever sought to go your own way, even when a loving God was beckoning you back to Him? If so, perhaps you can understand how God's heart is broken by our choices.

Jeremiah begins in hopelessness: "I am the man who has seen affliction."

In Lamentations 3, he then goes on to spend twenty verses outlining all his suffering: *skin and flesh grow old*—verse 4; *bitterness and hardship*—verse 5; *dwell in darkness*—verse 6; *unanswered prayer*—verse 8; *abandoned*—verse 11; *pierced heart*—verse 13; *mocked and become laughingstock*—verse 14; *deprived of peace*—verse 17; *hopeless*—verse 18; and *wandering*—verse 19.

But then Jeremiah chooses to place his hope in the only One worthy—God: "Yet this I call to mind / and therefore I have hope: / Because of the LORD's great love we are not consumed, / for His compassions never fail. They are new every morning; / great is your faithfulness. / . . . The LORD is good to those whose hope is in him, / to the one who seeks him" (Lamentations 3:21-25).

The season we are in now, Advent, is all about the future—the Christian hope for a new heaven and a new earth as a gift from God: "It is tied to Christmas because it is in the person and work of Jesus that we glimpse what God has in mind for the future. For that future we are to wait in hope. We are to pray for its coming as the Lord's Prayer teaches us to do. (The word 'advent' means 'coming.')"[37]

May you "overflow with hope" today.

My children, perhaps you, too, feel like a person who has seen more than your share of affliction. Whenever you begin to list them, I hope that you, like Jeremiah, will call to mind My faithfulness. My presence and power will bring you hope. And especially now as you are waiting.

21. widows

*True devotion, the kind that is pure and faultless before God
the Father, is this: to care for orphans and **widows** in their
difficulties.*

~ James 1:27 CEB

Do you ever skip over verses in the Bible because they don't seem important or relevant to you—perhaps even this verse? Do you think that if your life is not touched directly by an orphan or a widow, then perhaps it doesn't apply to you? Actually, we are told that these concerns, acted out in love, show our "true devotion, the kind that is pure and faultless before God the Father."

The holidays are an especially hard time for widows. My friend Gayle Roper put it this way after her husband, Chuck, died, "Christmas looms and my heart aches." With so much emphasis on family gatherings, such radical changes are jolting to a new widow: "The definition of family, our family, is painfully altered. There's no one to sit and stare at the tree with after we finish decorating it, no one to light the fire and put up the outside lights. The one who read the Story to us can no longer give voice to it. There's no one to start the wrapping paper fight with the kids and grand-kids after opening gifts."[38]

For Gayle, author of *A Widow's Journey*, the best thing her family did for her that first year was give her freedom not to celebrate: "I could remember and give thanks for the Christ Child who became the Savior of the world, but I couldn't celebrate."[39]

Do you know someone who is facing an empty Christmas?

My natural tendency is to want to cheer them up and invite them to every gathering so they won't feel so alone. But the truth is, sometimes those events make them feel all the more alone, emphasizing what they're missing. Perhaps a better alternative might be a one-on-one tea party together with music and conversation that they help direct. Offer them the option of talking about their loved one.

There are other simple ways to reach out to widows and widowers and other single parents:

- Offer to pick them up for the Christmas Eve service or concert and sit together.
- Deliver a tin of Christmas cookies, basket of tea, and a small devotional.
- Help them decorate for the holidays.
- Offer to take their young children on a shopping trip or other outing.

Just remember, they are still going to hurt. We can't change that.

The second year of Gayle's widowhood she learned how to celebrate her new normal and decided to purchase a smaller tree that she could handle alone: "I end up using only the top two tiers, and they are just right. I can put on the tree topper without climbing on a stool as I usually did, always fearing I'd lose my balance and fall into the tree. If I can reach the top of my new tree, can I also extend myself to grasp joy this Christmas?"[40]

Let's do whatever we can to help widows grasp joy this Christmas.

My child, there are so many people around you who are lonely. They are experiencing a loss that tears apart their soul. Whether or not you can understand, I am asking you to reach out. If you don't know what to say, just be there. And remind them of My love and presence. A promise you can both count on.

22. peace

*"**Peace** I leave with you. My peace I give you. I give to you not as the world gives. Don't be troubled or afraid."*

~ John 14:27 CEB

Are you tired of hearing news reports of violence around the world juxtaposed with carols that sweetly echo the words "sleep in heavenly peace"? Are you ever tempted to respond with "Bah, Humbug" when someone cheerily wishes you a Happy Holiday?

About a hundred years ago, Henry was also despondent on Christmas Day.

His wife, Frances, had just been killed in an accidental fire. His son, Charles, had joined the army without his father's blessing and now was severely wounded on the field. And to top it all, with the Civil War raging, no one felt much like celebrating Christmas.

Henry wrote down these struggles: "I heard the bells on Christmas Day, Their old, familiar carols play, and wild and sweet The words repeat Of peace on earth, good-will to men! And in despair I bowed my head; 'There is no peace on earth,' I said; 'For hate is strong, And mocks the song Of peace on earth, good-will to men!'"[41]

How can we find peace when there is only turmoil both outward and within?

By turning to the Source of all peace—Jesus, known as "the Prince of Peace." His parting words to his disciples in today's verse offered the gift of a different kind of peace than "the world gives." In the Scriptures, the word *peace* means more than the absence of hostility or enmity. The Hebrew word translated "peace" is *shalom*, which conveys wholeness, the perfecting of all that is broken or incomplete.

This kind of peace is what brings healing to our heart and soul: "Let the peace of Christ rule in your hearts, since as members of one body you were called to peace" (Colossians 3:15).

Perhaps you are also struggling this Christmas, wincing when you hear bells ring and others rejoice. How can you find peace in the middle of your own storm? "Christ is our peace" (Ephesians 2:14 CEB).

Christ is our peace. Not circumstances. Not world events. Not even our children's safety. Our peace comes from the One who promised peace and freely offers it to us. The question becomes, can we accept what He sends our way?

Amy Carmichael's powerful words often ring in my ears: "In acceptance lieth peace."

Henry Wadsworth Longfellow came to realize this before he finished writing his Christmas Day poem. And so he concluded with renewed hope, "Then pealed the bells more loud and deep: 'God is not dead, nor doth He sleep; The Wrong shall fail, The Right prevail, With peace on earth, good-will to men.'"[42]

Peace in our world is rare. But it is possible to discover this *shalom* and dwell in it. I've read the last chapter and God is victorious!

༽ⱴⱺ

My child, there will always be conflict and storms that threaten the peace that I have poured into your life. But, be of good cheer, I have overcome the world. The peace I give does not fluctuate with the tides of war. It is a parting gift that you can experience within and then spread without. Especially at Christmas.

23. light

*The people walking in darkness have seen a great **light**.*
On those living in a pitch-dark land, light has dawned.

~ Isaiah 9:2 CEB

Picture a large Victorian home deep in the Texas countryside—a retreat center where twenty-five women authors and speakers have just spent a week together. Tomorrow we have a crack-of-dawn bus ride to the Houston airport, but everyone has stayed up late for final chats.

Each of our rooms is filled to the brim with lovely antiques and collectibles. That's important to know because an early morning storm knocks out all the power and we awaken to do our final packing and dressing in the total darkness.

We can see nothing. Feeling around for random clothes and books is frustrating because of all the room decorations. Getting dressed is an exercise in making sure we don't forget something important before facing the public. As we stumble in the darkness we have things to do such as pack, connect with people, and catch a bus.

Soon our sleepy brains finally kick in, and we slowly begin to find and turn on our cell phones. Even those of us who don't have a flashlight feature discover that the glimmer from the LED face helps tremendously. We are on our way—a trickle of light helping us get there.

By the time the bus delivers us to the airport terminal, we are laughing uproariously. More than half of us are wearing our clothes inside out! This is definitely not our finest moment, but at least we made it here. Out of the dark into the light.

Only those who have experienced total darkness understand the importance of even a tiny bit of light. And sadly too many of us have a history with the lure of darkness, the prison of darkness, or the secret of darkness.

This time of year I often feel like I did when all the lights went out in Texas:

- There's somewhere I must go.
- There are things to do—to gather and put together.
- There are people I need to connect with.
- But it's completely dark. And I'm stumbling, bumping around, worried about leaving something behind, and worst of all—that the bus will leave without me!

Where is your "dark place" today? Where do you need some light to shine?

Christmas is all about God's plan to dispel darkness—by sending His Son, the Light of the world: "I am the light of the world. Whoever follows me won't walk in darkness but will have the light of life" (John 8:12 CEB).

And even a small amount of light can make a huge difference. A candle. A flickering ember. Will you ask the Holy Spirit to breathe your almost nonexistent light into a spectacular bonfire that brightens up every single corner? In the process He will light your way for all that is ahead during this Advent season.

"Light and life to all he brings, Risen with healing in his wings. Mild he lays his glory by, Born that man no more may die: Born to raise the sons of earth, Born to give them second birth. Hark! the herald angels sing, Glory to the newborn King!"[43]

My child, how long have you been stumbling around in a darkness of your own making? Choosing the awful familiar over the risky new? It's time to emerge into the light, My Light. Sure, you may be a bit disheveled, but that doesn't matter to Me. Come into all I have for you this season. Light and Life are born today. For you.

24. shepherds

*Nearby **shepherds** were living in the fields, guarding their sheep at night.*

~ Luke 2:8 CEB

If royalty were scheduled to be in your home, who would be at the top of your guest list? The mayor, the governor, the president? Who would have the equal class and gravitas demanded on such an auspicious occasion? Someone of importance or wealth or influence?

Probably not your garbage collector. Or the dog catcher. And most certainly not those clerks at the DMV who keep you waiting. Now, while all these professions are perfectly worthy, few appear to qualify for the level of royalty.

And yet God invited shepherds to the birth of His most royal son.

Shepherds were dirty outcasts who lived in the rough. He did it to show us that humble and ordinary can be very holy:

> We may hope for visions and revelations and wonderful experiences, forgetting that the context of the revelation of God to each one of us is exactly where we are—here, on earth, in this house, this room, this work, this family, this physical body. Think of the revelation of the divine life to the Bethlehem shepherds: the sudden appearance of the angel of the Lord and the glory of the Lord, the song of high praise sung by the "multitude of the heavenly host"—certainly a most wonderful experience—but it came while they were faithfully doing their usual job, just where they belonged.[44]

What would that have been like for the shepherds? I was once privileged to witness Boston pastor Bryan Wilkerson dressed as a shepherd offering a monologue of that one glorious night:

There was . . . a shaft of light coming out of the sky and falling on a patch of ground right in front of us. . . . The next thing I know I'm down on my knees . . . and with a voice like a song he said, "Don't be afraid. . . ." He told us we would find a baby wrapped in cloths and lying in a manger.[45]

These ordinary men were at the top of the guest list for the royal birth.

Wilkerson's shepherd concluded, "God sent angels to us, a bunch of shepherds, to announce that Messiah had come. It seems like maybe God doesn't care what you're wearing or if you smell kind of funny, if you're willing to listen and believe."[46]

Did you know that you, too, are invited to the stable? "Led by the light of faith serenely beaming, With glowing hearts we stand by the Babe adored. O'er the world a star is sweetly gleaming, And come now, Shepherds, from your flocks unboard. The Son of God lay thus within lowly manger; In all our trials born to be our Lord."[47]

My child, are you currently doing what you're supposed to be doing? If so, that is the very place that I will appear to you. And invite you to join me in witnessing all of the glory and beauty and compassion and grace that Jesus has for you. It doesn't matter how you dress. Or how you smell. Just that you are willing to leave your place and follow. And you will receive the Gift.

25. birth

*And she gave **birth** to her firstborn son and wrapped him in bands of cloth, and laid him in a manger, because there was no place for them in the inn.*

~ Luke 2:7 NRSV

The year 1809 was a bleak and dismal time for giving birth.

With ruthless dictator Napoleon determined to conquer the world, there was almost no hope left in anyone's heart. Yet in that one year alone, babies who were destined to change the world were born: Abraham Lincoln, Charles Darwin, William Gladstone, Alfred Lord Tennyson, Edgar Allan Poe, Cyrus McCormick, and Felix Mendelssohn.

While no one noticed.

Millennia before, very few noticed the birth of a baby to a young couple traveling to Bethlehem on a donkey and forced to spend the night in a stable. But God knew. And He orchestrated this humble birth as the beginning of life for a child who would literally change the course of history: Jesus Christ.

Do you ever wonder what this birth was really like?

Allow me to borrow the description of favorite storyteller Max Lucado:

> A more lowly place of birth could not exist. Near the young mother sits the weary father. If anyone is dozing, he is. . . . The mystery of the event still puzzles him. What's important is that the baby is fine and that Mary is safe. Wide awake is Mary. My, how young she looks! Her head rests on the soft leather of Joseph's saddle. The pain has been eclipsed by wonder. She looks into the face of the baby. Her son. Her Lord. His Majesty.
>
> At this point in history, the human being who best understands who God is and what he is doing is a teenage girl in a

smelly stable. She can't take her eyes off him. Somehow Mary knows she is holding God. So this is he. She remembers the words of the angel, "His kingdom will never end." He looks anything but a king. His face is prunish and red. His cry, though strong and healthy, is still the helpless and piercing cry of a baby. And he is absolutely dependent upon Mary for his well-being.[48]

This newborn baby is majesty in the midst of the mundane.

I picture that scene surrounded by the music of this fifth-century carol, "O that birth forever blessèd, when the virgin, full of grace, By the Holy Ghost conceiving, bare the Savior of our race; And the Babe, the world's Redeemer, First revealed His sacred face, evermore and evermore!"[49]

What difference will this birth make in your life each day?

At Christmas our pulses beat more quickly because we know the coming of that Baby has done more to soften the hardness of the world's heart, to bring hope in the midst of the world's despair, and to bring joy in the midst of sadness, than any event that has ever taken place since the beginning of time. . . . I wish we might think about that Baby every day of the year.[50]

Babies. Birth. Hope.

❧

My child, yes I came as a baby, a seemingly inauspicious beginning. Yet one more way to identify with you, My child. My humanity and divinity are a mystery but you need not concern yourself with that so much as to embrace the reasons for the Birth. Because I loved the world—you—so much. When you hold a baby next, never forget the promise of a future.

26. pondering

*But Mary treasured up all these things, **pondering** them in her heart.*

~ Luke 2:19 ESV

Sometimes it's what we *don't* share that's most precious.

Those moments and memories we keep to ourselves, taking out occasionally and reflecting on the glory of it all. Those times we don't even try to capture in a picture because the true beauty or meaning simply cannot be contained in two dimensions.

But we can treasure them privately, pondering.

After all that had happened in Bethlehem, Mary chose to keep her impressions, her experiences, and her joy quite close. If she had lived in the twenty-first century, I doubt she would have Tweeted or posted on Facebook. The whole miraculous glory of it all was too intimate.

In an age where many of us simply over share, perhaps we can learn something from Mary about the importance of pondering. Take time and place to think, reflect, observe, remember, and process all that has happened in our lives—the events, the conversations, the opportunities, the disappointments, the bad choices, and the untraveled roads. All are important in the living of our unique story.

Do you take time to search out meaning in your moments?

As the Christmas season draws to a close, perhaps now is a perfect opportunity to take up the spiritual discipline of journaling. This is defined as "being alert to my life through writing and reflecting on God's presence and activity in, around, and through me."

I sometimes call this "pondering with a pen."

Schedule a time and place where you can enjoy both solitude and silence. Pray and ask God to help you ponder the past year and look ahead. Here are questions to help you get started.

- What is my one prayer for this year that seems impossible, knowing that "nothing is impossible with God"?
- What is one thing I could do to improve the quality of my relationships this year?
- What is one area in my life that needs the most change, and what will I do about it?
- What is one thing I could do to enrich my spiritual legacy to my children and grandchildren?
- What is an important financial goal this year, and how will I meet it?
- How will I care for my soul this year?

Conclude your time by singing this or another favorite carol: "How silently, how silently, the wondrous Gift is given; So God imparts to human hearts the blessings of His Heaven. No ear may hear His coming, but in this world of sin, Where meek souls will receive Him still, the dear Christ enters in."[51]

My child, sometimes it's good to pull away. From people, places, and posts. At the end of this full season, perhaps this is just what your soul is longing for. Come to Me and I will help you remember and reflect. Turn to Me and seek My face for the unknown future. I am already there and will never leave you. Take time to ponder.

27. king herod

*After Jesus was born in Bethlehem in the territory of Judea
during the rule of **King Herod**, magi came from the east to
Jerusalem. They asked, "Where is the newborn king of the Jews?
We've seen his star in the east, and we've come to honor him."
When King Herod heard this, he was troubled.*

~ Matthew 2:1-3 CEB

There will always be evil men—Adolph Hitler, Pol Pot, Ivan the Terrible, Idi Amin, Nero, Osama bin Laden. Tyrannical rulers, power hungry and desperately insecure, ruthlessly seek out anyone who might threaten the kingdom they have fashioned.

To destroy them.

Because evil and good cannot reign together.

This is exactly what King Herod did when the magi unwittingly let it be known that there was another king on the horizon. While asking them to keep him informed so he could worship the new king as well (Matthew 2:8), Herod formed his own plan (Matthew 2:16).

He ordered all baby boys under the age of two to be executed.

And we shouldn't have been surprised. The "slaughter of the innocents" was only one in a long line of wicked acts. Under this cruel ruler, lives were disposable, promises broken, politics dangerous, and trusting others extremely risky. Herod killed his father-in-law, several of his ten wives, and two of his own sons. He ignored the law of God to suit himself and chose the favor of Rome over his own people.

Jesus and his family escaped Herod. The wise men also avoided him on their return trip. God had warned them all and protected them. And Herod came to a ruinous end himself. After reigning thirty-seven years, he died from a painful disease that causes breathing problems, convulsions, rotting of the body, and worms.

How do we handle bad news of yet another person doing evil and destructive things to innocents? Yes, some current rulers come to mind, but there are also incidents of teenagers and seniors and military leaders who one day decide to wreak havoc and destruction at will.

How do we live in a world like that?

By trusting that God will be with us and those we love: "Don't fear, because I am with you; / don't be afraid, for I am your God. / I will strengthen you, / I will surely help you; / I will hold you / with my righteous strong hand" (Isaiah 41:10 CEB).

And also by being wise to the ways of those who influence our culture. In a day when young people are vulnerable to the recruiting tactics of terrorists, all should heed King Solomon's warning:

> Don't go on the way of the wicked;
>   don't walk on the path of evil people.
> Avoid it! Don't turn onto it;
>   stay off of it and keep going!
> They don't sleep unless they do evil;
> they are robbed of sleep unless they make someone stumble.
> They eat the bread of evil,
>   and they drink the wine of violence.
> The way of the righteous is like morning light
>   that gets brighter and brighter till it is full day.
> The path of the wicked is like deep darkness;
>   they don't know where they will stumble.
> (Proverbs 4:14-19 CEB)

Herod did not have the last word in the Christmas story. And neither will wicked people today. God is triumphant.

My child, how I long to calm your anxious soul. I understand your fears for the young, the vulnerable, those easily influenced and enticed by promises of glory or power or even just fifteen minutes of fame. And yet, I implore you to remember that I am in control. I am Sovereign. I am your God and your Protector. Though some skirmishes are lost, ultimately, evil will not win.

28. treasures

On coming to the house, they {Magi} saw the child with his
mother Mary, and they bowed down and worshiped him. Then
*they opened their **treasures** and presented him with gifts of gold,*
frankincense and myrrh.

~ Matthew 2:11

How many gifts have you returned since Christmas?

Perhaps the garment didn't fit, or you already had one of those devices, or it just wasn't what you wanted. With gift receipts and digital accounting, it's easy to totally undo what the giver intended. Did that sound snarky?

Pardon, but it seems to me we've gotten too directed on our choices. I'm one of those people who finds it increasingly frustrating to be told what gift to pick. I would so much rather surprise you.

Perhaps we could all learn something from the wise men who gave baby Jesus treasures that had been carefully selected and divinely appointed for this birthday of a king.

Magi is derived from the Greek word *magoi*, which can refer to priestly men of Persia. Both Matthew's Gospel and Old Testament prophecy indicate that the magi were Persian priests, educated in astrology and astronomy, who interpreted the star's appearance as a sign of the new Messiah's birth.

Since they have traveled long and far to worship the new king, it is no surprise they have brought customary treasures with them.

There is much confusion about their names and gifts. But a seventh-century work by St. Bede, "The Excerpta et Collectanea," documents that "the first magi is said to have been Melchior, an old man with white hair and a long beard who offered gold to the Lord as to a king. The second, Caspar by name, young and beardless and ruddy complexioned, honored

Him as God by his gift of incense, an oblation worthy of the divinity. The third, black-skinned and heavily bearded, named Balthasar, by his gift of myrrh testified to the Son of Man who was to die."[52]

From ancient times, gold has been associated with rarity and royalty, and because of its endurance, gold also represented immortality. An essential gift for a king, Melchior's gold symbolized the magi's acknowledgment that Jesus was a divine king whose kingdom could not be destroyed by earthly powers.

Frankincense was not native to Israel and was thus considered precious and expensive to import. This resin or gum was used for both medicinal purposes and incense. Frankincense is also a symbol of holiness and righteousness. The magi Gaspar (also known as Caspar) gave frankincense to the Christ child to recognize His role as priest and His willingness to become a sacrifice.

In Jesus' time, myrrh was actually more precious than gold. It was an exotic spice used in embalming and was acquired from trees that grow in southern Arabia and Africa. It was sometimes mingled with wine to form a sedative drink—gall, which was offered to Christ on the cross. Balthazar's gift of myrrh symbolized bitterness, suffering, and affliction and was later used to anoint Christ's body after death.

Did Mary and Joseph totally understand the important symbolism of each of these treasures? All we know is that they graciously received them on behalf of the baby Jesus.

What are the treasures you take away from your own Christmas season? Long after the thank-you notes have been written, sizes exchanged, and packaging recycled, which gifts will you take with you into the New Year?

My child, "I will give you hidden treasures, / riches stored in secret places, / so that you may know that I am the LORD" (Isaiah 45:3). Receive from Me with open hands. Know that all of life is a gift and learn to treasure each one that comes your way.

29. word

*The **Word** became flesh and made his dwelling among us. We
have seen his glory, the glory of the one and only Son, who came
from the Father, full of grace and truth.*

~ John 1:14

God has now made His dwelling place among us.

The New Testament Greek word here for *dwell* is *skenoo*, which, properly translated, means "to pitch a tent," denoting much more than the mere general notion of "dwelling." When Eugene Peterson wrote his paraphrase, The Message, he put it this way, "The Word became flesh and blood, / and moved into the neighborhood."

Jesus' birth was the equivalent of God putting skin on and joining us next door.

In fact, John begins his Gospel with the Word: "In the beginning was the Word / and the Word was with God / and the Word was God. / The Word was with God in the beginning" (John 1:1-2 CEB). The New Testament Greek word for *word* is *logos* and was used by theologians and philosophers many different ways. In the Old Testament Hebrew "the Word" was an agent of creation (Psalm 33:6). In Greek philosophy, "the Word" was the principle of reason that governed the world. So to Greek readers "the Word became flesh" was unthinkable.

The Bible teaches that Jesus, is both fully human and fully divine (Colossians 2:9-10). Jesus didn't lose His divine status as God when He came to earth. He was born as a human, into a specific place and time in history, even though He's existed for all time and lives for eternity. All the massive, powerful, divine nature of God can be clearly seen in Jesus.

We, too, "have seen his glory." We saw that He was full of grace and truth. His Incarnation was nearness and allowed us to move in for a closer look: "We saw it in . . . laugh lines on his face, in the healing touch of his hands, in his tears and teaching, in his broken body and shed blood. We saw it when he looked into our eyes and said the words we needed to hear most: you are forgiven. This is close."[53]

Before Christ was born, people could know God partially, but now we can know God fully because He became visible and tangible in Jesus Christ—the perfect expression of God in human form.

Has Jesus moved into your heart and home? Has He come that close? If not, what could you do to be more in community with Him this year?

One Seattle graduate student answers this way: "Like Christ in His advent, it seems to me that we are called to move into wherever our neighborhood may be and we are called to transform it, to love it, to get closer than is comfortable. Because it's in the coming close that we are like Christ."[54]

Celebrate the Word today by offering a good word (and action) to the neighbor you meet.

My child, it wasn't enough for Me to be your God, I also wanted to be your Savior. And so I sent Jesus, the third person of the Trinity, to live among you. Close. And now you are called to live as an extension of Christ's body on earth as you reach out in your own neighborhood and life. And you can only do it up close. Incarnate my love. I'm with you.

30. new life

*The old life is gone; a **new life** has begun!*

~ 2 Corinthians 5:17 NLT

September 11, 2001, changed the world for everyone.

But for those of us living in the Northeast—near New York City and Washington—it was especially traumatic since most of us knew victims of the terrorist attacks. Three people from my own little town in Connecticut died in the World Trade Center. I can remember experiencing a low-grade depression most of that fall. By Christmas, we were all ready to turn the calendar to a New Year.

~~~~~~~~~~

This is my journal entry on December 27, 2001 ~ "Gracehaven" Wethersfield CT:

> With each New Year I am prompted to begin a new life.
>
> In my "new life" there would be no hastily spoken words that can never be retracted, no moments of opportunity lost forever due to fear or laziness, and no choosing of the urgent over the best. There would be—by God's grace—a moment-by-moment intimacy with my Lord, a life attitude of gratitude and grace shown through my words and actions, and a deliberate decision to make every moment of living count.
>
> 2002 will be a new year in only four days. But where is the "new me"? This morning I found the old one hiding under her quilt, weary of struggling to make sense of a senseless challenge. Tonight she is rallied and ready to gather for the family celebration in a world that offers few reasons to celebrate.
>
> Dare I hope that tomorrow she will rise early and be positive and productive? By New Year's Eve, she should be ready

(more than ready) for a transformation. Cocooning since the aftermath of 9/11 must certainly give way to a butterfly soon!

What will it take to fulfill my heart's desire in 2002?

- A spiritual filling of God's power and promise in my worn-out life
- More fuel from God's Word for incentive and direction
- A mind that makes decisions and follows through on them, regardless of extenuating circumstances
- An urgency to make each moment count
- HOPE based on my God who is Enough

Oh Father, please help me. Revive me, renew me, refresh me, restrain me, recharge me, reignite my passion for You and Your kingdom. This I humbly pray in the Name of God the Father, God the Son, and God the Holy Spirit. Amen.

~~~~~~~~~~

Fourteen years have now passed since that journal entry.

As I remember what I was experiencing back then, I am filled with gratitude that God met me in that place but loved me too much to leave me there. The following year, 2002, was a challenging one, but also a fruitful and formative time for me: "He brought me out into a spacious place; / he rescued me because he delighted in me" (2 Samuel 22:20).

How do you feel about the year that has just passed? Would you like a new life in the New Year that is ahead? Write down your thoughts and prayers. God will answer.

My child, "Behold, I make all things new" (Revelation 21:5 NKJV). The past has passed, and you now have a clean slate. I will bring you into a spacious place because I delight in you. What story will you live? Allow Me to be the Author and Finisher of your faith. Now, let's begin again.

renew

LENT

◈◈◈◈◈◈◈◈◈◈◈◈◈◈◈◈◈◈◈◈◈

But our today is all athirst for Thee,
Come in the stillness, O Thou heavenly Dew,
Come Thou to us—to me—
*Revive, **renew**.*

~ Amy Carmichael
"Today"

1. return

Yet even now, says the LORD,
  ***return** to me with all your hearts,*
  with fasting, with weeping, and with sorrow;
tear your hearts
  and not your clothing.
***Return** to the LORD your God,*
  for he is merciful and compassionate,
  very patient, full of faithful love,
  and ready to forgive.

~ Joel 2:12-13 CEB

Christina couldn't wait to leave home and see the world.

Though she had a loving mother, life in her poor Brazilian village provided only a pallet on the floor, a washbasin, and a wood-burning stove. Christina dreamed of more. And she expected to find it in the Big City: Rio de Janeiro.

It broke her mother's heart. Maria knew that her beautiful daughter had no way of making money and would be forced to do whatever was required when pride meets hunger. So she packed a small bag, bought a bus ticket, and stopped briefly at the drug store photo booth for lots of small photos of herself.

This desperate mother walked through the city, stopping in the worst places—bars, nightclubs, seedy hotels—anywhere that prostitutes might frequent. And in every location, she taped on the mirror a small picture of herself with a note on the back. And prayed. Soon out of money and pictures, she took the bus back home to her village.

Weeks later, a disillusioned and broken down Christina descended some stairs in the latest hotel, feeling exhausted and fearful, living a nightmare instead of a dream. How many times had she wished she could trade any of those countless beds for that safe pallet back home? But she could never go home again. Not now. As she walked to the door her eye caught sight of a picture of her own mother on the lobby mirror.

What in the world?

Written on the back she read, "Whatever you have done, whatever you have become, it doesn't matter. I love you. Please come home."

And she did.[1]

Have you wandered far in search of more?

Were you seeking a path of sensation, significance, or security? Only to discover the price was far too dear; you had to forfeit your scruples, your self-esteem, and perhaps even your soul. But now you realize that going it alone is highly overrated. Listening to the world's views will only confuse and confound.

Is it too late to return to the God who knows you best and loves you most?

Absolutely not.

Now is the perfect time to "return to the Lord your God." He is waiting to welcome you home. But it does require a choice.

During this season, there is ample opportunity to offer up your own tears and sorrow, your broken heart and shattered dreams, your disobedience or shame. God still loves you. He still wants you. And His arms are open to receive, "for he is merciful and compassionate, very patient, full of faithful love, and ready to forgive."

For those reading "Renew" during Lent, today is Ash Wednesday. It is a good time to return to the Lord in contrition and repentance. We have strayed and turned our attention to other pursuits. We have too often neglected to provide our children and the world an example of Christianity. But today we begin anew.

Today, we return.

∽❧∾

My child, you need wander no more. As the days lengthen, so will be the process of coming closer and closer to Me. Just take it a day at a time. Study My words. Soon you will find them to be life-giving sustenance for all that is ahead of you. You've done the hardest part already: returning. Let's journey forward together.

2. renewed

*Put on your new nature, and be **renewed** as you learn to know
your Creator and become like him.*

~ Colossians 3:10 NLT

Round Top, Texas, is home to the "Junk Gypsies," and whenever I'm
there, I like to pop in and see what latest "junk" they have transformed
into "treasure."

These two sisters, hosts of their own television show, see old horseshoes
and envision a chandelier. With a bit of welding, those used-up, thrown-out
pieces of rusty metal become a shabby chic light fixture for a fancy barn party.

I love this concept. Looking at the old and tossed-aside remnants of a
life. And then, with love, creativity, and hard work, repurposing it into a
unique and beautiful new creation.

God does this with souls. He renews us.

He sees far more potential in us than we ever can because He knows our
hearts. And, more than that, He knows what a bit of love, grace, and attention can do to renew us from the inside out. To make us into something
like "junk jewels."

In our verse today, the New Testament Greek word *anakainoo'* is best
translated as "to renew, make new again, amend, or change." This is referring to how God transforms a believer. This word *renew* is specifically used
for causing something (or someone) to become better or superior to what
they were before.

God can do the same thing with our lives: repurpose us as an authentic
soul who dwells in the power and presence of Christ.

Here it is used in the present tense to mean we are "constantly being
renewed," to a new quality of life. This is a marathon, friends, not a sprint,
and will continue the rest of our lives—the process of sanctification or con-
forming to the image of God's Son.

Paul used *anakainoo'* in referring to our physical bodies: "Even if our bodies are breaking down on the outside, the person that we are on the inside is being renewed every day" (2 Corinthians 4:16 CEB). And he used it referring to our minds: "Don't be conformed to the patterns of this world, but be transformed by the renewing of your minds" (Romans 12:2 CEB).

Are you ready for renewal?

We can choose to "renew" any time, but the days building up to Easter Sunday are an especially appropriate season for repenting and reflecting on what Jesus Christ has done for us. The season of Lent derives its name from the old Saxon word *lencton*, which literally means "length." Even as the cold, winter days are gradually lengthening, so are our souls moving from winter into the spring of new life and hope. This practice of a forty-day preparation began in the third century and is a great way to seek God in a fresh way.

In the ensuing days, may we choose to walk by faith not sight, by grace not law, by the Spirit not the flesh, by relinquishment not resistance, by wisdom not folly, and by losing our lives for Christ's sake instead of always looking out for number one.

In this way, may we "learn to know your Creator and become like him."

My child, life is an adventure. And in these next days I hope you will discover more and more of who you are in Me. It doesn't matter what happened before. Today I choose to take you as you are and repurpose and renew you into someone who will live a unique story of grace and glory. I am with you each step of the way. All you have to do is offer yourself to My keeping and care.

3. pray

*If my people who belong to me will humbly **pray**, seek my face,
and turn from their wicked ways, then I will hear from heaven,
forgive their sin, and heal their land.*

~ 2 Chronicles 7:14 CEB

"I pray because I can't help myself," C. S. Lewis once said to a friend.

"I pray because I'm helpless. I pray because the need flows out of me all the time—waking and sleeping. It doesn't change God—it changes me."

God never tires of hearing us pray to Him.

Prayer is one way we draw closer to God and dwell in Him. What a great reminder in today's verse that He will take action as a result of our prayers: "For reasons we may never fully understand, God chooses to use our prayers—chooses to respond to our prayers—as a means of achieving or accomplishing His purposes. He has given us the privilege and responsibility of partnering with Him in His work through the power of prayer."[2]

Someone once told me, "Prayer is work." And it's true. We don't just pray when we feel like it; we pray intentionally as a discipline and a privilege.

Do you believe your prayers to be more important than your activities?

To pray is to wage warfare against the enemy as vividly shown in the movie *War Room*. I interviewed Karen Abercrombie, who plays "Miss Clara," a woman who takes prayer seriously. She believes and shows that she can help move heaven and earth through the strategic work of powerful prayer.

Prayer that changes us and the world doesn't just happen. It takes commitment and a deep belief that it is the greater work, that we are engaging with the Almighty in *His* ultimate work.

"Devote yourselves to prayer with an alert mind and a thankful heart" (Colossians 4:2 NLT). Why is it so hard to be devoted in prayer—to have an alert mind and thankful heart? Prayer is hard because it calls for attentiveness, tuning out the world, and turning to God. We take the attention off ourselves to focus on others and pray for a greater cause. Another obstacle can simply be that in order to communicate intimately with God, we must be completely honest.

If you aren't sure how to pray today, why not ask God to teach you, using this prayer:

> Every day I see again that only You can teach me to pray, only You can set my heart at rest, only You can let me dwell in Your presence. But Lord, let me at least remain open to Your initiative; let me wait patiently and attentively for the hour when You will come and break through all the walls I have erected. Teach me, O Lord, to pray. Amen.[3]

I have often found that sitting beside an empty chair and pouring out my heart to Jesus as though He were sitting right there next to me, is a good place to begin.

God will answer. He will "forgive their sins" and "heal their land." But first we must do the hard work: we must pray.

My child, I delight in your coming to Me with your praise, your concerns, and your requests. I am always right next to you, willing to act on your behalf. By praying for others you are laying down your life as an offering that will not go unnoticed. I will hear. And I will act. Your prayer is warfare and there will be victory in your humble persistence.

4. called

*I, the Lord, have **called** you for a good reason.*
I will grasp your hand and guard you.

~ Isaiah 42:6 CEB

During the memorial service, ten different people spoke of their relationship with the deceased. And, though they knew her in different ways, there were remarkable similarities in their comments about her legacy. It occurred to me that this person absolutely knew who she was and who she was not.

She had lived her true calling.

A pastor recently posed this question: "What is the core part of you that people will talk about at your funeral? If you're not clear on this, ask those who know you well to describe why they think God put you on earth."

How can we know what God has called us to be and do?

I like what author Frederick Buechner says: "The place God calls you to is the place where your deep gladness and the world's deep hunger meet."[4]

Mark Labberton, author of *Called*, brings it into real time: "The vocation of every Christian is to live as a follower of Jesus today. In every aspect of life, in small and large acts, with family, neighbors and enemies, we are to seek to live out the grace and truth of Jesus. This is our calling."[5]

Labberton calls that "first things." *How* this is manifested in the varying details and seasons of our life is secondary. These "next things" matter, but specific job titles are not our primary calling. Jesus called each of His disciples, "Follow Me." Each had the same vocation, but they followed Jesus in a manner unique to their own lives.

My primary calling is to live as Christ's beloved.

As I live into this primary calling—my "first thing"—I am empowered also to love God and my neighbor. I often call the unfolding of such things my "marching orders." Throughout my adult life my calling has remained the same—to be a disciple of Jesus Christ. But my marching orders have varied greatly: journalist, radio broadcaster, missions pastor, mother, teacher for the blind, conference speaker, magazine editor, high school teacher, pastor's wife, and even tea parlor hostess!

No matter what "hat" I was wearing, it was important to view my primary call as Christ follower. And yet, due to the demands of each profession, it is natural for us to fall into the habit of making "next things" first things: "So we go to work and forget or neglect who we are, what our life is really about, how we seek to love and serve. We enter the subculture of our activities, and soon that reality begins to define and shape us, rather than the other way around. In Scripture, God seems far more passionate about first things—how we live and love Him and our neighbor—than about next things—what our set of daily tasks is."[6]

May you and I live out the extraordinary call of following Jesus (first things) amid our daily lives of ordinary works (next things).

৩৩৩

My child, I called you by name and you responded with courage and faithfulness. No matter where you are or what you do, remember that I hold you by the hand and will never let you go. Don't let go of Me either, no matter how demanding your placement is. Remember that your most important identity is as My beloved. It is good.

5. winter

*Here, the **winter** is past;*
the rains have come and gone.
Blossoms have appeared in the land;
the season of singing has arrived.

~ Song of Solomon 2:11-12 CEB

New England winters can be brutal. This year, we in Connecticut experienced twenty major snowstorms and a total of sixty-four inches of snow. Not to mention the ice.

But the really great news is that winter always, *always* turns into spring. And spring is a time of hope and new beginnings. As our verse says, "blossoms have appeared in the land; the season of singing has arrived."

But we must keep believing that under that snow, the bulbs and seeds hidden deep down in the cold ground are actually in the process of emerging into those as-yet-unseen blossoms. In our Lenten preparation, we have to keep reaching out, even when it's cold and dark, hoping for signs of new life.

That's why my friend Vicki gives out winter hats lovingly made by God's people for those in Hartford who need warmth and hope.

One day, she graciously offered the McDonald's drive-thru window attendant one of the new warm winter hats, wished her good day, and drove away. Sewn inside each hat was a tag saying, "God Loves You. Camp Hope" (Camp Hope is where volunteers made the hats). Doing such random acts of kindness is one way to fight the cold of winter and of life for so many in the city.

Weeks later, Vicki was stunned to receive a message forwarded from the folks at Camp Hope. Turns out, it was written by the window attendant from that McDonald's encounter:

> Hello, my name is _____. Today I received a winter hat
> working in the McDonald's drive-thru by a lady whom I wish

I had asked her name. On the inside of the hat it said "God loves you. Camp Hope." And I hope I'm writing to the right place. If I am and if you happen to know who this woman is, I'd like to thank her. I've always been strong in my faith even with my share of trials. But for the past year or so I've suffered from major anxiety and depression. **This morning I woke up with the intention of not living another day.** My boss called saying he needed me early so I decided I was gonna do it (kill myself) after work. It is true that God comes at the right time. **Seeing that message at that moment served as a reminder that I am loved.** And not just by anyone but by God, creator of EVERYTHING! Sometimes we forget about something so amazing as that. I just want to thank her for letting God use her in such a way that seems small, but for me it was great. **God used her to save my life.**

I hope this story encourages you to keep believing in the hope of spring. In new life. In renewal. Especially if you are reading this during winter. Amy Carmichael once said, "All weathers nourish souls." It's true. Every season has its purpose.

Whatever you are experiencing, may God provide the right person to reach out and give you hope. And may you be that right person for someone else today.

My child, I long to bring warmth to your cold places. One of the hardest things about winter is believing in the unseen growth occurring below the surface. I suspect this is happening in your heart as well. As you make your journey with Me to the cross, keep drawing near. I will hold you in My arms and surprise you with loving serendipity.

6. sees

*Thereafter, Hagar used another name to refer to the LORD, who had spoken to her. She said, "You are the God who **sees** me."*

~ Genesis 16:13 NLT

Hagar felt used.

Which is totally understandable. Because, quite simply, she *was* used—to provide a child for her master and mistress, Abram and Sarai.

God had promised them many children, but it hadn't yet happened. Impatient with the waiting, they came up with their own plan for having a child: "Now Sarai, Abram's wife, had not been able to bear children for him. But she had an Egyptian servant named Hagar. So Sarai said to Abram, 'The Lord has prevented me from having children. Go and sleep with my servant. Perhaps I can have children through her.' And Abram agreed with Sarai's proposal" (Genesis 16:1-2 NLT).

Of course, since childbearing was the mark of true womanhood in those days, as soon as she became pregnant, Hagar felt superior to her mistress, Sarai: "Then Sarai said to Abram, 'This is all your fault! I put my servant into your arms, but now that she's pregnant she treats me with contempt.' . . . Then Sarai treated Hagar so harshly that she finally ran away" (Genesis 16:5-6 NLT).

Can someone say, "It's complicated"?

Hagar felt like a pawn in a dangerous game, and so she chose to run away, hoping for a new life when her baby was born. But there was nowhere to run except the wilderness. And she found herself with no food, no protection, no husband, and no future. Forgotten.

But God had not forgotten her. He was not blind to her need and desperation. He sent an angel who "found Hagar beside a spring of water in the wilderness, along the road to Shur. The angel said to her, 'Hagar, Sarai's servant, where have you come from, and where are you going?'" (Genesis

16:7-8 NLT). After saying she had run away, Hagar was astonished to be told by the angel that God had heard her cry of distress; that she should return to her mistress; and that she would have a son and name him Ishmael. And that he would always be at enmity with his relatives.

From then on, "Hagar used another name to refer to the LORD, who had spoken to her. She said, 'You are the God who sees me'" (Genesis 16:13 NLT). Stunned that the God of the universe cared enough to comfort and provide for her, Hagar turned now to *El Roi*, the God who sees.

Did you know that God sees you in your wilderness? "From His dwelling place He watches all who live on earth—he who forms of the hearts of all, who considers everything they do" (Psalm 33:14-15). He sees what's really in our hearts: "He sees unforgiveness, unconfessed sins, the habits we cling to, the questionable shows we watch, and the literature we read. He sees the failures that we try to hold behind our backs, and He lovingly invites us to come out of hiding so He can clean up the mess we've made."[7]

In parts of South Africa, a common greeting is *"Sawubona!"* which means, "I see you!" and the response is *"Yebo!"*—"Yes!"

Will you say yes today to *El Roi* when He greets you?

─────────── ✺ ───────────

My child, there are many injustices in life. And whether we choose the wrong path or it is thrust upon us, there are always consequences. The two sons of Abraham, Ishmael and Isaac, were destined to become lifetime antagonists and their descendants today—the Arabs and the Jews—are still at odds. But I see each person as a unique individual. I will provide springs of living water.

7. forgiveness

If you kept track of sins, LORD—
my Lord, who would stand a chance?
*But **forgiveness** is with you—*
that's why you are honored.

~ Psalm 130:3-4 CEB

"I forgive you," Nadine said to the young man in the courtroom, her voice breaking with emotion. "You took something very precious from me. I will never talk to her again. I will never, ever hold her again. But I forgive you. And have mercy on your soul."

Nadine's mother, Ethel Lance, was one of the nine people killed by an angry young man during a Bible study at Emmanuel AME Church in Charleston in the summer of 2015.

I'm not sure I could forgive like that.

> Such forgiveness is illogical in the rational world and nonsensical to common human nature. Such forgiveness is humanity at its most human, or perhaps its most divine. . . . Good sometimes overcomes evil via counterintuitive forces: compassion, mercy and forgiveness.[8]

Those who have received God's abundant forgiveness are usually the ones best able to reach out and forgive, leaving the results in God's hands: "The victims' families are not saying that the terrorist should escape without penalty. . . . When we forgive, whether in the wake of an enormity such as this one or in the more mundane ways we have been hurt, we are not saying vengeance is not due. We are saying that vengeance is God's, not ours (Romans 12:19)."[9]

Are you amazed and humbled by this extraordinary act of forgiveness? I certainly am.

One of the words used in the New Testament for forgiveness is the Greek *charizomai*, meaning "to deal graciously with." But sometimes this seems so unfair! Forgiving others means releasing them from any obligation to make up to me what they have taken from me. And yet, there is also redemption: "When you release the wrongdoer from the wrong, you cut a malignant tumor out of your inner life. You set a prisoner free, but you discover that the real prisoner was yourself."[10]

In the Old Testament, we find two Hebrew words used for forgiveness. *Nasa* means "carry, bear, lift up, or forgive." *Salah* means "to forgive or be forgiven." Our verse today reiterates that because of God's great compassion and desire to restore our vital connection to Him, He graciously extends forgiveness to all who ask.

And He calls us to do the same.

I only hope that if similar circumstances ever occur, I will be able to say what my sister in Christ Nadine said after the murder of her mother. For I must. It won't mean that I pretend that the wrong didn't matter. Forgiveness is my willful decision to treat another person with the same mercy and grace that I have received.

Yes, it is costly to acknowledge the hurt and live with the consequences of other people's sin, but our friends in Charleston know that it is the first step toward healing.

Who do you need to forgive? God is our model and will help us.

My child, I know you are hurting and bewildered by the pain and senselessness of that person's actions against you. And you wonder if you will ever be able to move forward. The first step is to make a conscious decision to forgive them. You don't have to see them or reconcile with them. Just on your own, release them to Me. You can do this because I have already forgiven you.

8. hold

If I could fly on the wings of dawn,
stopping to rest only on the far side of the ocean—
even there your hand would guide me;
*even there your strong hand would **hold** me tight!*

~ Psalm 139:9-10 CEB

Henri Nouwen once told his father that he always wanted to be a trapeze artist.

Having become friends with The Flying Rodleighs, Henri enjoyed their performances around Europe.

> "As a flyer, I must have complete trust in my catcher," Rodleigh told him. "The public might think that *I* am the great star of the trapeze, but the real star is Joe, my catcher. He has to be there for me with split-second precision and grab me out of the air as I come to him in the long jump.
>
> "The secret is that the flyer does nothing and the catcher does everything. When I fly to Joe, I have simply to stretch out my arms and hands and wait for him to catch me and pull me safely in. . . . A flyer must fly and a catcher must catch, and the flyer must trust, with outstretched arms, that his catcher will be there for him," Rodleigh concluded.[11]

In a similar way, God is always there to catch us—and hold tight.

We do nothing, except reach out. He does everything.

"The eternal God is your refuge and dwelling place, / and underneath are the everlasting arms" (Deuteronomy 33:27 AMP). He is our dwelling place. No matter where we go in the world, God is the One who will provide a home and safe refuge.

Our verse today is from one of the most beloved psalms in the Bible. It begins with David's startling realization of God's intimate knowledge of us and constant presence with us: "You surround me—front and back. / You put your hand on me. That kind of knowledge is too much for me; / it's so high above me that I can't fathom it" (Psalm 139:5-6 CEB).

Did you know God holds you?

I love nothing better than to hold my precious grand-girl in my arms and read her a book, such as *The Runaway Bunny* by Margaret Wise Brown. Written in 1942, it's a classic for children of any age.

Of course the little bunny, like many of us, wants to run away from home and experience a grand adventure. But no matter how or where he decides to go, his mother is always there—for she loves her little bunny very much.

When the bunny says he'll become a rock on a high mountain, the mother replies that she will then become a mountain climber and climb to where he is. When he decides to hide in a garden as a crocus, she declares that she will become a gardener and find him. After several more scenarios the little bunny realizes the relentless love of his mother and decides, "Shucks, I might just as well stay where I am and be your little bunny."[12]

Where can you go from His presence?

Nowhere. God's hand will be wherever we are—to lift us up, to hold us tight.

Shucks, we may as well rest in the dwelling place of His love and care. And be His child.

———————————— ❧ ————————————

My child, I know that you have traveled far, if not in miles, in experience. But when you were in the pits, I was right there holding you. And when you flew to the heights, I held you fast. There is nowhere you can go—geographically, emotionally, spiritually, mentally—that I won't be. So come on home and rest in My everlasting arms.

9. *temptation*

{God} won't allow you to be tempted beyond your abilities.
Instead, with the **temptation***, God will also supply a way out*
so that you will be able to endure it.

~ 1 Corinthians 10:13 CEB

What was your biggest temptation this week?

That piece of cheesecake? That tantalizing website ad? That little black dress you saw on shopping TV? That drug-of-choice that has its tentacles around your mind and body?

Whatever your first thought, I daresay your and my temptations are nowhere near what our Lord endured. In fact, the word *temptation* is translated from the New Testament Greek word *peirasmós*, which means "trial" or "testing." The verb form is *peirazo*, rooted in "to pierce." I doubt our temptations pierce us in the same way as Christ was "pierced for our transgressions" (Isaiah 53:5).

What do you do when you are tempted?

Turn to the One who "will also supply a way out." God's indwelling presence offers us tactics to resist and respond to those areas where we know we are vulnerable. To rest in God's companionship in the midst of temptation provides a lifetime of strength.

Yet again, Jesus' life shows us the way.

At His moment of anointing for ministry—when His time had finally come and John had baptized Him and God had sent the seal of approval through a dove—He was led to the desert.

That's when temptations occur; tests come when we are focusing elsewhere and taken off guard.

Jesus prayed and fasted for forty days in the desert in order to prepare for this onslaught. And the enemy came at him with three different strategies to satisfy His needs: food, safety, and power. The devil, knowing how hungry He was, taunted Him to turn stones into bread. Then he took Jesus to the temple pinnacle and suggested jumping off so that angels would save Him. Finally, he led Him to a high mountain and offered power over all below if only Jesus would bow down and worship him.

And in each instance of temptation, Jesus fought back with God's Word. He knew that temptation would cause us either to turn toward God or to seek ways to hide from God.

If you are tempted right now, all you have to do is consult the One who has "been there" and understands: "We have a great high priest who passed through the heavens, who is Jesus, God's Son; because we don't have a high priest who can't sympathize with our weaknesses but instead one who was tempted in every way that we are, except without sin. . . . Let's draw near to the throne of favor with confidence so that we can receive mercy and find grace when we need help" (Hebrews 4:14-16 CEB).

Remember, you are not alone. We are all tempted.

Sometimes we rise above and are victorious; other times we give in. But we never give up!

We need the security of abiding in God's dwelling place: "I need Thy presence every passing hour. What but Thy grace can foil the tempter's power? Who, like Thyself, my guide and stay can be? Through cloud and sunshine, Lord, abide with me."[13]

◦◦◦

My child, there is much in your world that glitters and beckons. But it is not all from Me. The enemy of your soul would love nothing more than to tempt you as he did My Son—perhaps even with food, safety, and power. But you can resist and be strong, as you dwell in My constant presence and claim the Bible's promises for you. I have provided a way out.

10. wounds

But he was wounded for the wrong we did;
he was crushed for the evil we did.
The punishment, which made us well, was given to him,
*and we are healed because of his **wounds**.*

~ Isaiah 53:5 NCV

"Just assume that everyone within the reach of your words is wounded."

These were my words to the writers and speakers attending my seminar entitled "What Your Audience Desperately Needs." Because it's true.

We all carry soul wounds.

Scars from childhood family skirmishes. Scratches from professional rejection. Scabs from physical trauma we never saw coming. Limps from having fallen one time too many.

What are your souvenirs of suffering? And what do you do with them?

> There are two ways to receive wounds. One leads to larger life. The other leads straight to death, that is to destruction—of those we influence as well as of ourselves. No one has power to hurt us more deeply than somebody we loved and counted on to understand and support us. By grace we can receive the wounds of our friends in Christ's strength and for His glory. Or we can use the world's methods of anger, resentment and retaliation, which is natural but lethal. The choice is ours.[14]

Making this choice in the middle of woundedness is strategic: "Distress that drives us to God does that. It turns us around. It gets us back in the way of salvation. We never regret that kind of pain. But those who let distress drive them away from God are full of regrets, end up on a deathbed of regrets" (2 Corinthians 7:10 MSG).

Jesus knows we are wounded.

That's one reason He came and made the ultimate sacrifice for us on the cross: "he was wounded for the wrong we did; he was crushed for the evil we did. The punishment, which made us well, was given to him." He submitted to the lashes and the nails so that we wouldn't have to; "and we are healed because of his wounds."

Jennifer has a Y-shaped scar on her leg, which she says reminds her of Yahweh, one of the names of God: "Maybe we all need to feel along for our scars, to find the cherished mark of Yahweh upon our fragile personhood. Maybe we need to remember that though we were wounded, we have been healed and our scars are proof of a God redeeming all the broken things."[15]

But what if your wound isn't even a scar yet? Then be assured that our Lord is in the "binding up" aspect of restoration and healing: "God heals the brokenhearted / and bandages their wounds" (Psalm 147:3 CEB).

"Jesus mends. He sutures. He slathers salve on the injured area and wraps it in holy bandages presoaked in mercy. Then, under His divine touch, wounds heal. Even wounds that cut bone-deep or leave raised-welt scars. His mending is artistry. Restoring is His specialty. Renewing broken things is His heart. Reclaiming shattered souls—repairing tattered lives— His preoccupation."[16]

Like Thomas, perhaps we need to touch His hands and feet. He understands.

My child, My body and soul were broken too. And I cried out in pain, but I submitted because I knew My Father had a plan. My plan for you in the midst of your wounding and in the process of your healing is that you will turn toward Me and seek My face. And yes, it is a face that was despised and rejected by men. I understand. I'm here.

11. repentance

Godly sorrow brings **repentance** *that leads to salvation and leaves no regret.*

~ 2 Corinthians 7:10

Like many sons without fathers, young Robert fell in with the wrong crowd.

His gang of boys gambled, drank, and even went to hear George Whitfield preach in order to drown him out with their heckling. But the prophetic words of that preacher back in 1755 haunted Robert for several years until he finally turned his life completely around and followed Christ.

After becoming a minister, Robert Robinson wrote this hymn, in recognition of how far he had come: "Come, Thou Fount of every blessing, Tune my heart to sing Thy grace; Streams of mercy, never ceasing, Call for songs of loudest praise." And yet, embedded in the hymn was a knowledge of his own tendency toward unfaithfulness, "Prone to wander, Lord, I feel it, Prone to leave the God I love; Here's my heart, O take and seal it, Seal it for Thy courts above."[17]

Have you ever wandered astray? Away from wise family and friends? Away from your core values? Away from God?

Our verse today reminds us that if we have "godly sorrow," we can also turn our lives around. This process is called repentance, which is translated from the New Testament Greek word *metanoia*, which means "to change one's mind or purpose" or "to change the inner man."

It's never too late to turn around and change your total direction—spiritually, mentally, and emotionally. Jesus was especially drawn to those who need to repent: "I have not come to call the righteous, but sinners to repentance" (Luke 5:32).

Repentance is not an easy road. In a way, repentance is just another word for honesty—taking an honest look at yourself and recognizing what binds you to death. . . . Repentance is rethinking: it means reorganizing our patterns of sin instead of denying them.[18]

C. S. Lewis agrees that repentance is a process of dying: "Remember, this repentance, this willing submission to humiliation and a kind of death, is not something God demands of you before he will take you back and which he could let you off if He chose: it is simply a description of what going back to Him is like. If you ask God to take you back without it, you are really asking Him to let you go back without going back. It cannot happen."[19]

If you have godly sorrow you can change course.

Even twice, as Robert Robinson later learned. Unfortunately, he wandered away from his faith again as an older adult. But one day, while riding in a stagecoach, a woman asked him if he knew the hymn she was humming.

His reply: "Madam, I am the poor unhappy man who wrote that hymn many years ago, and I would give a thousand worlds, if I had them, to enjoy the feelings I had then."

And on that day, he repented yet again and experienced for the rest of his life "streams of mercy, never ceasing."

My child, is it time to turn around? You have been headed in one direction, and we both know that direction brings only pain and death. But as you face your poor choices with sorrow, you will find the courage to come back to Me. Lay all your wanderings at My feet and allow Me to send you in a whole new direction. That is why I'm here.

12. *restores*

He makes me lie down in green pastures;
He leads me beside quiet waters.
He restores my soul.

~ Psalm 23:2-3 NASB

When Lettie visited Africa, she wisely engaged a group of carriers and guides for her trek. On the first day, she was pleased that they covered many, many miles.

When she awakened the second day, eager for another leg of the journey, she noticed all the carriers she had hired remained seated and refused to move.

"Why aren't we ready to forge ahead?" Lettie asked the leader in an agitated manner.

His reply, "On the first day we traveled too fast. Now we are waiting for our souls to catch up with our bodies."

Devotional author Lettie Cowman reflected on this incident: "The whirling rushing life which so many of us live does for us what the first march did for those poor jungle tribesmen. The difference: they knew what they needed to restore life's balance; too often we do not."[20]

Our bodies and souls need rest. A good shepherd knows this, as the psalmist in today's verse so clearly states. And so our Good Shepherd does for us what is needed as "He restores my soul."

Those who are caregivers (including parents) and in the many helping professions (including ministry) are especially in need of regular restoration. One doctor offers these signs and symptoms that we may be lacking in self-care: "chronic exhaustion, sense that you can never do enough, work becomes the center of your identity (grandiosity), diminished creativity, inflexibility, guilt, fear, anger, relational problems, sleep problems, somatic complaints, lack of efficacy, helplessness, and hopelessness."[21]

When you and I ignore any of these symptoms we run the risk of causing problems and pain both to ourselves and those we serve. There is nothing wrong with taking care of ourselves. In fact, in that very act we are investing in becoming a person who is better able to take care of others.

For any who struggle with this self-care concept, may I direct us to the life of Christ.

"Then, because so many people were coming and going that they did not even have a chance to eat, he [Jesus] said to them, 'Come with me by yourselves to a quiet place and get some rest'" (Mark 6:31). Yes, our Lord and Savior, who was both human and divine, actually modeled the need to come apart and be restored.

> Jesus engaged in certain practices that allowed God's grace to keep replenishing his spirit:
>
> - He prayed.
> - He had a circle of close friends—the twelve who went through life with him.
> - He engaged in regular corporate worship at synagogue.
> - He fed his mind with Scripture.
> - He enjoyed God's creation—mountain, garden, and lake.
> - He took long walks.
> - He welcomed little children and hugged them and blessed them.
> - He enjoyed partying with non-religious types.[22]

If you are in need of restoration today, why not pick out one or two of the above practices and engage as Jesus would. It may just restore your soul.

My child, I know your greatest desire is to serve Me and those whom I have placed in your care. Your diligence is a great gift that I recognize and applaud. But you are exhausted. And it is also part of My purpose that you be restored and rested in order to face the tasks ahead. So, dear one, come apart. Do what is needed to refresh and replenish. I will be at your side all the way.

13. guide

I will make the blind walk a road they don't know,
*and I will **guide** them in paths they don't know.*
But I will make darkness before them into light
and rough places into level ground.
These things I will do;
I won't abandon them.

~ Isaiah 42:16 CEB

I was blindfolded every day for three months.

This was part of my training to become an orientation and mobility specialist for visually impaired people. In order to teach the blind, I first had to experience what they experienced.

One day, while tapping my white cane in front of me, a horn honked nearby, startling me. Then a dog barked, and I wondered if it was restrained. Such anxiety is common among people who cannot see. My cane also "told" me the sidewalk had become uneven as I precariously made my way toward my destination, the Hot Shot Café in the heart of Biltmore Village.

My trainer, Bette, told me of construction on this route but assured me the cane would "warn" me in time to avert potholes and newly dug ditches. "Just take it one step at a time," she instructed. "Your cane technique will give you the view of a single step ahead. The rest will be made clear as you progress."

But I wanted to know *now* where the obstacles were long before I encountered them, not just as I needed to alter my path. Similarly, I wanted to know the whole plan of my life while I was in my twenties—where to live and work, what graduate school degree to pursue, who to marry, and whether or not cowboy boots were a good investment.

Are you looking for a little guidance?

If so, you may have to be willing to "see" only one step at a time, rather than the whole picture. Eventually, God did indeed guide me to graduate school (in cowboy boots) up in New England. Upon arrival, my faculty advisor gave me today's verse as a promise for my time there.

The Hebrew word most often used in the Old Testament for guide is *nahal*. Though the Bible warns of snares, traps, and treacherous paths, it consistently portrays God as One who will counsel and safely guide all those who belong to Him.

There is absolutely nothing wrong with wanting to plan ahead.

God requires that we do our part (pray, make plans, and trust), and He will do His part (show us the way to go). If we take time to be quiet and listen, we may hear His voice, as the Israelites did: "If you stray to the right or the left, you will hear a word that comes from behind you: 'This is the way; walk in it'" (Isaiah 30:21 CEB).

Do the next thing.

When you can't see your way, know that you can dwell in God's presence and He will guide your path: "Wherever He may guide me, no want shall turn me back. My Shepherd is beside me, and nothing can I lack. His wisdom ever waking, His sight is never dim. He knows the way He's taking, and I will walk with Him."[23]

One step at a time.

∽∾

My child, I have a plan for where you are going, even if you can't see it. And I will reveal to you all you need to know—in My time and My way. Just trust Me and do your part in walking forward in the path you have been shown so far. One day you will turn around and see a grand plan for the journey—one that glorifies Me because of your faith and obedience. I am your Guide. Always.

14. wrestled

Your name is no longer Jacob. From now on it's Israel
*(God-Wrestler); you've **wrestled** with God and you've come*
through.

~ Genesis 32:28 MSG

Have you ever wrestled with God?

Struggling against where He was leading you or what He was requiring of you? Fearful of what might lay ahead on your journey because of what lay behind in your past?

Then perhaps you need to know Jacob, whose name was changed to Israel, which means "God-wrestler."

Jacob and Esau were the twin sons of Isaac and Rebekah. Prompted by his devious mother, Jacob stole his twin's birthright and blessing and ran for his life as Esau vowed to kill him. His next encounter was with his Uncle Laban who tricked Jacob into marrying daughter Leah before working seven more years to marry his great love, Rachel. This time he was the one who was tricked. Finally, he set off for home with a desire to reconcile with his brother, but he was also concerned what that might bring.

He sent gifts and offerings and kind words ahead to Esau to pave the way for forgiveness. But he still struggled with what might lay ahead. Hearing that Esau was approaching with hundreds of men caused Jacob a sleepless night as he had every reason to expect his brother to attack him. Still, he knew he needed to go to God before he went to Esau.

Left alone, Jacob was suddenly conscious of an assailant. A man wrestled with him until daybreak at the river named Jabbok (*yabok*), which means "wrestler" (*yaaveik*). The Hebrew word for wrestling is found only here and the next verse and nowhere else in the Hebrew Bible. The word itself comes from the root *avakthat*, mean dust. So the basic meaning of this word is to "get dusty while wrestling."

During the struggle Jacob was forced to face who he really was when the Lord asked him his name (Genesis 32:27) and then changed his name to Israel because he had persevered and overcome (Genesis 32:38). Jacob knew his past struggles and knew that God knew them as well, but he still sought a blessing so that a new chapter would begin when he finally saw Esau. That's when he cried, "I won't let you go until you bless me" (Genesis 32:26 CEB).

How long does God have to wrestle with you before you yield every area of your life to Him—past, present, and future?

Jacob met with God before he met with his brother. To Jacob's surprise, Esau's response to him was completely different from what he expected, and perhaps really deserved. In the intervening years Esau's heart had softened to God as had Jacob's.

The brothers wept and embraced. Miraculously, what had begun earlier in life as such a volatile relationship was now restored.

God longs to bless His children. But too often we find ourselves like Jacob and even Esau, clinging to old hurts and resentments, needing to work through the fallout of sin in the person we are today. Don't despair the struggle. Just cling to God and seek His face.

May He give you His blessing as well.

My child, I am with you in the dark when you are scared of confrontation because of past mistakes. I will stay with you and help you face the past and move into the future. But you need to persevere in prayer and even be bold enough to ask Me questions and demand a blessing. Israel went on to live a fruitful life. May you do the same.

15. godless chatter

*Avoid **godless chatter**, because those who indulge in it will become more and more ungodly.*

~ 2 Timothy 2:16

Today as I write, the Dow Jones has just plunged a thousand points. Planned Parenthood videos of baby parts are being shared on the Internet. ISIS is committing atrocities against women and children and executing Christians. Racism has prompted a slogan that should be a no-brainer, "Black Lives Matter" (because *all* lives matter). Gay marriage and LGBT issues are being debated everywhere from bakeries to colleges to the Supreme Court. Thousands of names have been published as subscribers to a prostitution service.

And everyone has an opinion! There is much "godless chatter" on social networking.

What is there about anonymity in technology that prompts people to say things they would never stand up and profess face to face?

Whatever it is, we better guard against it, as our verse says, because such Tweets and posts and blogs and shares rarely bring readers closer to God.

The apostle Paul wrote to "avoid godless chatter" in his final letter to Timothy. In some of his final words he reminds all of us of what's most important in carrying on the ministry of Christ. "For the time is coming when people will not endure sound teaching, but having itching ears they will accumulate for themselves teachers to suit their own passions" (2 Timothy 4:3 ESV).

Do you ever skim your news feeds to find words that suit your own passions?

What do you think Jesus really cares about: soapboxes or souls? "Jesus cares about truth. Jesus cares about love. Jesus cares about holiness. Jesus cares about the oppressed. But while everyone is yelling online what they think Jesus cares about, humble real-life meaningful conversations and relationships are fading," one blogger recently lamented.[24]

Don't you think we will love better online if we are loving others well offline?

That means reaching out to the unfamiliar and uncomfortable. Having those hard conversations. Listening hard and praying silently for the right words when it is time to offer them. Because "we are ambassadors who represent Christ. God is negotiating with you through us" (2 Corinthians 5:20 CEB).

Another young blogger I follow stated, "We are at an important time in our history. People need the hope that we have, and we know exactly where they can find it—in the heart of Jesus Christ as revealed in Scripture. But that means we have to choose our words carefully, deliver them prayerfully, and live out our messages faithfully."[25]

I love the paraphrase of today's verse: "Warn them before God against pious nitpicking, which chips away at the faith. It just wears everyone out. Concentrate on doing your best for God, work you won't be ashamed of, laying out the truth plain and simple" (2 Timothy 2:16 MSG).

Don't wear everyone out. Be a refreshing, winsome Christ-follower.

My child, thank you for caring so deeply about such important issues. I know they loom large and cover all the billboards of your mind. I know you harbor fear and anger and frustration and confusion as you consider the world today. Will you give it all to Me? And I promise I will help you process and proceed with love and truth and great compassion.

16. betray

After he said these things, Jesus was deeply disturbed and testified, "I assure you, one of you will betray me."

~ John 13:21 CEB

Have you ever been betrayed by someone you trusted? The wounds of an enemy are one thing; but the wounds of a friend—that's the worst.

And Jesus knows just how you feel.

Someone He had lived with, ministered with, traveled with—poured His life into—was about to turn Him over to be arrested by authorities. No wonder He was "deeply disturbed."

"This disciple asked, 'Lord, who is it?' Jesus answered, 'It's the one to whom I will give this piece of bread once I have dipped into the bowl.' Then he dipped the piece of bread and gave it to Judas, Simon Iscariot's son. After Judas took the bread, Satan entered into him. Jesus told him, 'What you are about to do, do quickly.' No one sitting at the table understood why Jesus said this to him" (John 13:25-28 CEB). But Judas knew.

Because of this one act, the name *Judas* continues to have the connotation of betrayal; we will say, "You're a real Judas," when someone has turned against us.

> Though Judas never deceived Jesus, he deceived their companions because the lure of money and power deceived him. Kissing Jesus on the cheek, he turned and handed Him over to the guards (Luke 22:39-53). The reality of Judas's betrayal sunk in soon after the cold silver filled his hands. He had committed treason toward the only man on record who called him 'friend.' The poison injected his soul, and he rushed out in despair and took his own life.[26]

Why do friends turn against us? It is said that Judas became upset with

Jesus after being chastised for criticizing a woman who honored Jesus by pouring expensive perfume on Him. Judas then went straight to the council and offered to turn Christ over to them in return for thirty pieces of silver, the price of a slave. Yet this reason doesn't justify the act.

Because even if we understand the reason for betrayal, it still hurts. And the consequences are still far-reaching. Betrayal is rarely contained between two people; like ripples in water, the hurt expands to others. The disciples scattered in fear, causing Jesus to feel more abandoned than ever before. And the atmosphere of mistrust and suspicion only deepened throughout the land.

When we are betrayed, we must relinquish our confusion, pain, and hurts to the Lord in prayer. We must work through the process of forgiveness, even if restoration is not possible. I cannot help but believe that if Jesus could forgive the two criminals on the cross next to Him, He most certainly would have forgiven Judas, had he turned to Him in repentance and remorse.

Betrayal does not have to be the end. We can move forward with the help of One who has experienced the greatest betrayal and still offers hope and new life.

My child, you have been deeply hurt. And it was by a friend or a fellow believer, not the enemy. That's what makes it betrayal—the worst sort of human rejection. Please know that I am with you in this pain. I understand all that you are going through. But in order to move forward, you must take some hard steps. Don't worry, I am right here, and renewal is on the other side.

17. engraved

I will not forget you!
*See, I have **engraved** you on the palms of my hands.*

~ Isaiah 49:15-16

She was waiting by the sink in the ladies room as I began washing my hands.

"Excuse me," she interrupted, "But the Lord has given me a word for you."

I was in Colorado Springs for meetings with my literary agent and publishers. Honestly, the meetings weren't going very well, and I had escaped our dinner table at the restaurant to have a moment alone.

The stranger continued as I stood there, too startled to speak; "God told me to tell you this: *You will not be forgotten*."

I gulped, "Okay. Thanks."

And then she interjected, "And, oh yeah, something about your stomach. Is there a medical problem? Well, God says that's going to be okay too." (Now I was *really* spooked; and it was years later until I finally understood that part of her word from God.)

But as she left the tiny room, she turned back with a smile, "Remember, *you will not be forgotten!*"

I never saw her again.

I also never shared this story. Until now, fifteen years later.

It seemed too far-fetched. Too "out there." Prophecies in bathrooms simply are not part of my normal life—even my spiritual journey.

But I did write it all down in my journal. And I did pray, asking God to show me what, if anything, this was to mean in my life. Because, honestly, sometimes I feel forgotten. By God and everyone else.

That's when He led me to today's verse: "I will not forget you!" In Scripture, when that promise is made, there are two rather interesting reinforcements: one before and one after. Leading into those words is an illustration that hits close to home: "Can a woman forget her nursing child, / fail to pity the child of her womb? / Even these may forget, / but I won't forget you" (Isaiah 49:15 CEB). As a mother who raised four children, I cannot imagine a world in which I would forget my nursing baby.

And though I don't have any tattoos, I have certainly written ink reminders on my hand. Sort of like the second reinforcement in our verse today: "See, I have engraved you on the palms of my hands." In biblical times a slave would often bear the brand of his master, but what a switch to have the Master inscribing his servant's name on His hand—a tangible reminder of the covenant between God and His people.

In order for God to forget us, the scars in the palms of His hands must disappear.

And that's never going to happen, as this old hymn affirms: "My name from the palms of His hands eternity will not erase; Impressed on His heart it remains, in marks of indelible grace. Yes, I to the end shall endure, as sure as the earnest is given; More happy, but not more secure, the glorified spirits in Heaven."[27]

Are you worried God might forget you?

I don't even need the gift of prophecy to reply, "God says *you will not be forgotten!*"

_____

⌒⌒

My child, how could I ever forget you? I thought you up. I made you. I am here to sustain you. I will never forget you. More than that, I will carry you in My heart and on My hands always. Cling to this promise and may it bring you peace and security. You are known. You are loved. You are not forgotten.

18. humility

*Don't do anything for selfish purposes, but with **humility** think of others as better than yourselves.*

~ Philippians 2:3 CEB

"We live in the culture of the Big Me," wrote David Brooks in the *New York Times* last week.

There is tremendous pressure to promote ourselves. Social media encourages us to broadcast a highlight reel of our lives. But our verse today reminds us that to live in humility is the better choice: "think of others as better than yourselves."

Are you seeking this quality?

In his book *The Road to Character*, Brooks suggests we do so:

> But all the people I've ever deeply admired are profoundly honest about their own weaknesses. They have identified their core sin, whether it is selfishness, the desperate need for approval, cowardice, hardheartedness, or whatever. They have traced how that core sin leads to the behavior that makes them feel ashamed. They have achieved a profound humility, which has best been defined as an intense self-awareness from a position of other-centeredness.[28]

The word *humility* derives from the Latin word *humus*, which we translate "earth." People with humility are down-to-earth types: "The humble live surprised. The humble live by joy. The humble are the laid-low and bowed ones, the surprised ones with hands open to receive whatever He gives. He hands them the earth. The earth. In the upside-down kingdom of heaven, down is up and up is down, and those who want to ascend higher must descend lower."[29]

Jesus was humble. Am I? Are you?

We are commanded in Scripture that the way to live fully is to "humble yourselves under God's power so that he may raise you up in the last day" (1 Peter 5:6 CEB).

How would that look?

Christ is the perfect model for us to emulate. His birth was humble, but so was his life. He had no home and was at everyone's beck and call morning and night. He encouraged his disciples that "the one who is greatest among you will be your servant." Yes, He definitely lived an upside-down life, declaring that "all who lift themselves up will be brought low. But all who make themselves low will be lifted up" (Matthew 23:11-12 CEB).

But the ultimate humility was when "he humbled himself by becoming obedient to the point of death, even death on a cross" (Philippians 2:8 CEB).

Christ is probably not asking you and me to literally die for Him today. But I believe He does require us to "die daily" in small ways as we forfeit our own desires and agendas so that we might look to another's interests first. We can turn the Big Me into the little me.

Do you want to dwell in a place of humility?

Let's let go of trying to orchestrate our own publicity and control our climb.

My child, I know you are paddling furiously, seeking to stay afloat in your hectic world. But it takes too much energy, doesn't it? And it's frustrating that you have no control over others' response to your best efforts. The better choice? Let go and leave it all in My hands. And keep reaching out to others, discovering what they have to offer. You will become salt of the earth in no time at all.

19. poured out

*I'm **poured out** like water.*
  All my bones have fallen apart.
  My heart is like wax;
  it melts inside me.
My strength is dried up
  like a piece of broken pottery.

~ Psalm 22:14-15 CEB

Have you ever experienced a "dark night of the soul?"

This term, first mentioned by sixteenth-century St. John of the Cross, has come to mean a season when one senses the total absence of God. Our prayers lack feeling and imagination. No insights carry us through the day; no sense of the holy emerges. It is an experience of dryness, darkness, and emptiness.

And it can come to anyone. Even a saint.

A few years ago the world was shocked to learn, through the publication of her private letters, that Mother Teresa of Calcutta experienced a dark night of the soul, which tormented her even in the midst of her amazing ministry to the poorest of the poor. "Over time, a spiritual adviser helped Teresa realize that her feelings of abandonment only increased her understanding of the people she helped. Ultimately, she identified her suffering with that of Jesus, which helped her to accept it."[30]

The psalmist in today's verse is experiencing deep emotional and spiritual trauma, which manifests itself in his body as well: "All my bones have fallen apart." One cannot read very far in Psalm 22 without realizing that these are the prophetic words of Christ's experience on the cross. No other Old Testament passage provides such a full picture of His suffering, beginning in dark anguish and ending in soaring hope. But even when He experienced a life "poured out like water," His passion was still to do the will of His Father, no matter how much it hurt, for the greater glory that would come.

If you are suffering, God is still at work in your life. In your soul. Cecil knows about dark nights:

> For Christians, those dark times may be a time for us to look deeply within ourselves and to examine our hearts. They may push us to overcome our complacency or to become aware of our dependency on God, or make us yearn for an even deeper commitment. Because of my period of darkness, I've come to realize that whether I sense the divine presence or I don't, it doesn't say anything about the Lord. When we've examined our hearts and believe we're as close to God as we know how to be, yet we have no sense of His presence, it may mean God is at our side, silently watching over us and always caring for us.[31]

But how can we find our way back into the joy of God's presence?

"What do we do in the dark night? We do nothing," suggests John Ortberg. "We wait. We remember that we are not God. We hold on. We ask for help. We do less. We resign from things, we rest more, we stop going to church, we ask somebody else to pray because we can't. We let go of our need to hurry through it. You can't run in the dark."[32]

My child, you will not stay in darkness. But if you have to dwell there for a while, know that I am with you, even though you may have no sense of My presence and My love at the time. Allow yourself to rest in Me, through faith, not sight. Remain in Me. I will bring you out into the Light.

20. fear

*There is no **fear** in love, but perfect love drives out **fear**, because*
__fear__ expects punishment.

~ 1 John 4:18 CEB

As Colleen spoke to me, I could see terror in her eyes. Instead of experiencing newlywed bliss, she was afraid of her new husband.

I was shocked because I had expected to see love.

Scripture reminds us that "there is no fear in love." And sadly, for good reason, that marriage was quickly annulled. I never saw Colleen again but often wondered (and prayed) that she found real love.

God is Perfect Love. The kind that "drives out fear."

How appropriate that these words were recorded by John, the disciple Jesus loved. We discover this in the upper room where John was reclining at the table, in the original language "his head upon Jesus' breast": "One of the disciples, the one whom Jesus loved, was at Jesus' side" (John 13:23 CEB).

Did you know that you, too, are the one Jesus loves?

In that room on that last evening together, John experienced Jesus as the human face of the God who is love. And in knowing he was loved, John lived his whole life in testimony to this, even as an old man writing today's verse.

> The night in the Upper Room was the defining moment of John's life. Some sixty years after Christ's resurrection, the apostle . . . recalled all that had transpired during his three-year association with Jesus. He made pointed reference to that holy night when it all came together, and he affirmed his core identity with these words: "Peter turned and saw the disciple Jesus loved following them—the one who had leaned on his breast at supper" (John 21:20).[33]

Those loved by God need not live in fear.

But as long as our view of God and others is that they are out to catch us in every mistake or sin, we will walk on eggshells like that emotionally abused young bride—"because fear expects punishment." How comforting that there are at least 365 verses in the Bible containing some sort of "fear not" phrase—one promise for every day of the year. Here are just a few:

- **Afraid of the world?** "Peace I leave with you. My peace I give you. I give to you not as the world gives. Don't be troubled or afraid" (John 14:27 CEB).

- **Afraid of financial ruin?** "Don't be afraid, little flock, because your Father delights in giving you the kingdom" (Luke 12:32 CEB).

- **Afraid of death or pain?** "Don't be afraid of those who kill the body but can't kill the soul" (Matthew 10:28 CEB).

- **Afraid of being left alone?** "Don't fear, because I am with you; / don't be afraid, for I am your God" (Isaiah 41:10 CEB).

Even those in the Bible who disappointed Jesus—Peter who denied Him, for instance—still raced to Jesus when given a miraculous opportunity to see Him again. They knew they were loved, and so they were not afraid.

Will you run to your Beloved today?

My child, I know there is much in the world to fear. But you never need fear Me, except only as experiencing the awe of My power. Love and fear cannot dwell together and I am perfect Love. More than that, I have chosen to call you My beloved and so it is My passion to deliver you from all fear. Believe that and do not go the way of the world. In this manner, you will shine brightly to others.

21. flame

He will not break the bruised reed, nor quench the dimly burning
flame. He will encourage the fainthearted, those tempted to
despair.

~ Isaiah 42:3 TLB

Is it starting to smolder, just a bit?

Your little flame. Of faith in God. Of passion for Kingdom work.

Wasn't it just yesterday you held a bright candle high, singing, "This little light of mine, I'm gonna let it shine. Let it shine. Let it shine. Let it shine"? Full of vision. And energy. And dreams of making a real difference in the world. Or even just your little world.

Only it's getting harder and harder to "fan into flame the gift of God, which is in you" (2 Timothy 1:6). Sometimes there are only embers.

Friend, the good news in our verse today is that God has not left you in this place—the place of the "bruised reed," the "dimly burning flame," the "fainthearted," and those "tempted to despair."

He does not come to break, but to build and encourage, to blow the sweet breath of His love and mercy into the dying embers of your hope and dreams.

Left alone, embers can burn themselves out, but they can also burn hot because they radiate a heat long after the actual fire has been extinguished. Inside, combustion is still happening. That's why embers are so dangerous in forest fires. There is still the potential for flame.

One of the strongest friends I have is Carol Kent, but even she confesses to times when her flame flickers.

> Over the years, I have come to realize that my Christian life
> has an ebb and flow to it. There are times I experience great
> joy in my relationship with God—when I sense His smile of
> approval on my life and ministry, and I'm encouraged by the

doors He is opening and the loving relationships I've been given. But there are other times, like my experience of humiliation in the courthouse [when jury duty revealed her as the mother of a man convicted of murder and other jurors shunned her], when I sense the fire of my faith slipping into a slow burn. I know God is with me. I'm not in crisis; and my fire hasn't gone out—but the intensity of my faith and my emotional connection to God seem to dwindle from high to low.[34]

Is your life today more smolder than burn?

This season of renewal is for you. Though you may feel powerless now, there is still the potential within you for a great flame of faith and life.

Prayer and time in God's Word are the greatest fuels for an unquenchable faith that will endure anything. So, share where you are with God, asking Him to stir up and bring forth all that is within you: "May Thy rich grace impart; Strength to my fainting heart, my zeal inspire! As Thou hast died for me, O may my love to Thee, Pure warm, and changeless be, a living fire!"[35]

Truly unquenchable.

─────────────────

My child, if today you find yourself in the dark, may I help bring you into the light? If you are cool, may I bring heat? And if all that you once believed, once cared about, once hoped for, is now dim, may I remind you that I alone can fan every flickering ember into a flame of holy passion. I am enough.

22. brokenhearted

*The LORD is close to the **brokenhearted**;*
he saves those whose spirits are crushed.

~ Psalm 34:18 CEB

Gwen's spirit was crushed after her abortion.

> How does a girl who loves God and comes from a loving, stable home find herself wading through muck and mire in the pit of brokenness? How is it possible that a girl who longed to do right and honor Christ with her life could end up in an abortion clinic at the age of twenty? And how is it conceivable that a young lady who made such horrible and murderous decisions could be reconciled to a holy God in heaven?[36]

Yet I can just imagine Gwen Smith's beautiful voice singing Fanny Crosby's words, "Trusting only in Your merit, Would I seek Your face, Heal my wounded, broken spirit, Save me by Your grace. Savior, Savior, hear my humble cry. While on others You are calling, Do not pass me by."[37]

Are you brokenhearted?

God will pick up the pieces of your shattered life. But "He doesn't put them back together as a restoration project patterned after our former selves. Instead, He sifts through the rubble and selects some of the shards as raw material for another project—a mosaic that tells the story of redemption."[38] You have purpose in life and one of God's greatest joys is to "[heal] the brokenhearted / and bind up their wounds" (Psalm 147:3).

Though she struggled with this part of her past, Gwen found courage to move forward into new life. But the brokenness maintained a grip until she was able to share it freely, first before God, and then carefully to others struggling in similar situations. Her message is clear: "Your past sins do not define you. Your painful scars do not define you. Your present sufferings do not define you. They are just shards of brokenness that God will use to lovingly refine your beauty. The restoration from broken into beautiful is neither easy nor instantaneous. It demands a yielded heart and can be quite painful, but it comes with great reward."[39]

Will you hand over your pieces for God to make the mosaic of His choosing?

"Jesus invites us to embrace our brokenness as He embraced the cross and live it as part of our mission. He asks us not to reject our brokenness as a curse from God that reminds us of our sinfulness but to accept it and put it under God's blessing for our purification and sanctification. Thus our brokenness can become a gateway to new life."[40]

My friend Gwen would agree, "Even to this day I get a bit nervous each time I take the stage to share my story. I have to swat away insecurities that fly in my face by reminding myself that God wants to reveal His love to others through me."[41]

Will you give Him your whole story?

かいの

My child, I know your heart is broken. And some of the pieces are from the pain and hurt inflicted by an imperfect world where things are not always fair. But some of what breaks your heart is from your own poor choices, perhaps the hardest to mend. Give all those pieces to Me and I will make something beautiful. For you. And for others.

23. freedom

*It is for **freedom** that Christ has set us free. Stand firm, then,*
and do not let yourselves be burdened again by a yoke of slavery.
~ Galatians 5:1

It doesn't exactly look like a place of total revolution. Total transformation. Freedom. Yet it is.

It is completely and utterly white. Puritan. No stained glass windows. No ornate decorations. Just a simple meetinghouse built in 1761.

I am standing in the same place that faithful patriots assembled one Sunday afternoon in order to pray before they marched off to Lexington, Massachusetts, to fight for freedom from England.

My home church is called the First Church of Christ Congregational in Wethersfield because it was the first church gathered in the colony of Connecticut back in 1635. Today, we still worship in the eighteenth-century building, and we still embrace freedom, surrounded by that great "cloud of witnesses."

Do you?

Our forefathers and foremothers were serious about freedom! They likened England's persecution of her colonies to the Old Testament persecution of the Hebrews by the Egyptians; and when war actually came, they saw divine intervention in all colonial victories.

> The Sunday following the Lexington alarm was a busy one in Wethersfield. The Broad Street or First Company of the Sixth Militia regiment prepared to march to Boston. They attended the morning service as a body and sat in the gallery. Dr. Marsh preached and everyone in the church was in tears. Final preparations were made and in the afternoon families and friends gathered in front of the Meetinghouse where Dr. Marsh offered a prayer.[42]

During the Revolutionary War, General George Washington worshiped here three times, including the 1781 meeting with the Count de Rochambeau to plan the Battle of Yorktown—"the most important conference of the war."

While wondering, "Is this the pew where George Washington sat?" I imagine that Sunday when so many were coming for spiritual sustenance before embarking on a journey from which they might never return. Were they excited? Were they exhilarated? They were going to fight for freedom! And they were willing to lay down their lives for freedom if that were required.

Our verse today encourages us to "stand firm, then, and do not let yourselves be burdened again by a yoke of slavery"

What enslaves you today? And how much do you want freedom?

Most important, what are you willing to do to throw off chains that bind so that you might dwell in the freedom Christ offers—freedom from anything or anyone who holds you captive? Imagine yourself as a patriot—a soldier in the militia—coming to church to pray to God before you head out in battle to fight for freedom. Thus fortified, you and I can face anything.

And sing, "Long my imprisoned spirit lay, Fast bound in sin and nature's night; Thine eye diffused a quickening ray—I woke, the dungeon flamed with light; My chains fell off, my heart was free, I rose, went forth, and followed Thee. Amazing love! How can it be That Thou, My God, shouldst die for me?"[43]

My child, slavery is not My plan. A life where you submit to binding addictions or tyrannical leaders is a slow death. I came to set you free. And if you bravely embrace My will and My way, you will be free indeed. Stand firm in the face of any enemy who tries to steal your freedom away.

24. near

*The LORD is **near** to all who call on him,*
to all who call on him in truth.

~ Psalm 145:18

They were so deep in thought that they never even looked up while walking. Even when the stranger asked to join them.

Sometimes we have no idea that the Lord is near to us. Especially in our darkest moments.

Heads hanging low, Cleopas and his companion were despairing of life itself. All their hopes had been on the Nazarene. Had they really dared to believe He might be the Messiah for whom they had long waited? And now, the whole world seemed to be going crazy after last weekend's crucifixion. The believers had scattered in fear, and no one seemed to know exactly what was going on. There was no one to lead. No one to follow.

Jesus, who was now walking in step with the men but unrecognizable, said "What are you talking about as you walk along?"

They stopped, their faces downcast: "Are you the only visitor to Jerusalem who is unaware of the things that have taken place there over the last few days?" (Luke 24:18 CEB).

They then began to explain all that had happened, ending with the fact that some women were now saying that Jesus had risen from the dead. They didn't know what to believe. So Jesus began to explain the fulfillment of all the prophecies of His life to them.

Even though they didn't realize at the time who He was, Christ's nearness made a difference, as they later reflected, "Weren't our hearts on fire when he spoke to us along the road and when he explained the scriptures for us?" (Luke 24:32 CEB).

What does it take for you to be near to God?

Just reach out. He's already there: "Come near to God, and he will come near to you" (James 4:8 CEB).

Praise God for having the ability to be everywhere at once ("omnipresent")—both vast and near at the same time:

> An astronomer who was also a Christian was asked a provocative question after his lecture: "How can a God big enough to manage the cosmos you just described possibly be involved in the personal lives of his followers—as you believe he is?" The scientist answered quietly, "The God I believe in is bigger than you think." God's love and wisdom are immeasurable, both in the extent he goes into space and the depth he enters into our hearts. A truly big God can do both.[44]

When we have been near Jesus, we want to share it. As Jesus accompanied the men into Emmaus and broke bread with them, they recognized the Messiah and ran to confirm to everyone that "the Lord really has risen!" (Luke 24:34 CEB).

Today, you and I can enjoy the nearness of God, wherever we are. His presence can bring us both comfort and renewal: "There is a place of quiet rest, Near to the heart of God, A place where sin cannot molest, Near to the heart of God. O Jesus, blest Redeemer, Sent from the heart of God, Hold us, who wait before Thee, Near to the heart of God."[45]

Today, will you draw near?

❧

My child, I am closer than you realize. Do you feel alone? Deserted? All you have to do is call out for Me to come near and I will. Some of the best beckonings sound a lot like the whisper, "help." So, look around. I am here. Right next to you. May this knowledge comfort your heart.

25. heart

*I will give you a new **heart** and put a new spirit in you. I will*
remove your stony heart from your body and replace it with a
living one.

~ Ezekiel 36:26 CEB

John and Charles desperately needed a change of heart.

These were the very two brothers who had formed the Holy Club while in school—covenanting to live disciplined Christian lives of serious Bible study, prayer, fasting, and charitable works. They had grown up in a strong Christian family and served in church leadership.

Still, it wasn't enough.

They longed for more assurance of God's love and grace.

Desiring to be used by Him, John and Charles even sailed to the colony of Georgia with General Oglethorpe. John served as a military chaplain, and Charles secretary to the governor. But their strict legalism made them view the natives as savage thieves, liars, and murderers. And there was opposition from the other white colonists who resented their rigid high churchmanship and many prohibitions.

The Wesley brothers returned home to England disillusioned. John even wrote, "I went to America to convert the Indians; but, oh, what shall convert me?"[46]

Have you ever found yourself going through the motions? Checking off a list of spiritual activity and involvement, but discovering no joy in the process? Doing all the "right things" but for all the wrong reasons?

Perhaps you, too, need a change of heart.

God "will give you a new heart and put a new spirit in you" if you turn to Him and ask. That's just what Charles and John Wesley did back in 1737 after they returned from America. They had witnessed a vibrant faith in a group of Moravians who spoke of the assurance of salvation that comes from a personal relationship with Jesus.

Then on Sunday, May 21, 1738, Charles had a spiritual experience that enabled him to be justified by faith. He wrote in his journal that the Spirit of God "chased away the darkness of my unbelief."

And then he went on to write more than seven thousand hymns reflecting his new heart, beginning with this one: "No condemnation now I dread; Jesus, and all in Him, is mine; Alive in Him, my living Head, And clothed in righteousness divine."[47]

A mere three days later, his brother, John, had what he called his own "heartwarming" experience. On May 24, 1738, he journaled, "In the evening I went very unwillingly to a society in Aldersgate Street, where one was reading Luther's preface to the Epistle to the Romans. . . . While he was describing the change which God works in the heart through faith in Christ, I felt my heart strangely warmed." He ran to his brother and declared, "I believe!" They prayed together and embarked on a very full life of international spiritual influence to this day.[48]

God is in the business of fanning the flame of cold hearts. If you are in need of a "heartwarming," just ask. And He will replace yours, too.

―――――――――― ✿ ――――――――――

My child, I love it when my children follow Me and do great things in My name. But I know that the doing of the ministry can sometimes overshadow the being in My presence. Know Me first. Allow Me to give you a heart to seek Me and find Me and spend time with Me. Out of the overflow, will come a life you never imagined. And you, too, can warm up a cold world.

26. heal

*I will **heal** their faithlessness;*
I will love them freely,
for my anger has turned from them.

~ Hosea 14:4 CEB

His wife had been unfaithful. She had done everything possible to reject him and flaunt her promiscuity to the world. Left alone with their three children, he lived in great pain and anguish.

Until he bought her back, out of slavery. Hosea (whose name means "salvation") found his wife Gomer, redeemed her, and brought her home again, fully reconciled.

Healing had begun.

Though I have never left my husband for another, I have certainly wandered away from God at times. Haven't we all?

The biblical love story of Hosea and Gomer is more than that; it's a story of what God's people have done and how He wooed them back to Himself. Israel had committed spiritual adultery through corruption, injustice, and willful idolatry. The people refused to repent; their hearts were hardened.

God became like a jilted lover: "The more I called them, / the further they went from me; / they kept sacrificing to the Baals, / and they burned incense to idols." God's holiness and justice required discipline, but out of compassion and love, He instead restored the people of Israel: "I took them up in my arms, but they did not know that I healed them. / I led them with bands of human kindness, with cords of love. / I treated them like those who lift infants to their cheeks; I bent down to them and fed them" (Hosea 11:2-4 CEB).

The Hebrew word *rapha* means "to heal or cure." In this story, as in many others in the Old Testament, God is known as *Jehovah Rapha*—the

God who heals. As God declared to Moses, "I am the LORD who heals you" (Exodus 15:26 CEB).

He is not just *a* healer; He is *our* healer.

In the New Testament, the Greek words *iaomai* and *therapeuo* mean "to heal or cure." In the Gospels we find Jesus Christ as the great Physician who cures souls as well as bodies. And He can do that for each of us today as well. In the seventh century Isaac of Syria said, "Do not fall into despair because of your stumbling, for you should not consider them incurable. There is indeed a healer: He who on the cross asked for mercy on those who were crucifying Him, who pardoned murderers as he hung on the cross."[49]

Do you need a healing touch today? Though deep healing hurts, each of us can walk that path in God's presence and the Holy Spirit's power:

> Remember that you aren't meant to travel the path to healing and transformation by yourself. We are never, ever meant to travel alone. God gives us the gift of His presence through the comfort and companionship of fellow believers—through friends, pastors, counselors, spiritual directors, teachers, and others who help us heal and grow. Don't walk this road alone. Please.[50]

Take a step toward healing. God will meet you there and "love you freely."

My child, some healing occurs on this side of heaven, and some healing occurs fully in My presence. But whether you are sick in body, soul, mind, heart, or will, I am the Lord who heals you. Don't run away; that will only cause more pain. Return to Me and reach out for all I have to give. I will heal every area that is tender and will love you in the process.

27. sheep

*Now when Jesus saw the crowds, he had compassion for them because they were troubled and helpless, like **sheep** without a shepherd.*

~ Matthew 9:36 CEB

Jesus says we are like dumb sheep. Troubled and helpless.

This stirs in Him compassion. He knows we need a shepherd. We need Him—the Good Shepherd (John 10:14).

Have you ever noticed how many times the Bible uses the whole sheep/shepherd word picture?

It's not something I'm proud of.

Because sheep are kind of pathetic; they're so dumb that they blindly follow the crowd, no matter where the crowd is going. I just read that recently in Turkey hundreds of sheep plunged off a cliff—one following the other. The first four hundred died and the next eleven hundred (yes, eleven hundred who followed them) just landed on a soft heap of sheep bodies and survived. Their shepherd, it seems, had gone off to breakfast. The loss to local farmers was $74,000.

Right about now I'm wondering whether this was the part of us that made Jesus think of sheep. How we can totally get carried away with the cause of the moment, the thrill of the week, the adventure of the season, and stupidly leave our brains behind.

Sheep are also wanderers, which we also know from biblical stories about the ones that got lost.

Because they look for grass in treacherous hills and through stony paths, the shepherd has to keep an eye on them all the time. It's easy for them to stray. Not only that, the shepherd must be a protector against wild animals and even robbers who want to steal the sheep.

Now I understand the analogy. After all, our world is scary and the path is narrow. We need a shepherd who protects:

> I am the good shepherd. The good shepherd lays down his life for the sheep. When the hired hand sees the wolf coming, he leaves the sheep and runs away. That's because he isn't the shepherd; the sheep aren't really his. So the wolf attacks the sheep and scatters them. He's only a hired hand and the sheep don't matter to him. I am the good shepherd. I know my own sheep and they know me, just as the Father knows me and I know the Father. I give up my life for the sheep. (John 10:11-15 CEB)

The most interesting thing I learned about sheep is that if they fall over on their backs, there is no way they can right themselves. They are helpless until someone comes to turn them over.

Have you ever fallen and been unable to retrieve your equilibrium on your own, either literally or figuratively?

Then you need a Shepherd too.

The great news today is that our Good Shepherd is compassionate, caring, and diligent to seek us out when we stray. The next time you say, "The Lord is my shepherd," may you be full of praise and gratitude. Because He has stooped down to scoop us up in His arms of care and protection.

My child, do you know My voice? Do you hear Me calling you back to the flock? To the narrow path? Do you hear Me directing you to follow Me and not the crowd? Do you feel Me turn you over and lift you up when you fall and are helpless? All these things I gladly do because you are Mine. I will always rescue you. You can never wander too far.

28. wisdom

*But anyone who needs **wisdom** should ask God, whose very*
nature is to give to everyone without a second thought, without
*keeping score. **Wisdom** will certainly be given to those who ask.*

~ James 1:5 CEB

"The one thing every Jesus follower needs every day is always the same: wisdom. In other words, we need an understanding of God's vision in action that will make a kingdom difference in people's lives," says Mark Labberton, president of Fuller Seminary.[51]

I totally agree.

In fact, I don't want just to grow older; I want to grow wiser. Every day.

"Get wisdom; develop good judgment. / Don't forget my words or turn away from them" (Proverbs 4:5 NLT). Just as the imagery in Proverbs suggests, wisdom calls out to us and to a world in need. Wisdom grounds our lives in communion with God and His Word. True wisdom is not just knowing the difference between right and wrong; it is knowing the difference and *choosing the right*.

That's why our wisdom must be fleshed out in our lifestyle.

> Wisdom calls out our identity and cheers our living response. Wisdom underscores that we are called to follow Jesus, who is wisdom incarnate, and to demonstrate wisdom by letting it become flesh in us. Biblical wisdom is not sage, religious advice that leaves action as an option for overachievers. It is character in action in the face of life's real needs. No action, no wisdom. God's wisdom is not a pathway of escape but a road of faithful engagement. Whatever our work or ministry may be, whether we're in the marketplace or in the nonprofit world, whether we're artists or pastors, we all need to know what gives life and how to share that with others.[52]

Do you want to be wise?

Then follow today's verse and "ask God, whose very nature is to give to everyone without a second thought, without keeping score." Daniel and his three friends—Shadrach, Meshach, and Abednego—asked God for wisdom while in Babylonian exile in the palace of King Nebuchadnezzar.

They knew and lived the most important thing: they were followers of the true God. And so, they practiced their identity as children of Yahweh every time they ate (Daniel 1). They also stepped up to the challenge of confronting an angry king who wanted impossible answers. They believed that "the LORD gives wisdom; / from his mouth come knowledge and understanding" (Proverbs 2:6 CEB). So they prayed and sought God's answer, even when it meant delivering bad news. As they interpreted his dream about a dissolving kingdom, Nebuchadnezzar received their words as truth (Daniel 2).

These four exiles were able to lead the most powerful man in the world to see the end of his own supremacy and to hear about the God who alone raises up and brings down rulers (Daniel 3). Die or live, they would not bow down and worship a false god. Nebuchadnezzar had power, but they had wisdom.

How do we know we have wisdom? One biblical definition states it well: "The wisdom from above is first pure, then peaceable, gentle, open to reason, full of mercy and good fruits, impartial and sincere" (James 3:17 ESV).

My child, I trust you are growing wiser every day. Even when you make mistakes. Especially when you make mistakes. Wisdom transforms your living into learning. And it's not what happens to you that matters as much as what you do about it. As you incarnate the wisdom I give you, you will truly help to change the world. When wisdom calls to you, be sure to answer.

29. name

*I have called you by **name**; you are mine.*

~ Isaiah 43:1 CEB

"Lucinda!" came the call from across the hotel lobby.

I turned and saw a woman I greatly admire but don't know very well. We hadn't seen each other for several years. Yet here she was remembering my name.

My heart sang.

Daddy taught me the importance of remembering to call people by name because "the sweetest sound to our ears is our own name."

When someone calls you by name, it's like they are saying, "You matter. You are important to me."

That's why it's even more remarkable that today's verse reminds us that the Creator and Sustainer of the universe knows our name. He not only calls me by name, but also claims me: "you are mine."

What could be better than that?

Well, perhaps this. God also knows the names we call ourselves—Loser, Failure, Ugly, Stupid, Fat, Worthless. But He loves us too much to allow us to own those names. He looks at us and sees a new name. In Simon He saw the potential and changed his name to Peter, a "rock." Abram became Abraham, which means "father of many," and his wife Sarai became Sarah, "mother of nations."

I remember identifying with the name of the little goat in Hannah Hurnard's allegorical story *Hinds' Feet on High Places*. Her name was "Much Afraid" because she lived in fear of all that she encountered on her journey from the valleys of life to the mountaintop of God's love. One of her most valuable lessons on her arduous climb was to rely on God's presence with her at all times. When she reached the peaks, her name was changed to "Grace and Glory."

In the last book of the Bible we read, "To him who overcomes . . . I will give him a white stone, and a new name written on the stone which no one knows but he who receives it" (Revelation 2:17 NASB). One day we will all receive a new name.

What do you think your new name will be?

What would you like it to be?

Personally I'd like to be known by some combination of these words: Peaceful, Compassionate, Kind, Empowering, Joyful, Grace, Wise, Serene, Gentle, and Strong.

Or perhaps I will be named Light. My actual first name, chosen just because Daddy liked it, is Lucinda, which derives from the word meaning "light." One could do worse than live up to that name.

Whatever my name—old or new—I'm thankful God knows it. That He recognizes me. And that He calls me His.

My child, I do know you. And you are mine. And yes, every day I call out your name and invite you to join Me in this grand adventure called life. To trust Me. To hold My hand. To follow Me. And to risk great things because you know I am beside you. Be confident. I know you will live up to your name: Christian.

30. suffering

*My **suffering** was good for me,*
* because through it I learned your statutes.*

~ Psalm 119:71 CEB

"No one participates in God's joy without first tasting His Son's afflictions," Joni Eareckson Tada says from her wheelchair on a vast stage during this memorial service for Elisabeth Elliot.

She has earned the right to speak. Having lived as a paraplegic for forty-five years, Joni is intimately acquainted with suffering.

She is also one of my heroes.

Today she is giving tribute to another woman who often said, also from personal experience, "Suffering is not for nothing."

Joni explains, "I thought I understood this when I first heard Elisabeth say it. After all, I had already lived in a wheelchair for ten years. I even wrote a book, summarizing all God had taught me about suffering—thirty-five biblical reasons to why God allows suffering and what we can learn from it." Joni sighs. "I'm afraid I had so much more to learn."

> Mostly that suffering means being pushed into, shoved, and literally pressed up against the breast of Jesus Christ until your heart lies beating in a rhythm with His. It's not a tidy list, but something messy. When you are decimated by affliction you learn that the Bible's answers are never, ever to be separated from the tender, sweet, holy, precious God of the Bible. Yes, after four decades of paralysis, chronic pain and cancer, those words "suffering is not for nothing" have made all the difference to me.[53]

Elisabeth Elliot once defined suffering to me as "having what you don't want and wanting what you don't have." When I was twenty-four years old, I wrote notes of our conversation down in my journal.

She said she did believe suffering was necessary for us to know the cross in our own lives (Philippians 3:10). That we must suffer for the Lord even though we don't seek out the suffering, nor do we have anything to do with choosing the fashion it will take. Sometimes this means allowing ourselves to be joyfully inconvenienced, not seeking our own way, but serving others. Daily prayers can be an opportunity of laying down our lives for someone else.

If you are suffering, will you offer that up to God? Ask Him to use this experience in your life and redeem it for good.

Malcolm Muggeridge looked back at his own eminently successful career with this insight: "I can say with complete truthfulness that everything I have learned in my seventy-five years in this world, everything that has truly enhanced and enlightened my existence, has been through affliction and not through happiness."[54]

"After you have suffered for a little while, the God of all grace, who has called you to his eternal glory in Christ Jesus, will himself restore, empower, strengthen, and establish you" (1 Peter 5:10).

My child, there is always a purpose in pain. Suffering is not for nothing, indeed. But in order to find the beauty in the ashes, you must submit to Me and trust that I am still Lord. And I am giving all you need to come out on the other side, radiant and renewed. I will truly "bring you safe through every loss."

31. unseen

*So we fix our eyes not on what is seen, but on what is **unseen**,*
*since what is seen is temporary, but what is **unseen** is eternal.*

~ 2 Corinthians 4:18

Today Dieter lives an unseen life.

But it was not always so. He pioneered one of the first GenX churches in America and was worship pastor at Willowcreek Community Church's Axis ministry for young adults. For years, he was in great demand as a musician, speaker, and author. Everyone wanted to listen to him perform and hear what he had to say.

Then Dieter suffered a major stroke, resulting in a coma. After six days, he emerged. Physically, he was no longer able to do the things he'd loved. He could no longer play piano, sing, or even speak. When he did, it took great effort and came out jumbled. It seemed as though all was lost.

> Yet, inside Dieter was still the same person. His brilliant and creative mind was completely intact. He had the same emotions, the same sense of humor, the same wit and eloquence, but he had a bungling mouth. It tired people out trying to understand him. One by one they went away. Isolation set in. He was sealed off from the rest of the world behind the wall that is called aphasia.[55]

Is our life worth living if most of it is unseen?

Our verse today says that we are to "fix our eyes not on what is seen, but on what is unseen."

Today Dieter Zander works in a back room at Trader Joe's and breaks down cardboard boxes. He also sorts through the shopping carts marked "spoils" and salvages food to deliver to the Salvation Army. "It will feed the hungry. . . . They don't care how it looks. They just want to eat." Dieter reflects, "I understand the spoils. I can relate. I used to be packaged as perfect. But now I am recycled Dieter."

In his private world of aphasia, Dieter heard the voice of God and felt His comfort, peace, and even laughter. Robert Murray McCheyne once said, "When the heart is at rest in Jesus—unseen, unheard by the world—the Spirit comes, and softly fills the believing soul, quickening all, renewing all within."[56]

What unseen things are important in your own life today—prayers, kindnesses, serving, giving, listening, sacrificing? Will you invest in such things, knowing that no one will know, except God?

Dieter has indeed changed. In addition to his stockroom job, he does photography and just finished a book with the help of a friend, *A Stroke of Grace*. Dieter is finally able to talk after years of therapy: "God was my boss. God is my friend now. Years ago, everything is dead. But now, my stroke is good to me and I am happy. I talk to God every day. I say, 'Thank you, I am alive again.'"[57]

Can we say the same?

My child, I know that the world reinforces all that is recognized and applauded. But I see the unseen. And that is important also. Maybe, sometimes even more important. During this season, why don't you work on those areas of your life and also try to appreciate them in others? Life really can be good even when it is simple. Perhaps because of simplicity.

32. power

*By his divine **power** the Lord has given us everything we need*
for life and godliness through the knowledge of the one who called
us by his own honor and glory.

~ 2 Peter 1:3 CEB

"As I travel around America, I'm struck by how utterly powerless most people feel."

Perhaps these words by Robert Reich, former U.S. Secretary of Labor, offer a dismal diagnosis. "A growing sense of powerlessness in all aspects of our lives—as workers, consumers and voters—is convincing most people that the system is working only for those at the top."[58]

Do you feel powerless today?

Jesus said, "My grace is enough for you, because power is made perfect in weakness" (2 Corinthians 12:9 CEB). He is enough.

And today's verse—one of my favorite promises in the entire Bible—confirms that God's divine power has "given us everything we need."

Not a little bit, not some, but *everything*!

> God's power is so great that no power in heaven or earth can compete with it. In so many ways, the strength that Christ has portrayed and that God promises is counterintuitive, a contradiction to the world's idea of strength. It is the power to control our appetites rather than to let them control us. It is the ability to keep gazing at God even when trouble and fear assail us. It is the patience to wait rather than run on ahead. It is the strength to be more than we are because God is more than we imagine. It is the power to ground ourselves in God's might and His power to help and save us.[59]

In the New Testament Greek, three words that we translate as "power" may seem familiar—*hyperballo*, *megathos*, and *dynamis*, which sound like "hyper," "mega," and "dynamite." And all three of these are used in this wonderful prayer that Paul prays for the Ephesians:

> I pray that the eyes of your heart will have enough light to see what is the hope of God's call, what is the richness of God's glorious inheritance among believers, and what is the overwhelming greatness of God's **power** that is working among us believers. This **power** is conferred by the energy of God's **powerful strength**. God's **power** was at work in Christ when God raised him from the dead and sat him at God's right side in the heavens, far above every ruler and authority and **power** and angelic **power**, any **power** that might be named not only now but in the future. (Ephesians 1:18-21 CEB)

Are you tapping into God's power today? If not, why not? If so, how is that working for you?

This power is mine and yours to claim today. "I sing the almighty power of God, that made the mountains rise, that spread the flowing seas abroad, and built the lofty skies."[60]

My child, you are not powerless. I who created the heavens and the earth imbue you with My power through the gift of the Holy Spirit. And this divine power will provide everything you need to live the life I have called you to. So, every time you have some heavy lifting to do, remember My strong hands are underneath to help in your own weakness. You can do far more than you imagine.

33. defeated

*You belong to God and have **defeated** them; because God's Spirit, who is in you, is greater than the devil, who is in the world.*

~ 1 John 4:4 NCV

I raised my fist to the sky and shouted, "In the Name of Jesus Christ, you will not have her!"

I am a Warrior Princess. Because we are in a battle—for the souls of those we love.

In addition to calling upon the Name of Jesus, I have also been known to sing these words in the face of a public heckler at a speaking engagement (angrily protesting my testimony at a recent court trial, she was escorted out by the authorities): "And though this world, with devils filled, Should threaten to undo us, We will not fear, for God hath willed His truth to triumph through us. The prince of darkness grim, We tremble not for him; His rage we can endure, for lo, his doom is sure; One little word shall fell him."[61]

Because there is indeed a villain in our life story: the enemy of our soul.

Satan wants to win. He wants to make life so miserable, so full of fear, confusion, worry, and doubt that we will simply become paralyzed and unable to move forward in a productive and redeeming way. If he can distract us from God's plan, he will have accomplished his purpose.

When my children were little I taught them that there was indeed evil in the world. That Satan has power: "But always remember, God has more power!" And then I would quote our verse today, reminding them that God's Spirit in us is far more powerful than any enemy from the world. I have read the last chapter of the Bible and God is victorious!

Is your enemy defeated? Or does he have a stronghold in your life?

Perhaps you haven't even given much thought to spiritual battle. While it's not something we need to constantly dwell on, I do recognize the dangers: "We must take this battle seriously. It is a war for the human heart. This is a Love Story set in the midst of a life and death battle. Look around you at all the casualties strewn across the fields, the lost souls, the broken hearts, the captives."[62]

How can we overcome and defeat the forces that are indeed aiming for our destruction? Only through God's strength and His methods: "Although we live in the world, we don't fight our battles with human methods. Our weapons that we fight with aren't human, but instead they are powered by God for the destruction of fortresses. They destroy arguments, and every defense that is raised up to oppose the knowledge of God" (2 Corinthians 10:3-5 CEB).

Today, stand strong and affirm your allegiance to the God who will fight for you:

- As I submit myself to God and resist the devil, he will flee from me. (James 4:7)
- I will be on the alert. I will resist my adversary, firm in my faith. (1 Peter 5:8-9)
- I will take up the full armor of God so that I can resist and stand firm. (Ephesians 6:13-18)

He will be defeated.

My child, there is no need to be afraid, but there is a need to be vigilant. One of the enemy's greatest strategies is to accuse you and distract you. Do not listen to his whispers and sneers. Listen only to My voice. I am calling you forth and girding you with holy armor. I will fight for you and with you.

34. new

It is what God is doing, and he is creating something totally
new, a free life!

~ Galatians 6:15 MSG

More than seven million acres in fifteen western states burned during one summer. It was a tragedy that came at tremendous cost: lives, homes, forests, and entire communities.

So many people were forced to start over, though not by choice. A new life and a new dwelling. The comment I heard most from interviews with the new homeless was, "At least we are alive."

Sometimes the new is forced upon us, and sometimes we choose to start fresh.

As you journey these days from winter into spring, are you longing for a new beginning in some area of your life—a new "dwelling place"? Instead of despair, hope; instead of chaos, calm; instead of me, others; instead of busy, intentional? The work of Christ that is celebrated in this season—reconciling us through His death and resurrection—offers in today's verse "something totally new, a free life!" Paul later reiterates, "The old things have gone away, and look, new things have arrived! All of these new things are from God" (2 Corinthians 5:17-18 CEB).

What needs to be destroyed in your life before you can fully embrace the new?

Many Southeast Native Americans, including the Cherokees, actually chose the purging by fire in their annual "Busk" ceremony. First, they made new clothes and home utensils and placed them all outside the village. Then they had spring cleaning.

Every corner of each Indian home was scrubbed. All the furniture was thrown out, and even children's toys were placed on the communal garbage heap. The dirt paths were swept, and the weeds were plucked up. Even the food left over from winter was thrown out. When all of the refuse in the village was gathered together into a pile in the center of the village, the chief set it on fire. As they watched it burn, everyone took off their clothes and tossed them into the fire as well.

Then the entire village washed and dressed in their new clothes. As they gathered, the chief started a new fire, and from those flames each family took burning sticks home to start their own fires. The old was gone; new life was beginning again!

I wish that new could come without loss.

But, isn't it worth it to release the old so that we can follow Christ more closely? "Just as Christ was raised from the dead through the glory of the Father, we too can walk in newness of life" (Romans 6:4 CEB).

I guess we have to want new more than we want safety: "Finish, then, Thy new creation; Pure and spotless let us be. Let us see Thy great salvation, Perfectly restored in Thee; Changed from glory into glory, Till in heaven we take our place, Till we cast our crowns before Thee, Lost in wonder, love, and praise."[63]

My child, I hope you are at a place on your journey where you are seeing that My great gift to you on the cross was to offer you a new life. Unfortunately, in order to "redecorate your dwelling place," the old has to go. May you find strength and courage to walk forth in your renewal of life, vision, and soul strength. I am with you all the way.

35. mercy

*But this is why I was shown **mercy**, so that Christ Jesus could show his endless patience to me first of all. So I'm an example for those who are going to believe in him for eternal life.*

~ 1 Timothy 1:16 CEB

If you've ever received an e-mail, card, or letter from me, you may have noticed my signature line is "under the mercy." Not "sincerely" or "fondly" or even "love and prayers." Why do you suppose I use this phrase, even in the sign-off for my weekly blog?

Because I am so very thankful to live every minute of every day *under the great mercy of God.*

What is mercy? I already defined its cousin—grace—as being the gift God gives us that we don't deserve and can never earn.

Mercy is God *not giving* us what we *do* deserve! Instead of justice—the appropriate sentence for our wrongs—He offers mercy, a second chance.

The biblical concept of mercy always involves help to those who are in need or distress. Though there are many words used to express these concepts, these two are translated into the English word *mercy*: Old Testament Hebrew *chesed* and the New Testament Greek *eleos*.

Chesed is best understood within the context of the covenant relationship God has with His people—one of love, faithfulness, devotion, loving-kindness, and mercy. *Chesed* is what tethers us to God, for without mercy the relationship between a holy God and a sinful people could not be maintained.

"*Eleos* is the New Testament Greek word that corresponds most closely to *chesed*. Jesus of Nazareth is God's mercy made visible. He shows God's faithfulness by saving us from our sins so that we may have eternal life in unbroken fellowship with God. 'Have mercy on us!' is a plea repeated by blind men, a tax collector, and desperate parents, all crying out to Jesus for His help."[64]

And this mercy is for those of us who know beyond the shadow of a doubt that we don't deserve it. Paul, who went from number one Pharisee to humble servant, reiterates this in today's verse: *"But this is why I was shown mercy, so that Christ Jesus could show his endless patience to me first of all."*

Have you done something so terrible you feel beyond God's mercy?

If you believe that, it is the guilt and shame (from the father of lies) that is speaking. He wants to convince you that your actions put you in a far worse position than anyone in the Bible—all the adulterers and murderers and slanderers who eventually were shown great love and mercy by a compassionate God.

Now is a perfect time for us to lay these at the foot of the cross and move forward "under the mercy."

"The question is: Are we like Judas, who was so overcome by his sin that he could not believe in God's mercy any longer and hanged himself. Or are we like Peter who returned to his Lord with repentance and cried bitterly for his sins? The season of Lent, during which winter and spring struggle with each other for dominance, helps us in a special way to cry out for God's mercy."[65]

My child, how often do people cry out for justice when what they really want— what they desperately need—is mercy? This I offer you today, freely and with great compassion. Let go of the guilt and shame. Embrace the gift. And then make sure you extend mercy to others. In My Name.

36. remember

After giving thanks, {the Lord Jesus} broke {bread} and said,
*"This is my body, which is for you; do this to **remember** me."*
He did the same thing with the cup, after they had eaten, saying,
"This cup is the new covenant in my blood. Every time you drink
*it, do this to **remember** me."*

~ 1 Corinthians 11:24-25 CEB

It was all so new and they didn't understand.

The twelve disciples had gathered in the upper room with Jesus, and He was talking with them about His body and blood as He passed around some wine and bread. What did it all mean?

This symbolic feast, which became a sacrament of the Church, was given in order that we remember Christ. And, in our remembering His sacrifice—His body broken and His bloodshed—we continue to be His hands and feet and mouth and heart to a hurting world.

Maundy Thursday is the day that commemorates the Last Supper of Jesus Christ with the apostles. It is also the night in which Jesus was betrayed by Judas in the Garden of Gethsemane (which we will examine tomorrow). The English word *Maundy* is derived from a Latin word meaning "mandate" because of our Lord's mandate to the disciples in the upper room: "I give you a new commandment: Love each other. Just as I have loved you, so you also must love each other" (John 13:34 CEB).

Our verse today includes the words of constitution in the service of *Eucharist*, a name derived from the Greek word for "giving thanks," which is exactly what our Lord did as He began the Last Supper. As we come to the table, may we also be filled with gratitude for what Christ has done for us. But, more than that, may we leave determined to also live *eucharistic* lives of gratitude.

This sacrament is also known as "Communion" (from the Latin meaning "union with") because it does indeed celebrate our union with God made available through Jesus' sacrifice on the cross. As such it is a meal of compassion, acceptance, and forgiveness.

"We taste Thee, O Thou living bread; And long to feast upon Thee still; We drink of Thee, the fountainhead; And thirst our souls from Thee to fill."[66]

"This ancient pattern for worshiping God and celebrating the Eucharist is the basis of our common life. The faithful have been practicing this same rhythm of worship since the first or second century after Christ. . . . At its heart, it is the same—gather, praise, read, exhort, bring gifts, offer thanksgivings, share the meal, say our prayers, offer up resources, take care of the poor."[67]

What are some ways you can prepare to remember Christ through communion this week? Times of silence and listening; confession and repentance; a sacred concert; a Tennebrae (dimming of the lights) service; a vigil?

Robert Benson urges us to never forget the story of *God with us*. "We are called upon to remember that everything changed after that night. We are called upon to remember Him as we take the Body and Blood. . . . We are called to remember that to do so in this mysterious sacramental act is a call for us to be broken and poured out as well."[68]

Always remember.

─────────────────

My child, may the partaking of communion be for you both a sober time of remembering your Lord and Savior, but also a time of gratitude for all you have been given. And may it fortify you spiritually to reach out in care and concern to those around you. May you know My presence and peace in a tangible way during these next days. I am with you.

37. with me

*Then he said to them, "I'm very sad. It's as if I'm dying. Stay here and keep alert **with me**."*

~ Matthew 26:38 CEB

They're not the same trees, but they could be.

While walking in the Garden of Gethsemane, I studied the ancient olive trees. Recent scientific tests prove that these current trees date back to the twelfth century and do contain the DNA from the original "mother tree," one believed to have witnessed Christ's human struggle that evening.

Just outside the Church of the Agony, I am hushed with wonder and a strange sense of remorse. I know Jesus experienced his deepest anguish and greatest feeling of abandonment here. Yet here, too, was where He totally entrusted himself to the will of His Father.

All He asked was for his closest friends to "stay here and keep alert with me."

And yet they all fell asleep.

After all they had gone through together—and especially at the Last Supper, Jesus washing their feet and reminding them that He was going ahead to prepare a place for them—here in the garden, Jesus needed close friends to sit with Him, the ministry of presence. But even though He tried to waken them twice, all humans let him down.

I find a tone of sadness and disappointment in today's words. In one sense, the Lord Jesus knew the disciples were not able to cope with the situation. He had told them in advance that they would desert Him. He still longed for them during this excruciating struggle.

Have you ever felt abandoned by those you thought would always be there for you?

Then perhaps you can understand how important it is to "carry each other's burdens" (Galatians 6:2 CEB). We must come alongside our sisters and brothers, where they are, speaking the Word of God and lifting loads for the sake of Jesus.

> This ministry of presence means that we will serve people even when it might make us uncomfortable. We will stand with people in the midst of anxiety and fear. Most importantly, in these difficult times we will be realists. We will not pretend things are better or worse than they actually are. We will address the situation appropriately, pointing people to the fact that Christ makes all things new.[69]

In the Garden of Gethsemane, I wondered what I would have done that night. Stayed awake? Run away?

As Jesus wrestled through the night, begging God to take away the cup of suffering, longing for his disciples to stay awake, He finally surrendered His will. And then Judas betrayed him. This frightening night ended in ultimate abandonment as "all the disciples left Jesus and ran away" (Matthew 26:56 CEB).

"'Tis midnight, and for others' guilt, The Man of Sorrows weeps in blood; Yet He who hath in anguish knelt, Is not forsaken by His God."[70]

God was still there. With Him.

My child, I hear you calling out for companionship, for empathy and consolation. And I know that all too often there have not been sisters and brothers there to join you in your struggle, your sorrow, your pain. Do you know now that I understand exactly how you feel? And I want to remind you that even if everyone else falls asleep on you, or deserts you, I will always be there. With you.

38. death

*{Christ} humbled himself by becoming obedient to the point of
death, even **death** on a cross.*

~ Philippians 2:8 CEB

In Old Jerusalem, I knelt down where Jesus was crucified on Golgotha.

It is located right in the middle of several different worship areas for
various religions contained in the Church of the Holy Sepulchre. Closing
my eyes, I also closed out all the people and sounds around me.

And then, as I pictured Christ's Passion, I softly sang every verse to the
twelfth-century hymn "O Sacred Head, Now Wounded": "O sacred Head,
now wounded, with grief and shame weighed down, Now scornfully surrounded with thorns, Thine only crown; O sacred Head, what glory, what
bliss till now was Thine! Yet, though despised and gory, I joy to call Thee
mine."[71]

Jesus was born to die.

> The crucifixion was no surprise to Jesus. He knew it was
> coming all along. From the beginning He understood what
> He would suffer. Yet He deliberately chose the path that
> would lead to the cross. He willingly laid down His life to
> save us. The blood of Jesus was shed for us. That day on the
> cross, He paid the ultimate price in order to reconcile God
> and man—to make peace between the two. What appeared
> to be a tragedy borne of hate was in fact love's greatest
> triumph.[72]

Perhaps that's why we remember today as Good Friday.

But how could such a brutal death have been good? Death by crucifixion
was, in every sense of the word, excruciating (Latin, *excruciatus*, or "out of
the cross").

It was the most painful method of public death in the first century. The victim was placed on a wooden cross. Nails were driven into the hands and feet of the victim, and then the cross was lifted and jarred into the ground, tearing the flesh of the crucified. . . . Historians remind us that even the soldiers could not get used to the horrible sight, and often took strong drink to numb their senses.[73]

These brutal images cause my tears to flow and my guilt to surface afresh as I continue softly singing, "What Thou, my Lord, hast suffered, was all for sinners' gain; Mine, mine was the transgression, but Thine the deadly pain. Lo, here I fall, my Savior! 'Tis I deserve Thy place; Look on me with Thy favor, vouchsafe to me Thy grace."[74]

What was the cost of this ultimate obedience to His Father? Today's verse says, "by becoming obedient to the point of death." And why would Jesus pay such a price?

Only for love. Love for you and for me.

What is your response to such love?

"What language shall I borrow to thank Thee, dearest friend, For this Thy dying sorrow, Thy pity without end? O make me Thine forever, and should I fainting be, Lord, let me never, never outlive my love to Thee."[75]

My child, I love you so much that I sacrificed My only Son to an excruciating death on the cross, to pay the penalty for your sin and die in your place. But even in this process, death was conquered! And you can have forgiveness, redemption, and live with Me for all eternity in heaven. Yes, this is a somber occasion to remember, but even in your tears, may you find deep gratitude.

39. wept

Then Peter remembered the word Jesus had spoken: "Before the
rooster crows, you will disown me three times." And he went
*outside and **wept** bitterly.*

~ Matthew 26:75

You'd cry, too.

If you had just publicly disowned your very best friend and then watched Him die an agonizing death.

Yes, Peter—the Rock on whom Jesus would build His church—turned out to be a sandpile. Though he boasted of unbending loyalty to Jesus, he later denied ever knowing the Nazarene.

Three times.

I love the way Eugene Peterson captures today's verse in the Message paraphrase, "He went out and cried and cried and cried" (Matthew 26:75 MSG).

Can you recall the last time you "cried and cried and cried" or "wept bitterly"?

Did you know that crying can actually be a part of our healing and eventual restoration? Centuries ago, many of our spiritual fathers considered tears as the ultimate sign of true repentance. They believed that without tears, there could be no possibility of going deeper into the heart of God: "Those who sow with tears / will reap with songs of joy" (Psalm 126:5).

We don't know where Peter spent that horrific weekend. It must have been one of the loneliest, most desolate times in his life. Quite certainly he believed that there was no longer any opportunity to right the wrong he had done to the One he loved most. No wonder he wept.

And yet, even this time of brokenness was significant in helping to turn Peter into the amazing Rock that emerged on the other side. No matter what the catalyst for your own tears, if offered back to God, they can water the soil of your faith and produce new fruit.

When my friend Jane was going through an ongoing family crisis she once confided in a friend, "I'm on the tears-every-day diet. But I think it's keeping me alive." She eventually realized that her tears connected her to her soul and to the God of the universe. "That virtual tethering saved my life. Morning after morning I encountered God's new mercies through the Scriptures. Through tears I wrote in my journal, 'Feeling sad, tired, lonely, like a blown-out Easter egg. Very fragile. My heart is trying to tell me something, and the only language it has right now is tears.'"[76]

When he stopped crying, Peter chose to do the next thing. We discover him back on a fishing boat. Perhaps he defaulted to his past, unsure if he could ever be used as a fisher of men again.

The cause of our tears often makes us feel unworthy, doesn't it?

And yet, Jesus waited for Peter on the shore. Given a miraculous second chance, Peter swam toward his Master and then impatiently confirmed his love. Three times. At this point, perhaps even weeping tears of joy, Peter was given the mandate to "feed My sheep." And he spent the rest of his life doing just that.

But I suspect he was a much more empathetic and kind soul. Tears can do that, you know.

My child, feel free to cry. Your heart is broken or you feel remorse or you are confused and distressed. All of these are valid emotions. I wept, too. I know the pain you feel. And I long for you to come to me for forgiveness or renewal. Not only will I offer you comfort but also I will restore your soul and give you a new vision for service and love to others who are also hurting.

40. resurrection

*May the God and Father of our Lord Jesus Christ be blessed! On account of his vast mercy, he has given us new birth. You have been born anew into a living hope through the **resurrection** of Jesus Christ from the dead.*

~ 1 Peter 1:3 CEB

The old cemetery is cold and dark.

I climb slowly up the hill, clad in snow boots and a winter coat covering a bright spring dress underneath. Grasping my daughter's hand, I weave through eighteenth-century tombstones, up to the summit of the Ancient Burying Ground.

We are waiting for the sunrise.

As light filters over the hill a full brass band plays "Jesus Christ Is Risen Today" and about a hundred people sing to commemorate that first Resurrection Sunday—Easter!

Shouts of "The Lord is Risen," followed by "He is Risen, Indeed," accompany our worship and joy. When the service is over, we make our way carefully back down to the church—this time in the light. And gather for a hearty New England breakfast.

And now folks' faces are shining like the sunshine that appeared. We had experienced the dark together, encountering obstacles but always waiting for the promise.

And He came.

Is this what it was like for the women who visited the tomb at sunrise so long ago? Daring to believe that indeed the One they loved and followed had conquered death and come back to life, just as He said?

Within me comes a renewed hope, a renewed vow to always be an Easter person. As today culminates in the end of our season of repentance and renewal, where does the Risen Lord find you in the Easter story?

Are you the one who goes to sleep in the garden? Are you the one who helps Jesus carry his cross? Are you the enthusiastic follower who falters when the going gets tough? Are you one of the first at the tomb? Are you the one who doesn't even recognize your companion on the road?

Jesus knows who we are. And still He loves us and reminds us in today's verse, "You have been born anew into a living hope!"

Almighty Father,
who in your great mercy gladdened the disciples
with the sight of the risen Lord:
give us such knowledge of his presence with us,
that we may be strengthened and sustained by his risen life
and serve you continually in righteousness and truth;
through Jesus Christ your Son our Lord,
who is alive and reigns with you,
in the unity of the Holy Spirit,
one God, now and forever.[77]

"Don't be afraid! I am the First and the Last. I am the living one. I died, but look—I am alive forever and ever! And I hold the keys of death and the grave" (Revelation 1:17-18 NLT).

He will have the last word. Hallelujah!

My child, I am alive. The greatest miracle of all is that you believe and live in this renewed life I offer. Don't let the lessons of this season be forgotten. You have been loved deeply, healed thoroughly, and now launched adventurously to share My grace and mercy with a hurting world. Remember, I am with you always.

grow
SUMMER

⟨⟨⟨

---

*O there was never a blossom
That bloomed content as she,
In the heart that burned, and lived, and learned
Of the Man of Galilee.
And plant her high, or plant her low,
In a bed of fire, or a field of snow,
There **grows** she.*

⟨⟩

~ Amy Carmichael
"Heart's Ease"

1. grow

*Instead, **grow** in the grace and knowledge of our Lord and
savior Jesus Christ.*

~ 2 Peter 3:18 CEB

Barry sat in a coffee shop looking outside the big window next to his table: "I remember thinking about the fact that it had been twenty years since I had become a Christian. As I sat there, one particular thought rolled around in my head. I thought, *God, it's been twenty years. I thought You would have fixed me by now!*"[1]

Are you "fixed" by now?

Are you still waiting to be "all grown up" in Christ? How long does that take, anyway—twenty years? Fifty years? Forever?

Spiritual growth "in the grace and knowledge of our Lord and savior Jesus Christ" is a process called sanctification. It is a process that lasts a lifetime, and even into eternity. But along the way, great strides can be made, even if some days it feels like we are advancing in maturity "three steps forward, two steps back."

Summer is a season of gardening and growth. It is a time to dwell in beauty and majesty of God's vast creation, appreciating nature and the everyday wonder of ordinary days. God has created us in His image and throughout His Word we are compared to blossoming wildflowers (Matthew 6:28-30 MSG), roses blooming in the desert (Isaiah 35:1 NKJV), and even a lily among the thorns (Song of Solomon 2:2 CEB).

But growth takes time and patience. And because there are so many variables, we grow at different rates, and it doesn't help to compare ourselves with others.

In Arnold Lobel's children's story "The Garden," Toad decides that he likes Frog's garden and wants to have one, too.

So Toad plants some seeds, puts his head close to the ground, and yells loudly, "Now seeds, start growing!" Of course, when he looks, it doesn't appear that the seeds are growing.

Frog comes along and encourages Toad to be patient: "Leave them alone for a few days. Let the sun shine on them, let the rain fall on them. Soon your seeds will start to grow."

But Toad is convinced his seeds are afraid of the dark so he stays up all night reading, singing, and playing music for his seeds. Still they do not appear to grow. Exhausted and disillusioned, he falls asleep.

"Toad, Toad, wake up," says Frog. "Look at your garden!"

Toad looks at his garden. Little green plants are coming up out of the ground. "At last," shouts Toad, "my seeds have stopped being afraid to grow!"

"And now you will have a nice garden, too," says Frog.

"Yes," says Toad, "but you were right, Frog. It was very hard work."[2]

Like Toad I have tried to cajole my way into godliness. Impatient with my own spiritual growth, I practically shout, "Now Cindy, start growing!"

But God keeps showing me that it takes a combination of planting the right seeds in fertile soil plus resting in His love and care—dwelling places—to produce fruit that will last.

In the next days I hope you and I will discover the joy of flourishing in God's dwelling place.

❧

My child, welcome to this season of growth. Of soaking up sunshine and drinking in life-sustaining water. Of rooting yourself deep into the soil of My love and wisdom. Of experiencing pruning, knowing the purpose is for richer fruit. Be deliberate, yet patient. You will grow. And I will never leave you alone.

2. thirsts

*My whole being **thirsts** for God, for the living God.*
When will I come and see God's face?

~ Psalm 42:2 CEB

Buckets and buckets of water could not quench her thirst deep inside.

Neither could the many men she had encountered, always hoping that perhaps *this one* would be different, this time he would love and cherish her. But, of course, each furtive liaison left her feeling used and dirty. Shamed and scarred.

And so very, very dry and thirsty.

That day, when she saw another man approach the well, all she could think was, "Oh no, here we go again."

Only this time was entirely different. She knew it the minute she looked into his eyes. They were not lustful; they were kind, almost tender. A spark of hope flashed within as he asked her for a drink of water.

And when he started talking about giving her "living water" for her soul, she determined to find out more.

> Jesus answered, "Everyone who drinks this water will be thirsty again, but whoever drinks from the water that I will give will never be thirsty again. The water that I give will become in those who drink it a spring of water that bubbles up into eternal life." The woman said to him, "Sir, give me this water, so that I will never be thirsty and will never need to come here to draw water!" (John 4:13-15 CEB).

Are you thirsty? Suffering from spiritual or emotional dehydration?

Do you know how dangerous it is to become dehydrated? Deprive your soul of spiritual water, and it will tell you. "Dehydrated hearts send desperate messages. Snarling tempers. Waves of worry. [Growing] guilt and fear. . . .

Hopelessness. Sleeplessness. Loneliness. Resentment. Irritability. Insecurity. . . . [But] you don't have to live with a dehydrated heart."[3] Visit the well and drink deeply.

When we go to the well, we meet "a man who has told me everything I've done! Could this man be the Christ?" (John 4:29 CEB). This man is the Christ, and He knows our hearts and what has made us dry. And He invites us to come to His well: "All of you who are thirsty, come to the water!" (Isaiah 55:1 CEB); "Let the one who is thirsty come! Let the one who wishes receive life-giving water as a gift" (Revelation 22:17 CEB).

Will you come and drink? Will you know the satisfaction of dwelling in the presence of a living God?

Jesus stood up on the last day of the great feast and shouted an audacious invitation: "All who are thirsty should come to me! / All who believe in me should drink! / As the scriptures said concerning me, / 'Rivers of living water will flow out from within him'" (John 7:37-38 CEB).

We long for the presence of God, the reign of God, and the peace of God. Saint Augustine famously summed it up well, "You have made us for yourself, O Lord, and our hearts are restless until they find their rest in You."

Come and drink. Thirst no more.

My child, yes I do know all about you. I know where you have sought respite from the parched life you sometimes lead. I know that those places never truly satisfy the longing in your soul. To be cherished. To be accepted. To be protected. To be given a purpose and passion for life. Come to the well of Mine, today, and I will offer you the best gift of all: living water. It's never too late.

3. children

See what kind of love the Father has given to us in that we
*should be called God's **children**, and that is what we are!*

~ 1 John 3:1 CEB

I will never forget the day I adopted my first three children.

After our court appearance, I mailed engraved announcements that included this verse: "Here am I, and the children the LORD has given me!" (Isaiah 8:18).

Because once they were not my children, but now they are. I am reminded of Peter's similar words, "Once you weren't a people, but now you are God's people. Once you hadn't received mercy, but now you have received mercy" (1 Peter 2:10 CEB).

All four of my children are a great mercy to my life.

The whole adoption process helped me better understand today's verse about the Father's love making us "God's children." We are no longer orphans; we are allowed to call the Creator of the universe *Abba*, the most intimate Aramaic word for "Daddy."

Do you ever still act like an orphan, like you have no heavenly Father and it's all up to you?

That is not your destiny! "God destined us to be his adopted children through Jesus Christ because of his love. This was according to his goodwill and plan" (Ephesians 1:5 CEB).

When God offers us new birth and adoption into His family, we receive all the rights of sons and daughters: "You received a Spirit that shows you are adopted as his children. With this Spirit, we cry, 'Abba, Father'" (Romans 8:15 CEB).

And the most important (and miraculous) thing of all? He wants us as His children, not because of anything we've done for Him, not because of how we look or how smart we are or because we have gotten everything just right. He calls us His children because of love, mercy, and grace.

In fact, we can never be worthy of a place in the family. But we have one.

Even though I don't possess material wealth, all I have is fully available to my children. Because of my great love for them, I willingly give of my resources, my strength, my creativity, my wisdom, my encouragement, and my possessions each day. How sad I would be if they acted as if I'd never come along. How useless I'd feel if they never came to me for all the blessings I so desire to give them.

If I feel this way, how much more so must my heavenly Father when I run around acting like an orphan, and not His child.

Why don't you crawl up into your heavenly Father's lap today and allow His mercy to wash over you?

> We are children, perhaps, at the very moment when we know that it is as children that God loves us—not because we have deserved His love and not in spite of our undeserving . . . but simply because He has chosen to love us. We are children because He is our Father; and all of our efforts, fruitful and fruitless, to do good, to speak truth, to understand, are the efforts of children, who, for all their precocity, are children still in that before we loved Him, He loved us, as children through Jesus Christ our Lord.[4]

Thank you, Abba.

My child, how my heart sings when you call Me "Abba." For truly I am your heavenly Father. And yes, you are My child. All who call upon Me are welcome in My family. Will you live today as a daughter of the King, a son of the King—Princesses and Princes who will carry out My reign in this world on earth? We are family.

4. unplowed

*Break up your **unplowed** ground;*
*   for it is time to seek the Lord,*
until he comes
*   and showers his righteousness on you.*

~ Hosea 10:12

Are you coasting through life?

You know the symptoms: lacking energy or enthusiasm for pursuing new things; feeling jaded or lethargic when you hear others speaking of a new vision or passion in their lives. Sometimes you just want to say, "Been there, done that, bought the T-shirt."

If so, then God has a word for you, through the prophet Hosea.

It's time: "Time to seek the Lord."

And He will do whatever is necessary to stir things up in order to make that happen. So I strongly suggest you become proactive and break up your own "unplowed ground." Because a field unplowed is an opportunity squandered.

And opportunities are what God is all about.

The phrase "unplowed ground" is the Hebrew noun *nîr*, meaning "the tillable or fallow ground." It is land that *could* be productive but has not yet been broken up, tilled, plowed, and prepared for planting.

Are there whole parts of your life that are unused?

The reason fallow ground is unusable is that it has not been prepared for planting. There are still obstacles. Sometimes we hold back from life because of similar obstacles. The stones in your field might be all those cutting remarks people made about you as a child—too dumb, too slow, too awkward. Or they might be burdens dropped on you every time you assumed guilt for other's choices.

But those stones must go.

And the soil must be loosened and plowed. It may be hard-packed. You may have worked all your life building up those protective defenses against being hurt again. But God wants to plant seeds of healing and hope in the hard soil and so you must allow the breaking of the ground.

Is there hardness of heart that needs loosening?

Finally, you need to do something that my daddy did every spring at our south Georgia farm: controlled burning. Thorns and weeds choke any possibility of new growth. They will prevent the promise of passion to fully bloom in your life. So throw them in the fire. Let go of all that entangles your heart and threatens your freedom. It might be a relationship, a habit, or an idol. But it's time to let the flames devour those fast-growing weeds.

And now the Lord can "[establish] your steps" (Proverbs 16:9). This word in Old Testament Hebrew, *kun*, also means "prepares," or "makes secure." And God wants to do just that as you grow in Him. Mark Batterson says, "God wants us to get where God wants us to go more than we want to get where God wants us to go. And He is awfully good at getting us there."[5]

Will you allow Him to redeem your past experiences and recycle them for future opportunities?

> God is the Composer. Your life is His musical score.
> God is the Artist. Your life is His canvas.
> God is the Architect. Your life is His blueprint.
> God is the Writer. You are His book.[6]

God is the Farmer. You are His field.

My child, be planted in the rich soil of My love and grace. It is time. Time to move forward and seek My face. Time to discipline yourself for new growth and new adventures. But, do not be afraid, for remember, I am with you always. And I will never call you to anything that I do not also equip and empower you to do. Seek Me, for I am seeking you.

5. worry

*Therefore, I say to you, don't **worry** about your life . . . Look*
at the birds in the sky. They don't sow seed or harvest grain or
gather crops into barns. Yet your heavenly Father feeds them.
Aren't you worth much more than they are?

~ Matthew 6:25-26 CEB

"Worry does not empty tomorrow of its sorrow, it empties today of its strength."

This wisdom from Corrie ten Boom is the very reason we are advised "don't worry about your life."

Choosing to worry is pointless and makes us weak.

As a child I learned a term for worrying about what might happen tomorrow: "borrowing trouble." Why borrow it? Chances are most things we dread never come to pass.

> Today's care, not tomorrow's, is the responsibility given to us, apportioned in the wisdom of God. Often we neglect the thing assigned for the moment because we are preoccupied with something that is not our business just now. Direct your time and energy into worry, and you will be deficient in things like singing with grace in your heart, praying with thanksgiving, listening to a child's account of his school day, inviting a lonely person to supper, sitting down to talk unhurriedly with wife or husband, writing a note to someone who needs it.[7]

The New Testament Greek word for worry here is *merimnaó*, which means "to be distracted" or "divided." Isn't that what happens when we choose to dwell in worry? We have a divided mind and a divided heart. Just like God's people who turned away from Him and went after idols: "Their heart is divided" (Hosea 10:2 NKJV).

Worry pulls us in opposite directions: part of us wants to trust God, but the other part is listening to the enemy's whispers of doubt and distress.

Is worry an affront to your heavenly Father? In our verse today, Jesus tells us to "look at the birds in the sky." We could learn a lesson of trust and carefree living from such creatures.

Hear from a man who took time to consider the birds:

> Hardly a day goes by that I don't notice the birds. They make me smile. They invite me to pause and breathe in God's beauty. . . . The birds inspire me not to worry, but instead to listen to Jesus and to place myself in his kingdom of the heavens as I go about my day. The birds inspire me to sing praise to my Heavenly Father. . . . Right now, somewhere near you, birds are singing: "Be still and know that the Father cares for you." Smile and sing along![8]

If God cares for birds, be assured He will certainly care for you and me.

My child, do you hear the birds singing? When was the last time you actually looked at a bird? I notice them all the time. I also notice every single hair on your head. You see, I care deeply about all that concerns you and those you love. And so I have it under control. You can trust Me to be on the job, even when you don't see anything happening. Do not worry. Sing.

6. garden

The Lord will guide you continually
and provide for you, even in parched places.
He will rescue your bones.
*You will be like a watered **garden**,*
like a spring of water that won't run dry.

~ Isaiah 58:11 CEB

My Mama has a green thumb. Mine is definitely brown.

I take one look at plants and they wilt. This is truly unfortunate because I love gardens of all kinds—flowers, vegetables, and herbs.

When I was a teenager I asked God for a "life verse." To my surprise, the clear answer was the garden-themed Isaiah 58:10-11. The promise of light and water and sustenance to keep me going for the long haul.

Looking back over all these years I can say today that God has truly *guided*, *provided*, and *rescued* me. He has made me a "well-watered garden" my whole life long, "even in parched places."

The Bible is full of gardens. From the Garden of Eden to the Garden of Gethsemane we find God's dwelling place that beckons us to come. To dig in the dirt. To sit in the shade. To listen for the still, small Voice. To stop and smell the flowers.

When was the last time you drew strength from a garden? They can be a place to go for rest and spiritual renewal as Emilie Barnes says:

> In the freeway of my life, I love to find an exit ramp that leads to a green retreat. There I can sit still or stroll slowly or dig in the soil and let the serenity of shrub and vine begin to grow inside me. For me, the garden path has always led to serenity, peacefulness, beauty, and yes, sometimes tears. If I want to get away and my heart is hurting, I take a walk out among the orange trees or in the rose garden and let my tears flow. I inevitably return with a sense of comfort, a renewed perspective,

and fresh energy to try again. I felt safe, comforted, reminded of God's presence. There I could gather strength to go on. There, somehow, my spirit would be renewed . . . recreated.[9]

Perhaps God wants to meet you in a garden today.

The great news is that we don't have to be expert gardeners in order to enjoy them! Whether it's that small spot of grass in your backyard or the lovely village green, or Central Park, why don't you go?

Here are some life principles I've learned from gardens, as listed in Barnes's book:

- Begin early. But it's never too late to start.
- If it doesn't work, try something else.
- Life is fragile. Protect it.
- Life is enduring. Trust it.
- Life is daily. Water it. Weed it. Prune it.
- Life is indescribably beautiful. Enjoy it and say thank you.
- Growth takes time. Be patient. And while you're waiting, pull a weed.
- There's something for everybody—different blooms for different rooms.
- Pruning hurts. Pruning helps you grow.
- Sometimes the tiniest flowers smell the sweetest.
- Grow what you love. The love will keep it growing.
- You reap what you sow. But there will be surprises![10]

My child, draw near. I am waiting here for you. In the garden. And together we can experience how life begins and thrives through constant daily care. Come for beauty. Come for silence. Come to dig or plant or prune. Gather flowers or fruit or vegetables and then share them all around. As you experience the new living here, may it spill over to your soul.

7. for good

*You intended to harm me, but God intended it all **for good**.*
He brought me to this position so I could save the lives of many
people.

~ Genesis 50:20 NLT

Joseph certainly had a roller-coaster life—full of ups and downs. His mother died; his jealous brothers sold him; Potiphar's wife accused him; and Pharaoh pulled him from prison to interpret his dreams. Pharaoh was so impressed with his life-saving interpretations that he made Joseph prime minister of Egypt!

One day during the famine all his brothers (except the youngest, Benjamin) knelt at his feet and begged for food. It was an opportunity to even the score.

What would you have done?

Joseph inquired of their family and learned that Jacob and Benjamin were still alive at home. So he tricked the brothers into bringing Benjamin back to Egypt and then planted a silver cup in Benjamin's pack so that he would be arrested. The other brothers were convinced this was their punishment for what they had done to Joseph so long ago. They knew if they didn't bring Benjamin home, their father would die of despair. So they begged to take his place.

Joseph, moved to tears, could hide behind his status no longer.

He revealed himself to his brothers who were shocked and frightened and hardly knew what to say. Surely now they would be punished for the crime. Joseph said,

> Now, don't be upset and don't be angry with yourselves that
> you sold me here. Actually, God sent me before you to save
> lives. We've already had two years of famine in the land, and
> there are five years left without planting or harvesting. God

sent me before you to make sure you'd survive and to rescue your lives in this amazing way. You didn't send me here; it was God who made me a father to Pharaoh, master of his entire household, and ruler of the whole land of Egypt. (Genesis 45:4-8 CEB)

Joseph eventually settled his father and all his brothers and their families into the land of Goshen near him. But his brothers still had a hard time believing they had been forgiven. When Jacob died, a new dread emerged: surely now Joseph would punish them.

But no. "Joseph replied, 'Don't be afraid of me. Am I God, that I can punish you? You intended to harm me, but God intended it all for good. He brought me to this position so I could save the lives of many people" (Genesis 50:19-20 NLT).

Have you experienced false accusations? Neglect? Punishment for that which you never did? If so, you will understand how easy it could have been for Joseph to store up all that rage and bitterness through the years, waiting for just the right time to release his fury.

But during those times in the pit, Joseph called out to God and focused on trusting Him and experiencing His presence. Though everyone else may have forgotten him, he knew God was with him. That's because God always has a plan. For good.

Will you trust God with the roller-coaster ups and downs of your life today?

My child, there will always be some who intend evil for your life. And, every time it enters your life, please be confident that I am still in charge. I can work every disaster into an opportunity. Because of My sovereignty, I see the entire picture, whereas you only see what you are encountering today. I intend it for good. And all will be good. Trust Me.

8. mature

Let this endurance complete its work so that you may be fully
mature, complete, and lacking in nothing.

~ James 1:4 CEB

There is no such thing as standing still.

At least not as far as spiritual growth. If we are not moving forward, slowly and steadily, then we will begin falling behind and losing ground. God longs for us to "grow in the grace and knowledge of our Lord and savior Jesus Christ" (2 Peter 3:18 CEB).

If we live healthily, physical maturity is the natural result. We have to learn social maturity gradually. But spiritual maturity only occurs through obedience, exercising the spiritual disciplines, and sacrificially serving others.

In the process, we must depend on God's grace each step of the way.

And He is quite willing to give it to us: "When we reach the end of our hoarded resources; Our Father's full giving is only begun."[11]

Are you growing toward maturity?

Can you look back at your life one year ago and see that today you responded differently than you would have then? That today there is a change of heart on at least one important matter?

> Spiritual maturity is not a destination, it's a journey; and the journey doesn't end until we see Jesus—then a new journey begins. Mature people know themselves, accept themselves, improve themselves, and give themselves to the Lord to serve others. They know what they can do and where they fit in, and they don't campaign for authority and visibility. They just trust God to help them do their work well to the glory of Jesus.[12]

Paul grew in leaps and bounds from that day he was blinded on the road to Damascus until his final imprisonment. As a result of his own growth journey, he was able to assure us that "the One who started a good work in you will stay with you to complete the job by the day of Christ Jesus" (Philippians 1:6 CEB).

We aren't born mature and complete; we move in that direction.

What is the next step you could take to grow up in God?

Here are some lessons learned along the way:

> One thing I'd probably do differently would be to relax and try to glean from the here and now, knowing that God is always at work, no matter how things appear to me. I would remember that in His sovereign wisdom God personally directs the course of my life, determining what I need to learn and how I can best experience growth.[13]

Hang on to our word for today and know that eventually you will "be fully mature, complete, and lacking in nothing."

❧

My child, when I see your heart's desire to grow in Me, I am so thankful. May you continue to take steps forward in wisdom and maturity. May you not become discouraged when you learn lessons the hard way, and feel stupid. You are growing up in Me. There is no end to all you can be and do as you daily relinquish control of your life and soul into My hands. I am with you all the way.

9. seeds

*The one who sows a small number of **seeds** will also reap a
small crop, and the one who sows a generous amount of **seeds**
will also reap a generous crop.*

~ 2 Corinthians 9:6 CEB

John Chapman was a Revolutionary War veteran who helped build a new nation by scattering seeds. Yes, "Johnny Appleseed's" orchards transformed pioneer land into homesteads.

Imagine what a few little seeds can do.

I will never forget my first visit to Muir Woods to see those amazingly huge Redwood trees, many of which were almost two thousand years old. Often measuring twenty feet wide and three hundred feet tall, they are certainly some of God's most majestic creations.

Once each of these giant trees was only a small seed. But a single seed can produce phenomenal results. And one sequoia, when it matures, often produces four hundred thousand seeds of its own *every year*. Think of the potential!

We sow seeds every day as well:

> We either sow to please our sinful nature, or we sow to please the Spirit. We can't do both. Sowing to please the sinful nature means I cultivate those impulses that indulge myself and mock God. I treat lust as a flower, not a weed. I vent anger instead of controlling it. . . . We reap what we sow, and then we store what we reap.[14]

Planting a seed always involves elements of risk. It has to fall into the ground and die. It must be trusted to the elements and allowed to break open and change, to transform, in order to become what it was meant to be.

Will my actions and my words plant seeds of goodness and faith?

One of the parables Jesus taught about planting was the farmer sowing seeds that landed on several different kinds of soil: well-traveled path, rocky, thorny, and good.

Jesus later explained His story:

> Whenever people hear the word about the kingdom and don't understand it, the evil one comes and carries off what was planted in their hearts. This is the seed that was sown on the path. As for the seed that was spread on rocky ground, this refers to people who hear the word and immediately receive it joyfully. Because they have no roots, they last for only a little while. When they experience distress or abuse because of the word, they immediately fall away. As for the seed that was spread among thorny plants, this refers to those who hear the word, but the worries of this life and the false appeal of wealth choke the word, and it bears no fruit. As for what was planted on good soil, this refers to those who hear and understand, and bear fruit and produce. (Matthew 13:19-23 CEB)

What is the soil of your heart today? Will God's seed grow in you?

In the ancient Greek world, maturity was envisioned as a three-step process. First was knowledge, becoming acquainted with a truth. Then came understanding, which is the grasping of that truth and the ability to put it into words. Finally, maturity came in wisdom as one applied the truth to life.

May we also grow in this way.

My child, the seed planted in your heart, whether recently or long ago, is now deep in soil. Though you cannot see it, it is growing. Your job is to receive this seed with the healthiest atmosphere possible—open to a new mind and new heart. Taking your time to discover My will and My way. As the blossoms appear, you will then scatter seed far and wide for others. I am confident of this.

10. sea

The sea is His and He made it.

~ Psalm 95:5 KJV

This summer I hope you enjoy some time at the seaside.

For me, there is nothing quite like ocean waves, shells on the shore, and sand between my toes. Early mornings looking out at the vast expanse bring a calm and peace unlike any other place.

The sea restores my soul.

When I see the powerful waves roll in, I know God is here as well, and my heart sings with joy, "There's not a plant or flower below but makes your glories known; And clouds arise and tempests blow, by order from Your throne; while all that borrows life from You is ever in Your care; and everywhere that I may be, You, God, are present there."[15]

What I take from such focused and rare experiences is truly a gift, or, as Anne Morrow Lindbergh's book is titled, *A Gift from the Sea*. Lindbergh, a busy mother of five in mid-century America and wife of the world's most famous aviator, echoed many of my own thoughts each summer:

> My life in Connecticut, I begin to realize, lacks this quality of significance and therefore of beauty, because there is so little empty space. There are so few empty pages in my engagement pad, or empty hours in the day, or empty rooms in my life in which to stand alone and find myself. Too many activities, and people, and things. Too many worthy activities, valuable things, and interesting people. For it is not merely the trivial which clutters our lives but the important as well.[16]

Do you sometimes feel as though your life is too cluttered?

That's why it is so crucial to periodically take time to pull away, to unplug and just sit beside the ocean waves and drink in the silence of God's goodness and restoration.

"Are you tired? Worn out? Burned out on religion? Come to me. Get away with me and you'll recover your life. I'll show you how to take a real rest" (Matthew 11:28-30 MSG).

As I wander along the shore, I gather shells and give each one a name—someone for whom I am praying. A few are perfectly white and symmetrically shaped, obviously young and new. Others are chipped and weathered, witness to many storms already but nonetheless full of beauty. I lay them in a small pile at my feet as I read my prayer book and look out at the rising sun.

How will you spend this golden summer season? What is a prayerful goal for such days?

Is it at all surprising that one of God's greatest gifts from the sea is grace?

Why not pick up a shell and write on it the gift you receive from the sea? Place it on your desk, window sill, or home altar to always remember those whispers from that still small Voice.

∽✷↶

My child, I did create the sea. The waves, the shore, and all the creatures who swim in the deep and crawl in the shallow. When you are near the ocean, I hope you can appreciate that though it is vast, I am still concerned with the small. Each shell. Each sand crab. Each child. The sea may make you feel small, but I hope it also makes you feel loved and comforted. A gift from Me to you.

11. community

*The **community** of believers was one in heart and mind.*

~ Acts 4:32 CEB

She had just lost her father and was grieving.

But today her tears weren't about the grief over his death. She was crying because she missed *people* in her time of great need: "I got beautiful e-mail messages, and beautiful Facebook messages, and beautiful voicemail messages, and beautiful text messages. But nobody just came and sat with me and cried with me."[17]

We are made to live in community.

"If one part suffers, all the parts suffer with it; if one part gets the glory, all the parts celebrate with it. You are the body of Christ and parts of each other" (1 Corinthians 12:26-27 CEB). Christian life flourishes in community networks. And yet, even with our increased proliferation of online connections, we find we are sometimes missing the human touch.

Especially on those days we need it most.

It takes community to nurture growth: "God has created human beings in an interlocking system of relationships, apart from which we cannot flourish. The church is a gift from God in order that we might be provided with a community of faith that holds us accountable and encourages us in our spiritual journey. As others spur us on, so we also spur others on."[18]

Are you actively part of a community of faith, a local church?

In the New Testament Greek, the word *ekklesia* is translated as "an assembly," which could refer to political, social, or religious gatherings. Eventually, the word came to also mean "the body of Christ." But the word we translate into "community" is usually from the New Testament Greek word *koinonia*, meaning "fellowship and partnership": "The believers devoted themselves to the apostles' teaching, to the community, to their shared meals, and to their prayers" (Acts 2:42 CEB).

With whom do you experience fellowship, shared meals, and prayers?

Do you realize that these people are God's beloved, with great gifts and great faults? Just like us. That's what makes community messy: we are all sinners. But we come together, not expecting others to fill our emptiness (only God can do that) but hoping that our combined lives will complement each other and that together, we can do more for the Kingdom.

A Bible study I once wrote, *Better Together*, covers the many "one anothers" in Scripture and lifts up the importance of community: "And let us consider each other carefully for the purpose of sparking love and good deeds. Don't stop meeting together with other believers, which some people have gotten into the habit of doing. Instead, encourage each other, especially as you see the day drawing near" (Hebrews 10:24-25 CEB).

Are you still looking for the perfect church? If that's your reason for not being in a community of faith, may I just say that you will never find a perfect church. But you will find other sinners—God's people—seeking to love God and love others.

You need them, and they need you.

My child, the church is made of people. Broken people. Difficult people. Caring people. People just like you who are on the journey, but haven't arrived yet. And so, if you find problems in any community, that's only because community is made up of all kinds. But it also makes life worthwhile. We have so much to learn from one another. Reach out today. Commit to one another.

12. springs

What joy for those whose strength comes from the LORD . . .
When they walk through the Valley of Weeping,
  it will become a place of refreshing springs.
  The autumn rains will clothe it with blessings.
They will continue to grow stronger.

~ Psalm 84:5-7 NLT

He was just an old man people rarely saw. A quiet forest dweller, he lived up in the Alps and was known by his task as "the keeper of the spring."

This mountain man had been hired many years earlier by an Austrian village council to clear away the debris from the pools of water that fed the lovely spring flowing through their town. With faithful, silent regularity his work helped make the village become a popular tourist destination.

Years later, when the town council reviewed the budget, they questioned the expense of the keeper's salary: "How important could this obscure man be?" So they dispensed with his seemingly unnecessary services.

By early autumn the trees began to shed their leaves. Small branches snapped off and fell into the pools, hindering the rushing flow of water. A slight yellowish-brown tinted the spring. Within another week, a slimy film covered sections of the water along the banks, and a foul odor was detected. Swans and tourists left; disease and sickness arrived.

Embarrassed, the council called a special meeting. Realizing their gross error in judgment, they hired back the old keeper of the spring. Within a few weeks, the river began to clear up.[19]

Friends, we, too, are in desperate need of such springs.

And today's verse reminds us that God will bring us to them, even as we have journeyed through the "valley of weeping." We are also promised that as we linger by these thirst-quenching springs, we will "continue to grow stronger."

Do you long for refreshment today?

It will never happen unless we also give attention to that which clogs our souls and chokes our minds and hearts. Just as the keeper of the spring had a daily job to do, so must we as keepers of our souls. Strengthen ourselves through daily time in prayer and God's Word. Keep short accounts by confessing sin each day and receiving a cleansing forgiveness from God. This keeps the flow going so that our "strength comes from the Lord."

Have you allowed your soul and heart to become clogged?

So did God's people long ago. God lamented (through His prophet Jeremiah) the choices of Israel: "My people have committed two crimes: / They have forsaken me, the spring of living water. / And they have dug wells, broken wells that can't hold water" (Jeremiah 2:13 CEB).

Not only had they given up on God, who promised them life-sustaining water. But also they had decided that something else—broken cisterns—would be where they placed their hope.

> Although a cistern is the best provision a human can make on his own, it is a far cry from a flowing spring of fresh water. A spring gives constant fresh water that is pure, great tasting, and never ending.[20]

Come to the waters, friend.

∽∾⌒

My child, do you sometimes feel as though you are leaking? That perhaps you have indeed placed your hopes and faith in other cisterns—other sources? Please remember that I am the One who can bring springs into dry, parched desert places. And I promise to do that if you will just seek My face. Know that our relationship takes care. Keep it clear and free flowing. I will refresh and restore.

13. always

*And surely I am with you **always**, to the very end of the age.*
~ Matthew 28:20

Final words are important, aren't they?

I discovered the last words of some famous people:

- "All my possessions for a moment of time." (Queen Elizabeth I, d. 1603)
- "That was a great game of golf, fellers." (Bing Crosby, d. 1977)
- "Now comes the mystery." (Henry Ward Beecher, d. 1887)
- "Get my swan costume ready." (Anna Pavlova, d. 1931)
- "Don't let it end like this. Tell them I said something." (Pancho Villa, d. 1923)

I find such things fascinating. Confronting death certainly brings out different things in different people. I hope my own last words hold substance and encouragement for those left behind.

Before Jesus ascended to heaven, He carefully chose words that would both comfort and empower His followers: "I am with you always."

What strong and appropriate words for anyone seeking to dwell in Christ's presence each moment! And how desperately we need to embrace this truth as we encounter instances of tragedy and sorrow; violence and hatred; confusion and despair with each new day this side of heaven.

How does knowing Christ is "with you always" affect your daily life? Does it make you stronger? Brave? Nervous? Comforted?

Invest in your own final moments by dwelling in His presence today. It may just change the way you live:

After months and years of practicing the presence of God, one feels that God is closer; His push from behind seems to be stronger and steadier; and the pull from in front seems to grow stronger. At times the wandering heart snaps back into place and the oneness with God returns instantly. Ideas come welling up from the unconscious, as from a hidden fountain. God is so close then that He not only lives all around us, but all through us. We look forward to life in the hereafter with God, and in the meantime, we taste and see that the Lord is good.[21]

Because he embraced this life, the apostle Paul's final words were, "I have fought the good fight, finished the race, and kept the faith" (2 Timothy 4:7 CEB). As I desire to live well, right up to the end, I want to embrace these seven characteristics of those who "run with perseverance the race marked out for us" (Hebrews 12:1).

1. Intimacy with Christ.
2. Fidelity in spiritual disciplines
3. A biblical perspective on the circumstances of life.
4. A teachable, responsive, humble and obedient spirit.
5. A clear sense of personal purpose and calling
6. Healthy relationships with resourceful people
7. Ongoing ministry investment in the lives of others.[22]

These characteristics move from the inner life to the outer life. In like manner, the presence of Christ *in us* will affect the love of Christ that flows *out from us*. For always.

∽◌↶

My child, each person's days on earth are numbered. And that's why I want you to live every one to the fullest. Remembering My promise—that I am always right beside you. The more you "practice the presence of God" the easier it will be for you to turn to Me at every moment. Don't worry about the end. Just live today in complete confidence and care. And courage. I'm with you.

14. reconciliation

*God was reconciling the world to himself through Christ, by not
counting people's sins against them. He has trusted us with this
message of **reconciliation**.*

~ 2 Corinthians 5:19 CEB

Our world is in desperate need of reconciliation.

There is discord and even violence between people of the same faith,
same race, same nationality, and same political persuasion. But it's even
worse for people who start out from *different* faiths, races, nationalities, and
politics. It seems like every day there is some horrific news report illustrat-
ing such conflict.

Don't you just wish someone would *do something* about all this?

We can't push this off on someone else. In today's verse we are told that
God "has trusted **us** with this message of reconciliation."

Where do we begin?

The original Greek word used here is *katallagé*, which is translated into
"reconciliation" or "a restoration of favor." Jesus shows us how to restore
favor: "[God] reconciled all things to himself through [Jesus]— / whether
things on earth or in the heavens. / He brought peace through the blood of
his cross" (Colossians 1:20 CEB).

A good place to start is right where you are.

Have you ever thought of your local church as a trailer for the eternal
church, sort of a preview of coming attractions? "The eternal church will be
a reconciled, unified, multiethnic community reigning on the earth, ador-
ing Jesus. The church today is to be a movie trailer, enticing and drawing
people to take part in this future reality. How can such a beautiful church
be possible? When God's people set their minds on Christ (Colossians 3),
who is our life, we are empowered by the Spirit to progressively mature and
reflect that great day in the future."[23]

We each have the ability to be reconcilers in every area of our lives. Here are four proactive ways to resolve conflict:

- **Glorify God**—How can I please and honor God in this situation, and how can I give witness to what he has done for me through Christ?
- **Get the log out of your eye**—How have I contributed to this conflict, and what do I need to do to resolve it?
- **Gently restore**—How can I help others to understand how they have contributed to this conflict?
- **Go and be reconciled**—How can I demonstrate forgiveness and encourage a reasonable solution to this conflict?[24]

Will you reach out as a reconciler today? Remembering that you have Christ with you—always?

The result may be nothing less than phenomenal.

> Through His passion and death Jesus made His pierced heart a safe place for every defeated cynic, hopeless sinner, and self-loathing derelict across the bands of time. The Cross reveals that Jesus has conquered sin and death and that nothing, absolutely nothing, can separate us from the love of Christ.[25]

⌒⌒⌒

My child, there is nothing that can separate us. Cling to Me and I will bring you into places of community among believers. Stop looking for a perfect anything. My church is made up of people just like you. Broken people. Caring people. Difficult people. It is a hospital for sinners, not a hotel for saints. So you will fit right in. Keep reaching out—everyone needs somebody. I gather you all.

15. rooted

*So live in Christ Jesus the Lord in the same way as you received
him. Be **rooted** and built up in him, be established in faith, and
overflow with thanksgiving just as you were taught.*

~ Colossians 2:6-7 CEB

It's called the Big Oak.

It is my Georgia hometown's most popular tourist attraction. This
Southern live oak tree dates back to 1680 and is currently 68 feet tall and
has a limb span of 165 feet.

It also stands on the property where my mother was born, at the home
of my great-grandparents Chastain who lived there from 1906 to 1966.

The tree is magnificent. The heavy limbs are now held steady by support
cables, and an underground watering system as well as an above-ground
sprinkler system all work together to maintain health and endurance. It is
preserved as a landmark of the International Society for Agriculture.

But it's the roots that tell the full story.

A mature live oak can have roots that spread underground totaling
hundreds of miles. The system is intricate and interwoven. At the beginning of an oak's life, when an acorn first sprouts, most of its energy is
spent on root development, with little growth above ground. The initial
root is the taproot, which grows deep underground, seeking a dependable
supply of moisture. Once this is accomplished, greater foliage and branch
growth can begin. Soon the taproot is surpassed by an extensive root system spreading horizontally, which provides moisture and nutrients for the
tree's lifetime.

Standing next to the Big Oak I am reminded of today's verse: "be rooted
and built up in him, be established in faith." I know that Paul was emphasizing that the only way we can grow strong and endure the storms of life is
if we have a deep root system. Planted in the soil of God's love. Watered by

His grace. Providing shelter for others in on the way. And extending quite a reach to a hurting world.

As a Southerner, family roots are important. And since mine started here, I wanted to return with Mama during her ninth decade. As we walk over to the Big Oak's trunk, she reminds me of her own mother playing in the center of that huge tree. Mama also played dolls in the Big Oak whenever she visited her grandparents' home. We have the faded black and white photos.

Walking along the heavy-laden branches, Mama—ever the master gardener—points out the lush resurrection fern growing out of the limbs. She explains this phenomenon: "Most of the time, Cindy, these leaves are brown and brittle. But when it rains they become green and vibrant and full of life. That's why this is called resurrection fern; it comes back to life if given nourishment and attention."

How true for people as well as leaves on an ancient oak.

We may (we *will*) experience those dry times of pain, disappointment, and weariness. We may often feel that life is over and we have nothing left to give.

But the truth is that God is always our Sustenance, our Source. When He looks at us, he sees "a planting of the LORD / for the display of his splendor" (Isaiah 61:3). The rain comes and we drink it in. And we, too, are resurrected.

Cherish your roots.

My child, be rooted in what's truly important. No one will see the care you take that is deeply underground, but I assure you that it is vitally important. During the inevitable storms of your life, it is the roots of My Word and your belief that will hold strong. These roots will help you grow tall and wide-reaching to some who live shallow. Never underestimate the power of strong roots.

16. path

Stop at the crossroads and look around.
Ask for the old, godly way, and walk in it.
*Travel its **path**, and you will find rest for your souls.*

~ Jeremiah 6:16 NLT

There are several routes to get to the top of Lookout Mountain in the little village of Montreat, North Carolina. When climbing Lookout was a regular occurrence for me, I never even thought about which path to take; my feet naturally defaulted to my usual route.

But it's been years since I was up there, and so I looked at the crossroads and wondered, "Which path?"

I remembered that one was steeper and came up the backside. No, not that one; I was too out of shape. I turned to the well-worn path and began my ascent. It was the right choice, especially at this season in my life. Soon I was enjoying the thrilling view of the Blue Ridge mountains and this little valley that was once my home.

As we seek to grow in our faith, there are many options offered to help us in the process. I've probably tried most of them, throughout the years.

And yet I still return to the "old godly way" and choose to "walk in it" and "find rest."

What is that sure path?

Daily prayer and time in God's Word.

That's the simple truth. You can call it anything you like—quiet time, devotions, or daily office. You can add to it many other spiritual disciplines: silence, worship, journaling, and fasting. But you cannot live a life in sync with God unless you spend time in daily prayer and the Bible.

Everyone can walk this path, no matter what shape we're in—physically, spiritually, or emotionally. We just begin. We set aside some time, and then we sit in stillness, open our Bibles, utter a prayer asking God to meet us, and receive.

Did you know that new research in the fields of neurology, psychology, and even theology shows evidence supporting the idea that if you directly infuse yourself daily with biblically based spiritual practices such as prayer, meditation, music, and worship, you will benefit immensely?[26]

This is the way God wired us. And it is essential to our growth.

God is "making a way in the desert, paths in the wilderness" (Isaiah 43:19 CEB). He has a way of slowing us down and making us new:

> We just have to be willing to take the older path that others have let grow over with thorns and weeds and neglect, a path God blazed by His Spirit and which remains under His eagle eye and protection. We need the ancient forests and mountains and streams, the good ways, whether they are the places of nature and creation we enter with a rod or camera in hand, or the spiritual places within our souls we enter with prayer and worship and questions. In these present times, we need these ancient pathways badly.[27]

Will you journey with me on this path? We have a terrific Companion.

My child, you are on the right path. I know that because you are seeking My face and reading My Word and coming to Me in devotion and prayer. This is the ancient path. But it is also the true path for modern times as well. I love to combine the well-worn ways with new innovations. I don't care when you come or how you come, but that you come. Journey to find rest for your soul.

17. moment

*But who knows? Maybe it was for a **moment** like this that you came to be part of the royal family?*

~ Esther 4:14 CEB

It was a moment that would change her life forever.

Winning a beauty pageant may have been what initially got her into the palace, but courage to act in God's power is what would keep her there.

Or cause her death.

She prayed. She prepared. And then Esther went forward to King Xerxes, unbidden, to plead for the life of her people.

It was indeed a "watershed moment."

> A watershed moment is a turning point brought on by circumstances that stop us in our tracks. Some call it an epiphany. A moment when everything changes. A point in time when nothing will ever be the same. Like a compass that provides direction, these are the moments that move us to new ways of thinking, relating, discerning, and accepting life's challenges.[28]

Can you think of a watershed moment in your own life?

When Esther came to the throne, trouble was stirring in the kingdom in the form of Haman, one of King Xerxes top nobles. Haman was furious that Esther's cousin Mordecai would not bow down to him, and he plotted to destroy Mordecai and all the Jews, little knowing that the queen was one of them. In desperation, Mordecai asked Esther to intervene on behalf of her people, even though it meant risking the king's wrath.

Esther requested that her people join her and her maids in prayer and fasting. She knew she had limited power as the queen but unlimited power as a daughter of the true God. Because of this, Esther felt secure in pursuing what she believed to be God's mission: "Even though it's against the law, I will go to the king; and if I am to die, then die I will" (Esther 4:16 CEB).

The king welcomed Esther, and she exposed Haman as the initiator of a plot to annihilate the Jews. As a result of her courage and quick intellect, the Jews were delivered, and Haman and all his family were killed, their land handed over to Esther and Mordecai. To this day, the Jewish people celebrate that deliverance with the feast of Purim.

Can you think of a time when you acted with courage and faith? Did it help you understand God's presence and provision and power?

In Esther's story we see loyalty, wisdom, humility, obedience, kindness, and discretion from her character, as well as bravery, concern for others above herself, prudence, and trust and faithfulness in her God. God used Esther to confront the enemy, approach the throne, and reverse a death sentence to a nation.[29]

When you encounter a pivotal moment in time, there are two ways you can respond: You can draw back in hesitation because you feel unworthy or unable to do what is required. Or you can pray and move forward on God's promises that He will guide and provide for all He calls you to do.

Perhaps you will change history as well.

My child, what do you learn from Esther? That when she was faced with a monumental task, she first called a prayer meeting? That courage will come when you call upon My name and go forth with conviction? I hope you will embrace pivotal moments that change you into all I planned for you to be and do.

18. scriptures

*Whatever was written in the past was written for our instruction so that we could have hope through endurance and through the encouragement of the **scriptures**.*

~ Romans 15:4 CEB

Mireille Dittmer was having an ordinary day when she became trapped during the devastating Haiti earthquake.

For five long days.

She had knelt to protect herself and thus couldn't move from that painful position. When asked how she kept from going crazy, she replied, "My faith in Jesus Christ. I have a very strong faith. I read my Bible every day. Whenever I started feeling weak, I started reciting psalms, and that gave me strength again."

Mireille counted on "the encouragement of the scriptures" to give her "hope through endurance" and literally keep her alive. She couldn't eat, drink, or sleep and even lost track of time in the total darkness and silence. Yet, she was determined not to lose faith. In an interview after her survival, she simply reminded everyone that "nothing is impossible with God."[30]

Do you know God's Word well enough to sustain you in such times when there is no other resource?

The Bible contains all we need for developing spiritual maturity. Peter encouraged others to love because of the seed that had been planted in them: "This seed is God's life-giving and enduring word" (1 Peter 1:23 CEB). The way to help that seed grow in our own lives is by daily attention. If we upload Scripture into our minds and hearts daily, we will be ready to download those life-giving verses at a moment's notice (and by heart, if we memorize).

Everything I write and say—all my "Encouraging Words" (the name of my ministry)—is based on the Word of God because I strongly believe that the Scriptures are relevant for each need and circumstance we face today. Even if your actual twenty-first-century experiences (or vocabulary) don't appear in the Bible, I assure you that the principles you need for living with them are there!

Never underestimate the power of the Scriptures: "God's word is living, active, and sharper than any two-edged sword. It penetrates to the point that it separates the soul from the spirit and the joints from the marrow. It's able to judge the heart's thoughts and intentions" (Hebrews 4:12 CEB).

Do you value God's Word?

If so, that is the beginning. Take and read.

Be convinced that there is something of worth to be had, and as an act of obedience pursue the riches in this book. You may just turn into a Word lover as well: "After a time, the choice to desire the Word, based on a decision to ascribe great value to that Word, transforms into pure delight. We start reading the Bible because we know it's good for us."[31]

May you take hold of the treasure of God's words today: "Holy Bible, Book divine, Precious treasure, thou art mine; Mine to tell me whence I came; Mine to teach me what I am."[32]

My child, I knew you would need instruction, encouragement, and support. So I breathed My Word into being through the faithfulness of My servants. Please don't let your Bible collect dust. Read it daily and learn these words by heart. They are a powerful weapon against the enemy of your soul and will both comfort and equip you in the days ahead. They are a light to your path.

19. *listens*

*The ear that **listens** to life-giving correction*
dwells among the wise.

~ Proverbs 15:31 CEB

I'm not a very good listener, I confess.

Especially with those closest to me, like my husband. In fact, because we know each other so well, I think that sometimes we just "tune out" the other's words, fast forwarding to what we *assume* the other will say.

There is a quote about listening that eloquently summarizes the nature of the process. The source of the words is unknown, but the message is universal: "God gave us two ears, but only one mouth. Some people say that's because God wanted us to spend twice as much time listening as talking. Others claim it's because God knew listening was twice as hard as talking."

Listening to others is an important skill. But listening to God is life-giving. In fact, today's verse says that the one who listens "dwells among the wise."

I definitely want to dwell among the wise!

But in order to hear God speaking wisdom to me, I must be quiet. And still. And expectant.

There is nothing more important in life than understanding when God is speaking to you: "If you are disoriented to God's voice, your life is dangerously vulnerable. The problem of not hearing God never lies with God. He does communicate His will. It is not a matter of us searching in vain for God's hidden will. He readily reveals it to those who show themselves obedient to do it."[33]

The more we dwell in God's presence, the easier it is to distinguish His true voice from all the others clamoring for our attention. When my kids phone me, they jump right into the conversation. They don't say, "Hi Mama, this is Maggie, you know, your daughter." Of course, I know her voice! All the time I have spent with her has tuned me in to her very heart. And that's what happens as we grow closer to God. We are able to hear and recognize His voice.

When was the last time you listened carefully to God?

> Allow God to soften your heart so you are ready to hear His voice and to respond in obedience. Continue seeking and listening until you have heard Him speak to you in His unmistakable voice. When He does, it will change your life.[34]

"O let me hear thee speaking, in accents clear and still. Above the storms of passion, the murmurs of self-will. O speak to reassure me, to hasten or control; O speak, and make me listen, thou Guardian of my soul."[35]

May we say like the boy Samuel, "Speak Lord, for Your servant is listening!"

My child, hush. Please stop talking long enough to listen to Me. For I am speaking to you in many ways and through many sources. But you simply must be quiet and still in order to hear. Do you know My voice? Your ear will tune to Me the more you spend time with Me. So, gather close and let Me share all the things I have for you—eye has not seen, ear has not heard. Oh yes. Listen!

20. trees

*They will be called righteous **trees**,*
planted by the LORD,
to glorify Him.

~ Isaiah 61:3 HCSB

Lori wasn't thrilled about moving into the fixer-upper across from the house where she had grown up. Until she saw the tree.

> One day I sat on the run-down front porch and took a long moment to look at the incredible tree, a Catalpa tree that spreads its beautiful branches over my front lawn. I saw the way the sun shines through the leaves, the graceful blend of its sturdy trunk, and the sheltering reach of its intricate weave of branches. Then I glanced across the street at the home where I grew up, and suddenly I saw what God had wanted me to see.
>
> This tree was no great wonder when I was a child . . . it was a young sapling I never noticed. But God knew, when I entered my fifties, my life would come unglued, and I would wonder if He even saw me anymore. He also knew that one morning I would sit on my porch and He could say, "I planned for this tree to be here for you before you ever dreamed you would need it. . . . I see you better than you see yourself. Years ago, when this seed fell into the earth, I knew it would one day speak to you of My provision and My long-range planning on your behalf. You didn't know you would be here, but I knew."[36]

Sometimes God gives us trees. And sometimes He *makes* us like trees.

Our verse today refers to us as "righteous trees" planted by the Lord with the sole purpose "to glorify him."

We grow when our roots go deep and we drink in the water of God's nourishment. My father was a forester and taught me about how to tell the age of a tree by the rings in its diameter. How the width of them indicated the past year's weather conditions.

When it's a dry season, we might find ourselves anything but strong, tall, and righteous.

That's the very time we must focus on God's majesty and power within us. The One who brings growth—sometimes wide rings of it, and sometimes very narrow—in each season.

> Trees are inherently marvelous. God pulled no stops when He made this part of His creation. . . . But trees grow seasonally, ring by ring. The line that marks the ring is . . . the scar of that year's dormancy. It's the epitaph on another death, the obituary on a brief life. And then, impossibly, life starts again. So those rings are also trumpet blasts of resurrection. We are trees. We grow seasonally too—spiritually speaking—and each season of flourishing is marked by another death, another dormancy, and then another resurrection.[37]

Trees point to God and lift our eyes upward, in hope.

෨෮

My child, I know the tree-rings of your life. Some years you grew so much and there is a width evidencing amazing spiritual strides. Other years were hard and lean, and those rings are barely visible. But they are there. You are growing into an oak of righteousness before Me. And you are launching toward the skies. May your majestic limbs reach far and wide in shelter and shade to all.

21. friends

*But you, dear **friends**: build each other up on the foundation of
your most holy faith.*

~ Jude 1:20 CEB

When did the word *friend* become a verb?

I guess it makes sense to "friend" someone. After all, I grew up hearing, "In order to have a friend, you must *be* one," which implies action. Thus, I have spent a lifetime "friending" a whole variety of people and finding myself greatly enriched in the process.

Along the way I've learned that both giving and receiving friendship take intentionality, humility, sacrifice, time, resources, and lots of forbearance. Psychological studies reveal that people with a healthy social support live longer and are healthier. My best friends and soul companions are those who point me to God and strengthen me on my faith journey. Today's verse gives a key action for such relationships: to "build each other up."

When was the last time you encouraged a friend—with hope or genuine affirmation?

"Spiritual friends help us pay attention to the work God is doing in each other's lives and help each other respond. They are a safe place we can fall into, where we can be undone, where we can be authentic. They spur us on to grow in the abundant life God has for us. They reflect to us the best of who God has us to be."[38]

But sometimes it's all too easy to substitute true friendship with a shallow version of it, found on today's social media sites.

Yes, there is potential danger that such practices may stunt a whole generation in the art of authentic friendship. However, there may be some positive benefits. In her book *Friending*, Lynne Baab says, "Two of the biggest friendship challenges of our time—busyness and mobility—have created distance between friends. Electronic communication, when used intentionally, can restore some of that lost connection. It can provide an immediacy that nurtures intimacy if the electronic communication is part of a broader, loving friendship."[39]

We must make sure that social networking is not the *only* way we interact with friends.

Jesus set the model for friendship with his disciples, but there were many others in the Bible: Paul had Silas and Barnabas, David had Jonathan, Moses had Aaron and Miriam, Elijah had Elisha, and Mary had Martha. And there are numerous Scriptural commands on our behavior toward "one another":

- Love one another (1 John 4:7)
- Accept one another (Romans 15:7)
- Serve one another (Galatians 5:13)
- Be kind to one another (Ephesians 4:32)
- Forgive one another (Colossians 3:13)
- Encourage one another (1 Thessalonians 5:11)
- Pray for one another (James 5:16)

Every act of friendship, large or small, builds a bridge. Every act of loving friendship brings healing balm to this broken world. . . . Every act of friendship, whether it is well received or not, transforms us into people who know a little bit more deeply what it means to be a neighbor to the people around us. Friendship transforms us, even as it brings healing, reconciliation and warmth to the world.[40]

❧

My child, I have called you to live your life for others—encouraging, loving, bearing, praying, serving, and building up. In the process you will meet so many people. And some will develop into friends. These are my gifts to you. You cannot live without them. But they need you as well, so continue to look for ways to build bridges and be there for others. I am always here for you.

22. prunes

He cuts off every branch of mine that doesn't produce fruit, and
*he **prunes** the branches that do bear fruit so they will produce*
even more.

~ John 15:2 NLT

It is incredibly hard to "quit while you're ahead." To be sidelined in the middle of living out your dream. For whatever reason.

And yet, we know from today's verse that God, the Master Gardener, sometimes "prunes the branches that do bear fruit."

I read the following from the author of one of the dozen or so blogs I follow that are written by very young and talented women, most of whom are also authors and mothers. On the eve of a brand-new book coming out, Emily Wierenga posted the following to Facebook: "Finally, I need to let you know that I'm going to be slowing down here on the blog, friends. In fact, it will feel like a complete stop for a while. I've written six books in seven years, and I'm tired. Needing rest. Longing for quiet. Wanting to soak up these three [accompanied by a photo of her three small children]."

For her, it is a time of pruning. I don't need to know how she made that decision, but I suspect it was a God-led choice. And I admire her for submitting to the process. You see, I too, well remember seasons of pruning. Of cutting back professional activities (sometimes at the height of success) in order to focus on mothering my own four kids. Or of restructuring my commitments in order to keep the most important at the forefront.

Are you in the midst of being pruned—cutting back?

God may do this for a number of very good reasons:

- **Remove Disease**—Often there must be surgery
  to remove something in our lives that is detrimen-
  tal and making us more vulnerable to sin.

- **Revive Fruit**—This process can actually help us produce a better quality of fruit. Pruning a plant in the right location can actually help propagate more new shoots. Our verse bears this out "so they will produce even more."
- **Redirect Growth**—Plants that are cut at one point stop growing in that direction and increase in another. God often does this in our lives to force us into new or healthier situations.
- **Restore Strength**—God's primary concern is our root system and if it is deep enough to receive nourishment. Sometimes He prunes the outer in order to strengthen the hidden work done in dark places.

As we grow in our Christianity, Christ prunes to cut away immature commitments and lesser priorities to make room for even greater abundance for His glory. May we offer up this interruption to Jesus and respond with joy and gratitude—not complaint or resentment.

Let the pruning begin; we will be better for it.

My child, I can almost hear you say, "Ouch!" Because I have had to prune back something in your life so that you are better able to focus on what matters most. Please know that it is never My intention to harm or squelch you. But you were made with limits, and by pruning back, your potential actually increases. Remember, it is only for a time. There will continue to be much fruit.

23. tests

Surely he knows my way;
*when he **tests** me,*
I will emerge as gold.

~ Job 23:10 CEB

Job was a godly man. Yet he still went through severe testing. His life filled with prestige, people, and possessions, Job was suddenly assaulted on every side and lost it all. But because his confidence was in God, he endured the tests and was able to "emerge as gold."

The word *Job* has now come to have two different meanings in the dictionary:

1. A Jewish hero in the Old Testament who maintained his faith in God in spite of afflictions that tested him.
2. Any long-suffering person who withstands affliction without despairing.[41]

Do you sometimes feel like a Job? Just remember, the word doesn't just mean you have crisis upon crisis, loss upon loss, pain upon pain; it means you are able to "withstand affliction without despairing."

Let's consider the story of this good man suffering for no apparent fault of his own. Job, a prosperous farmer living in Uz, had thousands of livestock, a large family, and many servants. Suddenly, Satan the accuser claimed that Job was trusting God only because he was wealthy and everything was going well for him.

That's when the testing began. Satan was allowed to destroy Job's children, servants, livestock, herdsmen, and home; but Job continued to trust in God. Next Satan attacked Job physically, covering him with painful sores.

Job suffered in silence and was told by his friends—Eliphaz, Bildad, and Zophar—that his sin was the cause of his own pain. The last friend, Elihu, said that God might be allowing the test in order to purify him. Do you find that everyone has an explanation for your troubles?

We demand an answer, don't we? But God does not have to give one: "Job asked God many questions about his problems. But not until Chapter 38 does God speak, and then, from the midst of a storm. It's all designed to teach Job a fundamental lesson: that God is other than we are. God wants Job to acknowledge His sovereignty."[42]

Job asked forgiveness for questioning God, repented of his attitude, and acknowledged God's great power: "I know you can do anything; / no plan of yours can be opposed successfully" (Job 42:2 CEB).

What will be the results of your testing? Will you emerge stronger on the other side?

> The Scriptures are full of how God patiently works in us and through us. How He teaches and trains us. How He prepares us for the battles He knows we will face. How He tries and tests us. How He strengthens and blesses us. . . . He was with you before. He will be with you again.[43]

My favorite verse is the one in which Job explains the fruit of his tests—his faith has gone from *head* knowledge to *heart-soul-and-experience* knowledge: "My ears had heard of you, / but **now** my eyes have seen you" (Job 42:5 CEB).

Job emerged as gold, confident it was more important to know God than know answers.

My child, you don't have to know all the reasons certain things come about in your life and the lives of those you love. All you have to know is Me. That if I allow hardship, I will also provide what is needed for you to pass the test. And coming through such things will strengthen you in ways you cannot imagine now. Instead of knowing about Me, you will know Me intimately. I am here.

24. foundation

*The rain came down, the streams rose, and the winds blew and
beat against that house; yet it did not fall, because it had its
foundation on the rock.*

~ Matthew 7:25

Bill and his wife were thrilled to buy the fixer-upper house in a lovely San Francisco neighborhood. Eager to renovate the cottage, this young couple worked day and night.

Until one day their dreams collapsed around them. Literally.

The foundation was too damaged to hold the weight of the small house, and the couple were lucky to get out alive from the rubble. Too bad they chose to ignore the real estate listing: "Major Fixer Upper needs everything. Buyers and agents beware of unstable building, floors, dry-rot and foundations. Enter at your own risk."[44]

Do you have a strong foundation to hold you together?

Our verse today warns that those who neglect such things are much more susceptible to destruction when the storms come. In a similar way, if we aren't working daily on building a strong faith and value system based on God's truth, then when crises come, we may crumble as well.

One ancient way of building a solid foundation for life is called the Rule of Life. Long ago people of faith centered their lives around the daily rhythms of three basic elements: prayer, work, and rest. These practices were intentional ways of staying connected with God and cultivating spiritual character growth in all of life—attitudes, behaviors, daily habits, and routine.[45]

In the past decade, I have greatly benefitted from having a basic Rule of Life. Without an intentional plan, I could easily squander my time and energies with no clear focus. Here's what I've decided to use to shore up my own "dwelling place"—my personal Rule of Life:

- Practice *Spiritual Disciplines* through daily office each morning and night, which incorporate silence, prayers, journaling, scripture, devotional reading, and hymnody.

- Observe *Sabbath* one day a week as a time for rest, reflection, and worship. Twice a year take a personal retreat of rest, reflection, and recreation in the presence of God.

- *Study God's Word* personally as well as participate in / teach regular group Bible Study for mutual support, accountability, and knowledge.

- Continue to invest time, energy, and resources in *Relationships* with family, friends, colleagues, neighbors, and church family. Look for ways to encourage, support, and connect.

- Fully engage in all my *Work* "as unto the Lord" and seek to practice the presence of God wherever I serve or labor. Grow in my skills as a writer, speaker, and teacher.

- Maintain physical *Health* through good food choices and regular exercise. Seek to stay balanced physically, spiritually, emotionally, and mentally.

- Expand my *Global Worldview* and discover ways to reach out in compassion, relief, and prayerful redemption to needy people locally, nationally, and internationally.

My child, those who build on sand sink quickly. And, unfortunately, things that trickle through our fingers, is exactly what the world is offering as an "insurance plan." But you can build a firm foundation for your life and those in your care by systematically building into it all that is most important. May your fruit grow and balance on the trellis of your own Rule of Life, close to Me.

25. transformed

*Don't be conformed to the patterns of this world, but be **transformed** by the renewing of your minds so that you can figure out what God's will is—what is good and pleasing and mature.*

~ Romans 12:2 CEB

Can you imagine walking into a room with over a thousand fluttering butterflies?

I did just that at the Cecil B. Day Butterfly Center at Callaway Gardens in Georgia, and it was quite a colorful experience. Not to mention hot and humid, out of necessity. In this glass-enclosed ecosystem more than fifty species of butterfly live freely among tropical plants. Butterflies arrive there in the chrysalis stage, purchased from family-run butterfly farms in economically challenged tropical countries.

These beautiful creatures start out as caterpillars, crawling along the ground, eating grass, and enjoying themselves. That is, until they go into a dark and tight place that feels like death: the cocoon.

What they think is the end of the world is actually the beginning of a whole new life.

After a period of time in the chrysalis, the caterpillar breaks through the covering and emerges. During this struggle a secretion is released that gives it the ability to stretch its new wings and fly. Unfortunately, if there were no struggle to emerge, there would also be no soaring. Now it has metamorphosed into a totally different creature: a butterfly with gorgeous markings and those incredible wings that enable it to fly!

In today's verse, God calls us to transform, not to just a better version of our old self, but to a totally new creation.

This miraculous process is called metamorphosis, which is derived from the Greek word *metamorphoo*, meaning "to change into another form" or "transform." Our verse today reminds us that this is exactly what God is doing with us: changing us from the inside out.

But the process may be slow and even painful at times. It may even seem like death.

Eventually our transformed heart changes us:

> Without even knowing it, we are practicing the presence of God. Formal times of prayer merely join into and enhance the steady undercurrent of quiet worship that underlies our days. Without even realizing it our heart is taking on a new character. Gone are the old impulses for manipulation, anger and revenge. Before we are aware of it, in slip new responses of love and joy and peace and patience and kindness and goodness and faithfulness and gentleness and self-control. (Galatians 5:22-23)[46]

"Then we shall be where we would be, Then we shall be what we should be, Things that are not now, nor could be, Soon shall be our own."[47]

How would you like God to change you today?

I desire what Thomas Kelly calls a life of unhurried peace and power: "It is simple. It is serene. It is amazing. It is triumphant. It is radiant. We need not get frantic. He is at the helm. And when our little day is done we lie down quietly in peace, for all is well."

Tired of crawling? Time to soar!

My child, conform or transform? Those are the two choices. And what I desire in you is that you become a totally new creature! Still, this changing is a process which happens in tight and dark places. And you may feel forgotten or useless during that season. Just know that in the end you will become more beautiful and free than you have ever been before. And it starts with your mind.

26. shade

You have been a refuge for the . . .
needy in their distress,
a shelter from the storm
*and a **shade** from the heat.*

~ Isaiah 25:4

At cool of day with God I walk in my garden's grateful shade.
I hear His voice among the trees, and I am not afraid.
~ Caroline Anderton Mason, 1823–1890

I love hydrangeas.

In fact, I think they look like bouquets of lace. So I was thrilled to receive a beautiful hydrangea plant for my birthday, which was immediately stuck in a hole in the ground outside. But I am not a gardener. Every time blossoms would appear, they turned brown almost immediately, and no amount of water could resuscitate them.

The problem was, of course, they had way too much sun. Hydrangeas grow best in the shade. I know that now. And our plant, repositioned by my gardener husband, is beautiful and thriving in the shadow of our porch.

Shade is not just for comfort; it's also for protection.

In fact, in our verse today the Old Testament Hebrew word connoting protection here is *tsel*, which is translated "shade" or "shadow." They are interchangeable as found in Psalm 91:1, "Whoever dwells in the shelter of the Most High / will rest in the shadow of the Almighty."

Whether in gardening or in life, we all need some shade. A respite from the heat of the sun or the heat of demands and pressures to perform or produce.

Shade evokes a sense of rest and peace.

When was the last time you sat in the shade and soaked in the presence of God?

The psalmist reminds us that "the LORD is your protector; / the LORD is your shade right beside you" (121:5 CEB).

May I suggest today that you go find some lovely shade and just sit still with open hands to receive the love, protection, mercy, and grace God has for you? After a few moments, here is a prayer you might want to offer up, in keeping with our growth theme this season:

> Lord God, I pray that You bear lasting fruit in my life through the gift of the Spirit. You are the fountain of life. Enliven and refresh my listless, thirsting soul and spirit through Your love and vibrant life that renews. You are the tree of life. Make strong the branches of my life that have been weakened by the storms of daily life. Keep me fresh and filled with Your life. Your Spirit is living water. Deepen the roots of my restless and weary life through the river of life in Your Word. . . . Amen.[48]

And remember, sunhats provide lovely shade, too.

My child, I want to be your ultimate Refuge. Your shade and your shelter. I know the beating of sun and the pressure of life can scorch even the heartiest of growing things. So you must learn how to retreat and rest. To come apart and just remain in Me. Under the shelter of My wings and in the shadow of My peaceful dwelling places. I am here now, waiting for you. Come to the shade.

27. fruit

*Even in old age they will still produce **fruit**;*
they will remain vital and green

~ Psalm 92:14 NLT

Jimmy taught Sunday school as usual this week.

Even though he is ninety years old and has been diagnosed with cancer, including four brain tumors. Yet on this day he was engaging, a good Bible teacher, personable in sharing his deep faith, and a true gentleman.

And one thousand people showed up to hear him.

President Jimmy Carter's life has not been a one-act play. After being the leader of the free world, the thirty-ninth President of the United States President chose not to rest on his laurels. Establishing the Carter Center, he and his wife of sixty-five years, Rosalyn, still work to eradicate diseases such as Guinea worm and river blindness as they champion human rights, journey to build houses in poor countries, and take part in other endeavors befitting the recipient of a Nobel Peace Prize.

London's *Guardian* called Carter "a man of modesty and principle. . . . He is a citizen of the world, shunning the exploitation of his political career via the pursuit of celebrity, wealth, and the acquisition of all the often ridiculous paraphernalia of visible affluence."[49]

I suspect President Carter fully understands our verse today: to "still produce fruit" and "remain vital and green." And, though he is currently fighting terminal cancer, his eyes are on God and the hope of heaven

Where are you in life? If you happen to be a "seasoned senior," then perhaps you have occasionally wondered what you have left to offer back to God and a hurting world.

Warren Wiersbe, in his eighties now, says,

> I can't do all the things I used to do, but by God's grace I want
> to keep doing the things He lets me do. The time of old age

reveals what is truly important to us and it gives us one more opportunity to serve the Lord and help to reach others. We can walk with the Lord and allow the rivers of water to flow and bless (John 7:37-39) or we can live selfishly and stop bearing fruit for His glory. Let's make the right decision![50]

But what if the limitations in your life (health, mental, physical, financial) prevent you from serving in those up-front active ministries mentioned?

God still has a place for you. "Even to your old age and gray hairs / I am he, I am he who will sustain you. / I have made you and I will carry you; / I will sustain you and I will rescue you" (Isaiah 46:4).

We are all in different seasons, but each is necessary for fruit-growing. In quiet ways your vibrant life and legacy are being passed on to others—as nourishment and wisdom. So continue to trust the One who is with you, and the fruit will spill out all over.

My child, if you are in a season of diminishing ability, please know that I am still with you. I continue to have a plan for you in My Kingdom work. Yes, even now. I will never forget you, though you may feel forgotten by a younger, distracted generation. You are so valuable to Me and have a lifetime of wisdom to share. So, be strengthened to live fully, for your fruit is still sweet nourishment.

28. story

*Tell the **story** of what God has done for you.*

~ Luke 8:39 CEB

He had quite a story to tell.

His memoir included living in a cave, running around naked, screaming because he was demon-possessed, breaking through his hand and foot chains, calling out to Jesus, and watching the demons take over a whole herd of pigs and throw themselves off the cliff. Eventually, he was "dressed and in his right mind" (Luke 8:35) and begged to go with Jesus.

Instead, Jesus sent him out into the world to "tell the story of what God has done for you."

What's your story? Did you know that Jesus wants you to share it?

> Maybe nothing is more important than we keep track, you and I, of these stories of who we are and where we have come from and the people we have met along the way because it is precisely through these stories in all their particularity, as I have long believed and often said, that God makes himself known to each of us most powerfully and personally.[51]

The world today is enchanted with stories. We want to read a good book or watch a thrilling movie; and we often become totally absorbed in the characters—both fictional and real. We're eager to see the plot resolved, journey completed, mystery solved, or lovers reconciled. Stories help us deal with life. Author Madeleine L'Engle wrote her first story at age five: "I knew that it was through story that I was able to make some small sense of the confusions and complications of life. . . . I was frightened and I tried to heal my fear with stories which gave me courage, stories which affirmed that ultimately love is stronger than hate."[52]

Christ's followers are no different. Christians long for meaning in our ministry, purpose in our passion, and worth in our walk of faith. Someone once called Jesus "a theologian who told stories." Eternal truths were communicated clearly through parables structured around everyday experiences, such as planting seeds, borrowing money, or welcoming home a rebellious teenager.

Musician Stephen Curtis Chapman says, "We are becoming a narrative nation—people starving for the authenticity of personal story. In the age-old continuum of 'show and tell,' our culture seems to be crying for a lot more *showing* (inviting) and a lot less *telling* (indicting)."[53]

Do you want to just continue reading stories, or watching stories; or are you ready to live your story—right in the middle of God's own Kingdom story?

I believe there is in each of us an innate desire to play a key role in the saga that is life. And though many of us merely muddle through our days juggling responsibilities and relationships mired in the mundane, we want more. We want the magnificent.[54]

And that's exactly your unique story that God calls you to share.

My child, your life story continues to unfold in surprising and amazing ways. Did you ever believe you would find yourself in this place? And yet, here you are. But always remember I am the Author and Director of this drama. I see the beginning and the end. And your story can help others discover their own, so please share it today.

29. flourish

They will again live beneath my shadow,
    *they will **flourish** like a garden;*
they will blossom like the vine,
    their fragrance will be like the wine of Lebanon.

                    ~ Hosea 14:7 CEB

Catherine studied the recent photo of herself in her favorite lavender jacket.

She was stunned at how she looked. Comparing it to an earlier photo in the same jacket, she realized that the stress and strain of life she'd been carrying inside was taking its toll on the outside.

> How did I allow myself to slowly wilt, letting the languishing deplete my best, most flourishing self? Where was the sparkle in my eyes, the playful, genuine happiness in my smile? I missed having exuberance for life and soul serenity. I wanted more than anything else to get back to the joyful, peaceful persona I had deep within me. No doubt I needed a fresh anointing, some deep soul renewal, and an extreme life makeover.[55]

Do you feel wilted? Do you long to flourish?

If so, you are not alone. In the *Journal of Health and Social Research*, results of the study "From Languishing to Flourishing in Life" reveal that only 18 percent of American adults meet the criteria for flourishing. And about 17 percent of adults fall into the category of languishing or being mentally unhealthy.[56] There is a sense of emptiness and feeling lost, and lacking purpose and fulfillment. Such people struggle with transition and change.

God promised His people that if they returned He would "heal their waywardness and love them freely" and to "be like the dew to Israel: he will blossom like a lily." As a result of pursuing God's way again, "His splendor will be like an olive tree, his fragrance like a cedar of Lebanon." Now they will "flourish like a garden" and "blossom like a vine" (paraphrase of Hosea 14).

What would it take for you to draw closer?

Spending time in prayer and God's Word is the only way we can truly flourish: "For Him shall prayer unceasing and daily vows ascend; His kingdom still increasing, a kingdom without end: The mountain dews shall nourish a seed in weakness sown, Whose fruit shall spread and flourish and shake like Lebanon."[57]

That woman in the lavender jacket, Dr. Catherine Hart Weber, now writes and speaks about her own journey of learning how to flourish so that others can enjoy that vibrant life that transforms us into people with the emotional virtues of love, joy, gratitude, peace, and hope:

> We flourish when we have a sense of well-being and can function positively in our spiritual, personal and social lives—when we experience high levels of emotional, psychological, and social well-being. It includes a life of vigor, vitality, goodness, generativity, and continuous growth. Flourishing means we are able to have close relationships and a meaningful and purposeful life where we contribute in productive ways.[58]

"Let the righteous flourish throughout their lives, / and let peace prosper until the moon is no more" (Psalm 72:7 CEB).

∾⟊⟋

My child, sometimes you get so caught up in living fast and furiously that you forget how to balance your activities and your rest. There is a price to pay for this kind of neglect of body and soul. So, if you find yourself not even recognizing yourself, please come to Me and let's work at restoration and renewal. My greatest joy is that you flourish in every way. I will help you to do so.

30. harvest

Let's not get tired of doing good, because in time we'll have a
harvest if we don't give up.

~ Galatians 6:9 CEB

As I write the final page in this book, the season of harvest is just now beginning.

It is a time of "gathering in." All the planting, all the nourishing, all the work, and all the joy have brought us to this place. And now we see the fruit of our lives laid bare for those who will come and taste.

Do you ever wonder what your own harvest will be?

Whatever we desire folks to say about us after we are gone, that is how we should be living this very day. Live your legacy *now*.

We don't get to choose our beginnings. Some start out in the rocky soil of poverty, family crisis, or disability. Others are born into a rich loam with resources and people to nourish and care. Most of us fall somewhere in between. But we all have to find our way, and I hope the words in this book have been a living encouragement to do just that—one word a day.

Because we do get to choose whether or not we will finish well: "No matter what season of life we are in, what developmental stage we are passing through, or what struggles we are facing, we can pause and intentionally choose who we want to be. We have an incredible opportunity to choose the pathway toward a flourishing finish."[59]

Do you realize that all that pain and patience in growth is helping accomplish an inner light in your soul?

That dwelling in the presence of God is forming you into a person of fruit and virtue and legacy. You don't need to be better than everyone else, just better—deeper—than you used to be. And that happens gradually.

Do not despair the process, for harvest is coming.

In his powerful commencement address to the Dartmouth College class of 2015 David Brooks urged the kind of growth that leads to harvest:

> We are not a society that nurtures commitment-making. But your fulfillment in life will not come from how well you explore your freedom and keep your options open. . . . By the time you hit your thirties, you will realize that your primary mission in life is to be really good at making commitments— falling in love with something, and then building a structure of behavior around it that will carry you through when love falters. . . . The highest joy is found in sending down roots.[60]

Brooks asked the graduates to picture their reunion twenty-five years into the future, gathered on the college lawn with their friends and family, thinking back over their lives so far. He concluded that your commitments are what define your maturity, what really "set you free."[61]

What have you committed your life to? This, friend, will be your harvest—your legacy.

My child, all your growth is reaping rewards. There is a harvest, only some of which you will witness on earth. Your legacy will influence those left behind. They will remember how you lived, what you cherished and fought for, and all you taught them through words, prayers, and extraordinary actions. So live your legacy. You can count on My presence always.

gratitudes

As a storyteller and a "word girl," I have been consumed with joy exploring all the dimensions of the 130 words in this book, including their scriptural context. My original vision was to lift up those biblical words that draw us deeper into the presence and peace of God, enabling us to *dwell* in His refuge and quiet beauty. But as the project evolved into words for *four* seasons, instead of just one, I discovered words that cause us to *shine* during Advent, more words helping *renew* us during Lent, and then even words encouraging us to *grow* as we witness God's natural majesty outdoors.

But there are so many more words! Perhaps this devotional will whet your appetite to explore some of them on your own. When God gave me my word-for-the-year *dwell*, it was a word I rarely used and had never studied. But my deep longings for sanctuary and serenity seemed to resonate with this concept. Almost immediately, I was invited to lead a silent retreat in Pennsylvania, which was just the impetus to spend a long winter month exploring what God had to say on this subject—silence, rest, refuge, listening. And that was just the beginning.

Through events that could only be orchestrated by a loving and sovereign Lord, *Dwelling Places: Words to Live in Every Season* is now in your hands.

My heart is full of gratitude to the many who have touched my life in such a way that enabled me to write this book:

"In the beginning was the Word . . ." So begins John's Gospel, and so begins my thanksgiving for the process that has brought about this book. I'm deeply grateful that Jesus Christ, the Word made flesh, and the Bible, the Word of God, have been my foundation and inspiration throughout the living and writing of *Dwelling Places: Words to Live in Every Season*.

To all those whose treasures I have shared in this book: If I quoted you, then consider yourself my teacher and I your grateful student. Special gratitude to the writers of the hymns I love and sang throughout my typing. Your words inspire my words. Thank you.

To my readers and my audience: What would I do if you weren't willing to read my books and listen to my "Encouraging Words"? I would never have written twelve books if you hadn't kept buying them and sharing them with others. And a special thanks to all those I meet at events for women, men, writers, and speakers. Your desire to learn and grow is what keeps me sharing the stories!

I'm extremely grateful to my editor Ramona Richards for believing in me and inviting me to Abingdon Press. Everyone there is lovely and special thanks go to Cat Hoort, Susan Cornell, Teri Wilhelms, Susan Salley, and the terrific sales, marketing, and publicity team.

We all need professional colleagues who nudge us to live a balanced life of physical, spiritual, mental, and emotional health. For me, these are the delightful women who are my SpaSisters. They embrace my authenticity and undergird me in prayer and I treasure each one—you know who you are! I also continue to learn from all my writer/speaker friends in AWSA (Advanced Writers Speakers Association).

My diverse and creative community—New England Christian Writers Retreat—is flourishing up here in the rocky soil of New England, and I could not shine a light without their support and desire to communicate Kingdom truth. Especially my very own phenomenal and prayerful writers group, Tessa Afshar and Lauren Yarger.

Our growth group—Bob/Vickie Anderson, Mark/Collette Charette, John/Kathy Cooper, Al/Helga Philips—has prayed diligently. My "Daybreak" prayer gals—Judy Franzen, Karen Memmott, and Jessica Parchman—kept me in lobster and laughter. And my faith community—First Church of Christ Congregational in Wethersfield—continues to be my favorite place for loving God and loving others, all the while singing amazing Hymns.

I will never understand the grace of God that placed me into such a loving family, which has only increased in breadth and depth over the years.

Hearty thanks to *everyone* who has or once had the last name of Secrest, Hasty, McDowell, van Seventer, Stallings, and Karpoff. Special gratitude to my praying mother, Sarah Secrest, and my two sisters who keep me sandwiched in my place as the middle daughter—Cathy Secrest Ray and Susan Secrest Waters.

I have been greatly blessed with precious friends—some for a lifetime. There is not enough space to list each one. But special thanks to best friend Maggie Rowe who knows exactly what it takes to do what I do in writing and has thus prayed me into the doing of it daily. And to Claire Whitfield Tucker with whom I share both childhood dreams and adult adventures. I'm so glad to be back with a publisher from your town: Nashville.

Portions of this book were written in the sanctuary of "Mountain Meadows," the country home of lifelong friends Newton and Barbara Schoenly. I am always grateful for their "nest."

I confess that I am a huge fan of all my young adult children. Seriously. Somehow they have turned out to be the most remarkable humans I have ever met. So it is with great humility and gratitude that I thank Justin, Tim, Fiona and Tim K., Maggie and Stephen for allowing me to gush, sing, ask technical questions, pray, give, applaud, and hang out with you throughout life! And hugs for my darlin' girl; just know Granny will always have books and books to read to you and stories to share.

This year has been a new season for my faithful husband, Michael McDowell, and I'm not sure he signed up to do *all* the housework, gardening, bill-paying, travel-agenting, cooking, and numerous runs for more ink and paper this summer, but that's exactly what he did while I wrote this book. Most important, he continues to show me what it means to "glorify God and enjoy Him forever" in all the dwelling places we are given. Thank you, hon, for being my better half and lifting me higher.

Epilogue

Secrets of the Nest

Lord, you have been our dwelling place
throughout all generations.

~ Psalm 90:1

As you come to the close of our one-word-a-day devotional, I hope you have been able to embrace the triune Lord God Almighty as your forever always dwelling place!

Be assured that these precious times of quiet reflection on how God's Word and our lives intersect do not have to end. In fact, this process of dwelling not only includes the drawing near but also offers the empowering to go forth!

May I share how God is still teaching this to me?

A few months after I finished writing *Dwelling Places* (but before the final edits) I was asked to speak words of greeting to a gathering of fellow authors and speakers who would be spending a week together focusing on the theme "Free to Fly." I knew that the atmosphere of this retreat always encouraged times of silence and prayer, listening to God and one another for the year of ministry ahead of us all. But it was also a time of drawing strength and purpose for carrying out specific tasks ahead. How would we seamlessly move from one into the other?

Isn't that often the struggle—balancing the *being with* God and the *doing for* God?

As I thought about what to say at our opening tea, I was immediately drawn to the image of a bird's nest. Remembering that the Hebrew word in the Old Testament for *dwell* is often translated as "nest," I pictured us all gathered in the nest eagerly seeking nourishment so that we could then fly away into Kingdom work.

Nests are where life begins and is nurtured. But their ultimate purpose is to eventually become empty—a launching pad out into the world.

Come close and I will share with you my three secrets of the nest.

1. The Nest Is a Place of REFUGE.

How priceless is your unfailing love, O God!
*People take **refuge** in the shadow of your wings.*

~ Psalm 36:7

God wants us to dwell so closely with Him that He becomes our default "safe place"—our true refuge. We can be our authentic self there and make our home in Him, even as we are protected.

It is no secret that we live in a dangerous world. Forces from without and within threaten to shatter our sense of calm, courage, and conviction. Confusion and chaos reign in a culture that is forever changing.

Do you ever want to just throw yourself into Mama's apron and hide your eyes? Do you ever want to just climb into Daddy's lap and snuggle close?

The little child within us all knows that only God can provide true security.

The psalmist actually talks about God covering him with "feathers" and offering secure refuge "under His wings" (Psalm 91:4). Can't you just imagine a bird, such as an eaglet, nestling into safety under his mother's wings?

Why, even King David was ready to "dwell" and "shelter" in that safe place (Psalm 61:4). And later, his son Solomon carried on the importance of knowing God as refuge: "The LORD's name is a strong tower; / the righteous run to it and find refuge" (Proverbs 18:10 CEB).

I, too, seek that kind of refuge.

2. The Nest Is a Place of RESIDENCY.

*{Make} the Most High your place of **residence**.*

~ Psalm 91:9 CEB

God doesn't want us to just visit Him, He wants us to make our hearts His home. If we will abide, He promises to reside.

In the dictionary, *residency* is defined as a period of time when you live somewhere. Another definition is "a period of advanced training" such as a medical residency in which you are already a doctor but you are still learning things before you go out on your own.

The nest is also a place of advanced training in preparation for the future.

The Old Testament Hebrew word used here is *yashab*, which is translated "to dwell or to remain." In the New Testament, Jesus calls this process "abiding" and the Greek word indicates continual action. It's not just once and done. We are to remain and abide in God's presence continually.

And as we do, we learn.

Eagles and other predators are born with instincts that urge them to fly and pounce, but precisely how to do these things is another matter. In the life of a young eagle, both parents are always showing their offspring how to grow into the magnificent and powerful creature they were intended to become.

It takes months of trial and error for an eaglet to acquire basic skills such as lighting on perches or stooping on prey. But their parents cannot tell them how to hunt. During this time of "residency" the young eagle must simply spend time observing the parent and practicing the behavior he sees.

Residency is a good time to learn how to incorporate spiritual disciplines into our everyday lives. While the non-negotiable basics are daily time in the Bible and prayer, other practices help us immensely in the process of becoming more and more like Christ: silence, worship, journaling, solitude, fasting, sacraments, and giving. We do what we observe our heavenly Father doing. And, just like the eagle, we learn how to come into our own.

I don't want to waste my residency in the nest. I long to nestle close, abide and dwell, learning all I can to prepare for what is ahead.

3. The Nest Is a Place of RELEASE.

But those who trust in the LORD will find new strength.
They will soar high on wings like eagles.

~ Isaiah 40:31 NLT

We were not made to stay in the nest forever but to fly out into the world.

The period when baby eagles leave their nest is called fledging. Male eagles fledge usually around seventy-eight days and females around eighty-two days. Up until that time they have been fed and sheltered by the mama and daddy eagle. But getting to this point is a process, and not always an easy one. The first few times a fledgling pops over the side of the nest, they are clumsy and often crash land on the ground.

What is perhaps most interesting is the process in which the parents urge the eaglet to fly.

The mother circles the nest with food, just out of reach. The eaglet is very hungry and reaches out, perhaps even hops up, to get the food, but the mother is only teasing and keeps it from her young. Sometimes the bird is so desperately starving that he roots around in the bones embedded in the nest for anything of nourishment. As days pass and the baby bird loses some of his body fat, he actually is able to move quicker and finds himself airborne occasionally, even if for a moment.

The parent continues to swing by near the nest dangling food and urging the eaglet to leave its aerie and fly. Eventually, everything comes together and he is out of the nest, seeking his own food and his own life.

For the first six months after fledging, eagles usually stay within a half mile of their home nest before they venture farther afield. Their parents' duty was to birth them, raise them, teach them, but then release them, even if it meant forcing them out of a comfort zone.

I wrote earlier in this book that our primary calling is to seek to live out the grace and truth of Jesus Christ. In all we do. Wherever we do it. This process can only happen as we are released to experience new adventures and new challenges that will enable us to go "with God" into every situation of life, for His glory.

I would never attempt such a thing without first spending time dwelling in the nest. Would you?

Refuge. Residency. Release. Secrets of the nest.

Where are you being released today? Whether it's a scary place or an exciting place, my prayer is that you have spent so much time soaking up God's presence, peace, and power that you simply cannot wait to fly out into a broken world with the healing and hope-filled words of Christ!

And may you know in a very real way that our Lord is with you in all the dwelling places you encounter.

Lucinda Secrest McDowell
"Sunnyside"
February 2016

notes

DWELL

1. Ruth Haley Barton, *Invitation to Solitude and Silence* (Downers Grove, IL: InterVarsity, 2010), 12.

2. Richard Peace, *Noticing God* (Downers Grove, IL: InterVarsity, 2012), 61.

3. Dallas Willard, *Renovation of the Heart* (Colorado Springs: NavPress, 2002).

4. Frederick Buechner, *The Alphabet of Grace* (New York: HarperOne, 2009).

5. Sharon Garlough Brown, *Sensible Shoes: A Story About the Spiritual Journey* (Downers Grove, IL: InterVarsity, 2013), 178.

6. Kevin P. Emmert, "He Suffers with Us and We with Him," *Christianity Today* (July/August 2015): 61.

7. John Ortberg, *Soul Keeping* (Grand Rapids, MI: Zondervan, 2014), 121.

8. Kent and Amber Brantley, *Called for Life* (Colorado Springs: WaterBrook, 2015), 2.

9. Brantley, *Called for Life*, 3.

10. Corrie ten Boom, *The Hiding Place* (New York: Bantam, 1974).

11. John Greenleaf Whittier, "Dear Lord and Father of Mankind," *United Methodist Hymnal* (Nashville: The United Methodist Publishing House, 1989), 358.

12. Jane Borthwick, "My Outlook," in *Gateway to Joy* by Elisabeth Elliot (Ann Arbor, MI: Vine, 1998), 85.

13. Sharon Garlough Brown, *Two Steps Forward: A Story of Persevering in Hope* (Downers Grove, IL: InterVarsity, 2015), 212.

14. S. Trevor Francis, "O The Deep Deep Love of Jesus," accessed December 17, 2015, www.hymnary.org/text/o_the_deep_deep_love_of_jesus.

15. Jane Rubietta, *Worry Less So You Can Live More* (Minneapolis: Bethany House, 2015), 73.

16. Amy Carmichael, "The Shell," in *Toward Jerusalem* (Fort Washington, PA: Christian Literature Crusade, 1936), 68. Amy Carmichael was a missionary to India at the beginning of the twentieth century. Amy, known as Amma, spent her life rescuing children from temple prostitution, at a time when sexual trafficking was rarely acknowledged. After a severe fall, Amy's own "dwelling place" was one of chronic pain the last half of her life. Though she uses antiquated and often mystic language, I draw great comfort from her poetry and share these verses with you in honor of her life and ministry.

17. Steve and Sharol Hayner, *Joy in the Journey* (Downers Grove, IL: InterVarsity, 2015), 140.

18. Jennifer Kennedy Dean, *Pursuing the Christ* (Birmingham, AL: New Hope, 2008), 23.

19. G. K. Chesterton, *Orthodoxy* (London: Catholic Way, 2013), 183.

20. Wade Goodwyn, "One Night Only: The Streets Meet the Opera House," National Public Radio, February 16, 2015, www.npr.org/sections/deceptivecadence/2015/02/16/386681308/one-night-only-the-streets-meet-the-opera-house.

21. Robert Boyd Munger, *My Heart—Christ's Home* (Downers Grove, IL: InterVarsity, 1986).

22. Richard Foster, *Sanctuary of the Soul* (Downers Grove, IL: InterVarsity, 2011), 153.

23. John Muir, *Our National Parks* (New York: Houghton, Mifflin & Company, 1901), 56.

24. Murray Pura, *Majestic and Wild* (Grand Rapids, MI: Baker, 2013), 153.

25. Jon Mooallem, "The Self-Storage Self," *The New York Times Magazine* (September 2, 2009).

26. Nara Schoenberg, "Behind the Zen of Decluttering," *The Hartford Courant* (July 4, 2015): B10.

27. Schoenberg, "Behind the Zen of Decluttering."

28. P. D. Eastman, *Are You My Mother?* (New York: Random House, 1998).

29. Hannah Whitall Smith, *The God of All Comfort* (Chicago: Moody, 1953).

30. Os Guinness, "The Shocking Weakness of God's Truth," *Christianity Today*, July/August 2015, 86.

31. Carolina Sandell, "Day by Day," 1865, accessed December 17, 2015, www.hymnary.org/text/day_by_day_and_with_each_passing_moment.

32. Sally Lloyd-Jones, *Thoughts to Make Your Heart Sing* (Grand Rapids: Zondervan, 2012), 28.

33. Jenn Graffus, "Voices on Stillness," *Fuller Magazine* (Summer 2015).

34. Brown, *Sensible Shoes*, 62.

35. Katharina von Schlegel, "Be Still My Soul," *The United Methodist Hymnal*, 534.

36. Foster, *Sanctuary of the Soul*, 150–51.

37. Leslie Vernick, *Lord, I Just Want To Be Happy* (Eugene OR: Harvest House, 2009), 15.

38. Elisabeth Elliot, *Be Still My Soul* (Grand Rapids: Fleming H. Revell, 2003), 71.

39. Elliot, *Be Still My Soul*, 78.

40. Elisabeth Elliot, *Gateway to Joy*, radio program #1697 (July 22, 1999).

41. Alan Burgess, *The Small Woman* (Ann Arbor, MI: Servant Publications, 1985).

42. Henry F. Lyte, "Abide with Me," *The United Methodist Hymnal*, 700.

43. Mark Batterson, *Draw the Prayer Circle* (Grand Rapids: Zondervan, 2012), 167–68.

44. Barbara Cooney, *Miss Rumphius* (New York: Puffin, 1982).

45. John Biersdorf, *Healing of Purpose* (Nashville: Abingdon Press, 1985).

46. Edgar P. Stites, "Trusting Jesus," accessed January 15, 2016, www.hymnary.org/text/simply_trusting_every_day.

47. Judith C. Couchman, *The Mystery of the Cross* (Downers Grove, IL: InterVarsity, 2009), 167.

48. Couchman, *Mystery of the Cross*, 169.

49. Kevin DeYoung, *Crazy Busy* (Wheaton, IL: Crossway, 2013), 118.

50. Foster, *Sanctuary of the Soul*, 105.

51. Lloyd-Jones, *Thoughts to Make Your Heart Sing*, 77.

52. Elisabeth Elliot, *Through Gates of Splendor* (Wheaton, IL: Tyndale, 1996), epilogue to 40th anniversary edition.

53. Isaac Watts, "O God, Our Help in Ages Past," *The United Methodist Hymnal*, 117.

54. Andrew Murray, *The Holiest of All* (Grand Rapids: Fleming H. Revell), 526–27.

SHINE

1. Mark Buchanan, *Spiritual Rhythm: Being with Jesus Every Season of Your Soul* (Grand Rapids: Zondervan, 2010), 238.

2. Ann Voskamp, *Selections from One Thousand Gifts* (Grand Rapids: Zondervan, 2012), 111.

3. Voskamp, *Selections from One Thousand Gifts*, 106.

4. Steve and Sharol Hayner, *Joy in the Journey* (Downers Grove, IL: InterVarsity, 2015), 126.

5. Joachim Neander, "Praise to the Lord, the Almighty," trans. Catherine Winkworth, *The United Methodist Hymnal* (Nashville: The United Methodist Publishing House, 1989), 139.

6. Jane Rubietta, *Finding the Messiah* (Indianapolis: Wesleyan, 2014), 11.

7. A. A. Milne, *Winnie the Pooh* (New York: Puffin, 2005).

8. Ann Voskamp, "A Sorta Guide for the Overwhelmed and Brokenhearted This Christmas," *A Holy Experience* blog, December 12, 2014, www.AHolyExperience.com.

9. Charles Wesley, "Come, Thou Long Expected Jesus," *The United Methodist Hymnal*, 196.

10. Larry James Peacock, *Openings* (Nashville: Upper Room Books, 2003), 374.

11. Allison Glock, "Family Matters," *Southern Living* (blog), January 2, 2014, http://thedailysouth.southernliving.com/2014/01/02/family-matters/.

12. Donald J. Selby, *The Unsettling Season* (Nashville: Upper Room, 1989).

13. Sharon Garlough Brown, *Two Steps Forward: A Story of Persevering in Hope* (Downers Grove, IL: InterVarsity, 2015), 245.

14. Phillips Brooks, "O Little Town of Bethlehem," *The United Methodist Hymnal*, 230.

15. Christina Rossetti, "In The Bleak Midwinter," *The United Methodist Hymnal*, 221.

16. Lucinda Secrest McDowell, *A Southern Style Christmas* (Colorado Springs: Shaw/WaterBrook, 2000), 52.

17. Jennifer Kennedy Dean, *Pursuing the Christ* (Birmingham, AL: New Hope, 2008), 107.

18. Brown, *Two Steps Forward*, 86.

19. Elisabeth Elliot, *God's Guidance: A Slow and Certain Light* (Grand Rapids: Fleming H. Revell, 1973).

20. Emily E. Elliot, "Thou Didst Leave Thy Throne," accessed January 19, 2016, www.hymnary.org/text/thou_didst_leave_thy_throne_and_thy_king.

21. Alexander, *Father Arseny—1893-1973: Priest, Prisoner, Spiritual Father*, trans. Vera Bouteneff (Yonkers, NY: St. Vladimir's Seminary, 1998).

22. Charles Wesley, "Hark! the Herald Angels Sing," *The United Methodist Hymnal*, 240.

23. Catherine Marshall, "My Most Memorable Christmas," *Guideposts* (1965).

24. Marshall, "My Most Memorable Christmas."

25. Buchanan, *Spiritual Rhythm*, 204.

26. McDowell, *Southern Style Christmas*, 39.

27. Peacock, *Openings*, 266.

28. Scott Sauls, "When You Want to Find Hidden Graces in the Dark Places," *A Holy Experience* (blog), July 16, 2015, www.AHolyExperience.com.

29. Sauls, "When You Want to Find Hidden Graces."

30. Elizabeth Howell, "How Many Stars Are in the Universe?" Space.com, May 31, 2014, www.space.com/26078-how-many-stars-are-there.html.

31. John H. Hopkins, Jr., "We Three Kings," *The United Methodist Hymnal*, 254.

32. Jason Lisle, "What Was the Christmas Star?" Answers in Genesis website, December 19, 2014, https://answersingenesis.org/holidays/christmas/what-was-the-christmas-star/.

33. Peacock, *Openings*, 397.

34. Dean, *Pursuing the Christ*, 89.

35. Cynthia Ruchti, *An Endless Christmas* (Franklin, TN: Worthy, 2015), 224.

36. C. S. Lewis, *The Collected Works of C. S. Lewis*, vol. 3 (New York: HarperCollins, 2007).

37. Laurence Hull Stookey, *This Day* (Nashville: Abingdon Press, 2004), 107.

38. Gayle Roper, "The First Christmas," *The Widow's Journey* (blog), December 10, 2012, www.WidowsJourney.com.

39. Gayle Roper, *A Widow's Journey* (Eugene, OR: Harvest House, 2015).

40. Gayle Roper, "Year 2," *The Widow's Journey* (blog), December 13, 2012, www.WidowsJourney.com.

41. Henry Wadsworth Longfellow, "I Heard the Bells on Christmas Day," accessed January 19, 2016, www.hymnary.org/text/i_heard_the_bells_on_christmas_day.

42. Longfellow, "I Heard the Bells."

43. Wesley, "Hark! The Herald Angels Sing," *The United Methodist Hymnal*, 240.

44. Elisabeth Elliot, *The Music of His Promises* (Ann Arbor: Vine), 177.

45. Bryan Wilkerson, "A Wonderful Night," sermon delivered at Grace Chapel, December 17, 2006, www.grace.org.

46. Wilkerson, "Wonderful Night."

47. John S. Dwight, "O Holy Night," accessed January 19, 2016, www.hymnary.org/text/o_holy_night_the_stars_are_brightly_shin.

48. Max Lucado, *God Came Near* (Portland: Multnomah, 2000).

49. Aurelius Prudentius, "Of the Father's Love Begotten," *The United Methodist Hymnal*, 184.

50. Charles L. Allen, *Christmas in Our Hearts* (Grand Rapids: Fleming H. Revell, 1957).

51. Phillips Brooks, "O Little Town of Bethlehem," *The United Methodist Hymnal* (Nashville: The United Methodist Publishing House, 1989), 230.

52. Father William Saunders, "Who Were the Magi?" accessed December 21, 2015, www.catholiceducation.org/en/culture/catholic-contributions/the-magi.html.

53. Ashley Van Dragt, "Moving into the Neighborhood," *The Well*, December 2, 2013 www.thewell.InterVarsity.org.

54. Van Dragt, "Moving into the Neighborhood."

RENEW

1. Max Lucado, *No Wonder They Call Him the Savior* (Eugene, OR: Multnomah, 1986), 158–59.

2. Christin Ditchfield, *Praying Ephesians* (Brentwood, TN: Worthy, 2013), 199.

3. Henri J. M. Nouwen, "Teach Me to Pray," in *The Pursuit of Wisdom* by Thomas Becknell and Mary Ellen Ashcroft (Valley Forge, PA: Judson, 2002), 35.

4. Frederick Buechner, *Wishful Thinking* (New York: HarperOne, 1993).

5. Mark Labberton, *Called* (Downers Grove, IL: InterVarsity, 2014), 45.

6. Labberton, *Called*, 89.

7. Gwen Smith, *Broken into Beautiful* (Eugene, OR: Harvest House, 2008), 41.

8. John S. Dickerson, "Charleston Victims Wield Power of Forgiveness," *USA Today* (June 22, 2015).

9. Russell Moore, "What Charleston Should Remind Us About Forgiveness and Justice," *Russell Moore* (blog), June 23, 2015, www.russellmoore.com.

10. Lewis B. Smedes, *Forgive and Forget* (New York: HarperOne, 2007).

11. Henri Nouwen, *Our Greatest Gift* (San Francisco: HarperSanFrancisco, 1995), 66.

12. Margaret Wise Brown, *The Runaway Bunny* (New York: HarperCollins, 1942).

13. Henry F. Lyte, "Abide With Me," *The United Methodist Hymnal* (Nashville: The United Methodist Publishing House, 1989), 700.

14. Elisabeth Elliot, *A Lamp for My Feet* (Ann Arbor, MI: Servant, 1985), 107.

15. Jennifer Dukes Lee, "Why Our Scars Matter," *Jennifer Dukes Lee* (blog), August 23, 2013, www.JenniferDukesLee.com.

16. Cynthia Ruchti, *Tattered and Mended* (Nashville: Abingdon Press, 2015), 13, 15.

17. Robert Robinson, "Come, Thou Fount of Every Blessing," accessed January 19, 2016, www.hymnary.org/text/come_thou_fount_of_every_blessing.

18. Fredericka Matthews-Greene, *Welcome to the Orthodox Church* (Brewster, MA: Paraclete, 2015), 166.

19. C. S. Lewis, *Mere Christianity* (New York,: Harper & Brothers, 1943).

20. Lettie Cowman, *Springs in the Valley* (Grand Rapids: Zondervan, 1939), 41.

21. Genalin Niere-Metcalfe, "Self-Care," in *Silencio*, a Resource of Leadership Transformations (August 2015).

22. John Ortberg, *Soul Keeping* (Grand Rapids: Zondervan, 2014), 129.

23. Anna L. Waring, "In Heavenly Love Abiding," accessed January 19, 2016, www.hymnary.org/text/in_heavenly_love_abiding.

24. Jennie Allen, "Leading Through the Culture Wars," *Jennie Allen* (blog), July 22, 2015, www.JennieAllen.com.

25. Jennifer Dukes Lee, "Planned Parenthood, the Value of Life, and a Grace That Finds You Wherever You Are," *Jennifer Dukes Lee* (blog), July 24, 2015, www.JenniferDukesLee.com.

26. Jane Rubietta, *Finding Life* (Indianapolis: Wesleyan, 2014), 79.

27. Augustus M. Toplady, "A Debtor to Mercy Alone," accessed January 19, 2016, www.hymnary.org/text/a_debtor_to_mercy_alone.

28. David Brooks, *The Road to Character* (New York: Random House, 2015).

29. Ann Voskamp, *Selections from One Thousand Gifts* (Grand Rapids: Zondervan, 2012), 118.

30. Shona Crabtree, "Book Uncovers a Lonely, Spiritually Desolate Mother Teresa," *Christianity Today* online, August 30, 2007, www.christianitytoday.com/ct/2007/augustweb-only/135-43.0.html.

31. Cecil Murphey, *Knowing God, Knowing Myself* (Ventura, CA: Gospel Light, 1996), 222–23.

32. Ortberg, *Soul Keeping*, 183.

33. Brennan Manning, *Abba's Child* (Wheaton, IL: NavPress, Tyndale, 2014), 105.

34. Carol Kent, *Unquenchable* (Grand Rapids: Zondervan, 2014), 66.

35. Ray Palmer, "My Faith Looks Up to Thee," *The United Methodist Hymnal*, 452.

36. Smith, *Broken into Beautiful*, 13.

37. Fanny Crosby, "Pass Me Not, O Gentle Savior," *The United Methodist Hymnal*, 351.

38. Ken Gire, *The North Face of God* (Wheaton, IL: Tyndale, 2006).

39. Smith, *Broken into Beautiful*, 113.

40. Henri Nouwen, *Bread for the Journey* (New York: HarperOne, 2006).

41. Smith, *Broken into Beautiful*, 170.

42. Lois Wieder, *A Pleasant Land—A Goodly Heritage* (Wethersfield, CT: First Church of Christ in Wethersfield, 1986), 68–69.

43. Charles Wesley, "And Can It Be?" *The United Methodist Hymnal*, 363.

44. Ben Patterson, *God's Prayer Book* (Wheaton, IL: Tyndale, 2008), 83.

45. Cleland Boyd McAfee, "Near to the Heart of God," *The United Methodist Hymnal*, 472.

46. Adapted from Roger J. Green, "1738 John and Charles Wesley Experience Conversions," in *Christian History Magazine* (1990).

47. Charles Wesley, "And Can It Be," *The United Methodist Hymnal*, 363.

48. Green, "1738 John and Charles Wesley Experience Conversions."

49. Shane Claiborne, *Common Prayer* (Grand Rapids: Zondervan, 2010), 426.

50. Sharon Garlough Brown, *Sensible Shoes: A Story About the Spiritual Journey* (Downers Grove, IL: InterVarsity, 2013), 229.

51. Labberton, *Called*.

52. Labberton, *Called*, 121–22.

53. From my notes at the live service, which can be found on YouTube, "Elisabeth Elliot Memorial Service at Wheaton College," July 26, 2015. Joni Eareckson Tada's eulogy is at 1:40:45.

54. Malcolm Muggeridge, *A Twentieth Century Testimony* (Nashville TN: Thomas Nelson, 1978).

55. Bill Gaultiere, "A Kingdom of Cardboard and Spoils," *Soul Shepherding* website, March 16, 2013, www.soulshepherding.org.

56. Robert Murray M'Cheyne, Sermon XIV "On the Close of a Communion Sabbath," www.mcheyne.info/sermons4.php.

57. Vicki Larson, "Stroke Leads Ex-Pastor Dieter Zander on a Different Path to Grace," *Marin Independent Journal* (April 14, 2014).

58. Robert Reich, "Why So Many Americans Feel Powerless," *The Baltimore Sun* online, April 29, 2015, accessed January 14, 2016, www.baltimoresun.com/news/opinion/bal-why-so-many-americans-feel-powerless-20150428-story.html.

59. Ann Spangler, *The Tender Words of Jesus* (Grand Rapids: Zondervan, 2008), 86.

60. Isaac Watts, "I Sing the Almighty Power of God," *The United Methodist Hymnal*, 152.

61. Martin Luther, "A Mighty Fortress Is Our God," *The United Methodist Hymnal*, 110.

62. John Eldredge, *Epic* (Nashville: Thomas Nelson, 2004), 100.

63. Charles Wesley, "Love Divine, All Loves Excelling," *The United Methodist Hymnal*, 384.

64. Spangler, *Tender Words of Jesus*, 127.

65. Henri Nouwen, *God's Abiding Love* (Fenton, MO: Christian Communications for the Parish, 2014).

66. Bernard of Clairvaux, "Jesus, Thou Joy of Loving Hearts," trans. Ray Palmer, accessed January 19, 2016, www.hymnary.org/text/jesus_thou_joy _of_loving_hearts.

67. Robert Benson, *That We May Perfectly Love Thee* (Brewster, MA: Paraclete, 2002),40–41.

68. Benson, *That We May Perfectly Love Thee*, 87.

69. R. C. Sproul, "The Ministry of Presence," *Ligonier Ministries* website, accessed December 22, 2015, www.ligonier.org/learn/devotionals/ministry -presence/.

70. William B. Tappan, "'Tis Midnight and on Olive's Brow," accessed January 19, 2016, www.hymnary.org/text/tis_midnight_and_on_olives_brow.

71. Paul Gerhardt, trans., "O Sacred Head, Now Wounded," *The United Methodist Hymnal*, 286.

72. Ditchfield, *Praying Ephesians*, 14.

73. J. Daniel Baumann, *Dare to Believe* (Glendale, CA: Regal Books, 1977).

74. Gerhardt, "O Sacred Head," 286.

75. Gerhardt, "O Sacred Head," 286.

76. Jane Rubietta, *Worry Less So You Can Live More* (Bloomington, MN: Bethany House, 2015), 109.

77. "Collect for Third Sunday of Easter," *Common Worship: Daily Prayer* (London: Church House Publishing, 2005).

GROW

1. Barry D. Jones, *Dwell* (Downers Grove, IL: InterVarsity, 2014), 212.

2. Arnold Lobel, *Frog and Toad Together* (New York: HarperCollins, 1979).

3. Max Lucado, *Come Thirsty* (Nashville: Thomas Nelson, 2006).

4. Frederick Buechner, *The Magnificent Defeat* (New York: HarperOne, 1985).

5. Mark Batterson, *Draw the Circle* (Grand Rapids: Zondervan, 2012), 24.

6. Batterson, *Draw the Circle*, 25.

7. Elisabeth Elliot, *Trusting God in Tough Times* (Old Tappan, NJ: Fleming H. Revell, 1989).

8. Bill Gaultiere, "Why the Birds Don't Worry," *Soul Shepherding* website, May 20, 2008, www.soulshepherding.com.

9. Emilie Barnes, *Time Began in a Garden* (Eugene, OR: Harvest House, 1995), 11.

10. Barnes, *Time Began in a Garden*, 44.

11. Annie Johnson Flint, "He Giveth More Grace," accessed January 19, 2016, www.hymnary.org/text/he_giveth_more_grace_as_our_burdens.

12. Warren W. Wiersbe, *Old Testament Words for Today* (Grand Rapids: Baker, 2013), 107.

13. Tricia McCarry Rhodes, *Sacred Chaos* (Downers Grove, IL: InterVarsity, 2008), 155.

14. Mark Buchanan, *Spiritual Rhythm: Being with Jesus Every Season of Your Soul* (Grand Rapids: Zondervan, 2010), 153.

15. Isaac Watts, "I Sing the Almighty Power of God," *The United Methodist Hymnal* (Nashville: The United Methodist Publishing House, 1989), 152.

16. Anne Morrow Lindbergh, *Gift from the Sea* (New York: Pantheon, 1955).

17. Jones, *Dwell*, 111.

18. Laurence Hull Stookey, *This Day* (Nashville: Abingdon Press, 2004), 80.

19. Adapted from a story in Peter Marshall, *Mr. Jones, Meet the Master* (Grand Rapids: Fleming H. Revell, 1950), 147.

20. Kathy Collard Miller and Larry Miller, *Never Ever Be the Same* (Abilene, TX: Leafwood, 2015), 18.

21. Jan Johnson, *Enjoying the Presence of God* (Colorado Springs: NavPress, 1996), 136.

22. Kenneth Boa, *Conformed to His Image* (Grand Rapids: Zondervan, 2001), 451.

23. Derwin L. Gray, "The Church Is the Greatest Movie Trailer Ever," *Christianity Today* online, June 1, 2015, www.christianitytoday.com /derwin-gray/2015/june/church-is-greatest-movie-trailer-ever-.html.

24. Ken Sande, *The Peacemaker: A Biblical Guide to Resolving Personal Conflict* (Grand Rapids: Baker, 2004).

25. Brennan Manning, *Abba's Child* (Wheaton, IL: Tyndale, 2015), 137.

26. Dr. Earl Henslin, *This Is Your Brain on Joy* (Nashville: Thomas Nelson, 2008), 19–20.

27. Murray Pura, *Majestic and Wild* (Grand Rapids: Baker, 2013), 189.

28. Gari Meacham, *Watershed Moments* (Grand Rapids: Zondervan, 2013), 12.

29. Lucinda Secrest McDowell, *Spa for the Soul* (Bloomington, IN: Cross-Books, 2009), 95.

30. Transcript of CNN broadcast, CNN News, January 24, 2010, www.cnn.com/TRANSCRIPTS/1001/23/smn.02.html.

31. Buchanan, *Spiritual Rhythm*, 262.

32. John Burton, "Holy Bible, Book Divine," accessed January 19, 2016, www.hymnary.org/text/holy_bible_book_divine_precious_treasure.

33. Henry and Richard Blackaby, *Hearing God's Voice* (Nashville: B & H, 2002), 264.

34. Blackaby, *Hearing God's Voice*.

35. John E. Bode, "O Jesus, I Have Promised," *The United Methodist Hymnal*, 396.

36. Lori Stanley Roeleveld, *Running from a Crazy Man* (Raleigh: Lighthouse Publishing of the Carolinas, 2014), 217.

37. Buchanan, *Spiritual Rhythm*, 249.

38. Catherine Hart Weber, *Flourish* (Bloomington, IN: Bethany, 2010), 122.

39. Lynne Baab, *Friending—Real Relationships in a Virtual World* (Downers Grove, IL: InterVarsity, 2011).

40. Baab, *Friending*.

41. "Job," definition, accessed December 22, 2015, www.vocabulary.com/dictionary/Job.

42. Joni Eareckson Tada, *Pain and Providence* (Torrance, CA: Rose, 2012).

43. Christin Ditchfield, *What Women Should Know About Letting It Go* (Abilene: Leafwood, 2015), 229.

44. Demian Bulwa, "'Dream House' Collapses on Sunnyside Hill," *San Francisco Gate* online, May 7, 2007, www.sfgate.com/bayarea/article/SAN-FRANCISCO-Dream-house-collapses-on-2596529.php.

45. N. T. Wright, "Comments on the Book of Colossians," plenary session at Following Christ 2008, www.InterVarsity.org.

46. Richard Foster, *Sanctuary of the Soul* (Downers Grove, IL: InterVarsity, 2011), 35.

47. Thomas Kelly, "Praise the Savior, Ye Who Know Him," accessed January 19, 2016, www.hymnary.org/text/praise_the_savior_ye_who_know_him.

48. Adapted by Dr. Catherine Hart Weber from "Intercession," *Magnificat*, vol. 12, no. 5 (July 2010): 271.

49. "Jimmy Carter: A Man of Principle—Still Active, Still Looking for Ways to Serve," *The Guardian* online, September 10, 2011, www.theguardian.com/commentisfree/2011/sep/11/jimmy-carter-human-rights.

50. Wiersbe, *Old Testament Words for Today*.

51. Frederick Buechner, *Telling Secrets* (New York: HarperOne, 1991).

52. Madeleine L'Engle, *Walking on Water* (Colorado Springs: Shaw, 2001).

53. Stephen Curtis Chapman and Scotty Smith, *Restoring Broken Things* (Brentwood, TN: Integrity, 2005), 18.

54. For more on this subject, see Lucinda Secrest McDowell, *Role of a Lifetime—Your Part in God's Story* (Nashville: B & H, 2008).

55. Weber, *Flourish*, 24.

56. Corey L. M. Keyes, "The Mental Health Continuum: From Languishing to Flourishing in Life," *Journal of Health and Social Research* 43 (2002): 207.

57. James Montgomery, "Hail to the Lord's Anointed," *The United Methodist Hymnal*, 203.

58. Weber, *Flourish*, 19.

59. Weber, *Flourish*.

60. David Brooks, "Commencement Address," *Dartmouth Now*, June 14, 2015, http://now.dartmouth.edu/2015/06/david-brooks-commencement-address.

61. Brooks, "Commencement Address."

about the author

Lucinda Secrest McDowell is a storyteller who delights in weaving grace and mercy into ordinary life situations. She is the author of twelve books, including *Live These Words, Amazed by Grace, Refresh, Quilts from Heaven, Role of a Lifetime*, and *God's Purpose for You*.

A graduate of Gordon-Conwell Theological Seminary and Furman University, Lucinda is known for her ability to convey deep truth in practical and winsome ways. She speaks internationally through her ministry "Encouraging Words." Her forte is creatively developing themed events that engage both heart and mind. Lucinda's favorites include tea parties, good books, laughing friends, ancient prayers, country music, cozy quilts, and musical theatre. She writes from "Sunnyside" cottage in New England.

MISSION: To glorify God and live in His grace and freedom, and through the power of the Holy Spirit to use my gifts to communicate God's faithfulness, extend His grace, and encourage others to trust Him fully.

> *Every word you give me is a miracle word—*
>   *how could I help but obey?*
> *Break open your words, let the light shine out,*
>   *let ordinary people see the meaning.*
> ~ Psalm 119:129-130 MSG

Website/Blog	www.EncouragingWords.net
E-mail	cindy@encouragingwords.net
Phone	860.402.9551
Twitter	@LucindaSMcDowel
Facebook	Lucinda Secrest McDowell
Mail	Encouraging Words, PO Box 290707, Wethersfield CT 06129 USA